WHAT LIES BENEATH

COLORADO

PIONEER CEMETERIES AND GRAVEYARDS

EILENE LYON

FOUNDING EDITORS,
GAIL L. JENNER AND CYNTHIA LEAL MASSEY

TWODOT®

ESSEX, CONNECTICUT
HELENA, MONTANA

A · TWODOT® · BOOK

An imprint of The Globe Pequot Publishing Group, Inc.
64 South Main Street
Essex, CT 06426
www.globepequot.com

Distributed by NATIONAL BOOK NETWORK

Map by Melissa Baker

British Library Cataloguing in Publication Information available

Library of Congress Cataloging-in-Publication Data

Names: Lyon, Eilene, author.
Title: What lies beneath Colorado : pioneer cemeteries and graveyards / by Eilene Lyon.
Description: Essex, Connecticut : TwoDot, [2024] | Series: What lies beneath | Includes bibliographical references.
Identifiers: LCCN 2024008734 (print) | LCCN 2024008735 (ebook) | ISBN 9781493076185 (paperback) | ISBN 9781493076192 (epub)
Subjects: LCSH: Cemeteries—Colorado—History—19th century.
Classification: LCC F776 .L96 2024 (print) | LCC F776 (ebook) | DDC 978.8—dc23/eng/20240403
LC record available at https://lccn.loc.gov/2024008734
LC ebook record available at https://lccn.loc.gov/202400873

♾™ The paper used in this publication meets the minimum requirements of American National Standard for Information Sciences—Permanence of Paper for Printed Library Materials, ANSI/NISO Z39.48-1992.

CONTENTS

CONTENTS

CONTENTS

CONTENTS

1 Mystic San Luis Valley
2 Canyons & Plains
3 Pioneering Plains
4 Denver & Cities of the Rockies
5 Pikes Peak Wonders
6 Rockies Playground
7 Mountains & Mesas
8 The Great West

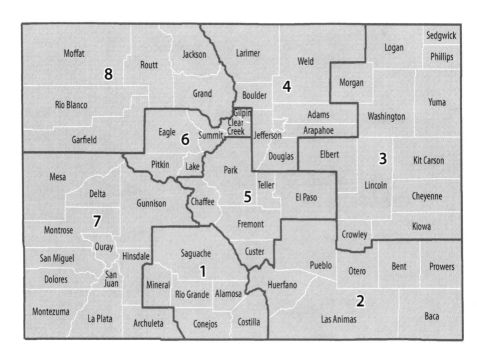

INTRODUCTION

When I was in college in Columbus, Ohio, I would walk past an urban cemetery on my way to work. I loved to stroll through the peaceful, park-like grounds, reading the epitaphs and dates, pondering the family groups, often with many members who died as infants or toddlers. Death was a mystery to me. In my experience, children survived childhood diseases, went to school, did homework and chores, enjoyed summer vacations, and everything else about growing to adulthood. So, who were all these people planted in this lush garden with stone markers? What had their lives been like, so different from my own? What had they enjoyed and endured in their lifetimes before being relegated to this final resting ground, perhaps to be ignored by the living world for an eternity?

I never lost my curiosity about the lives of those who went before, though I failed to pry much information from my grandparents about their lives. I wish I had asked them more questions—and taken care to record the answers. Instead, I must rely on the artifacts that remain: official records, newspapers, letters and diaries, old family photographs. Even cumulatively, they do not tell the whole story.

So much is lost forever—the personalities and emotions. Even what a person looked like is often a mystery.

As I wander my now-home state of Colorado, visiting small towns, large cities, ghost towns, and rural open space to find state pioneers, I realize I can only provide a glimpse into their lives, and never the full breadth of their existence. Much has been written about the politicians, outlaws, city founders, and railroad and mine developers. While I will touch on some of these, my goal is to reveal more about the "ordinary" people. They, too, made Colorado a settled place, built towns and farms, established schools, churches, fraternal lodges . . . and cemeteries. They performed the day-to-day work of building businesses and families, without which none of us would be here today.

Why should you care about these ordinary people? They lived quiet lives, and in most cases had quiet deaths. Their experiences epitomize what it meant to be a pioneer. Not someone who had the means to bring eastern comforts with them, but who settled for what the mountains, plains, and canyons had to offer. Who left behind a life, not necessarily of ease but of establishment. To understand this, it's necessary to study the lives and deaths of those who crossed the plains to start all over from scratch.

Pioneer life was harsh, and this is reflected in the number of graves belonging to children and young adults. Someone who died in their fifties was described as an "old-timer." People in their thirties were called "Aunt" and "Uncle." Living in transient mining camps or on a remote homestead meant little access to health care. Pioneers did dangerous work such as mining and railroad building. Many young women died of childbirth complications. Fires and blizzards took their toll. Diseases that can now be prevented by vaccination or cured by antibiotics—such as diphtheria, measles, sepsis, and scarlet fever—killed many. Cholera could kill an adult quickly; tuberculosis might take years. What is rare in pioneer cemeteries is to find someone who lived into their eighties or nineties.

When writing about the dead, stating the manner in which they died is almost inevitable. Sometimes how they died overshadows how they lived. This, too, is of interest. Death in the nineteenth century was vastly different from today. In the 1800s and earlier, nearly every parent suffered the loss of not just one but usually several children. Rearing all one's young to adulthood was the exception. Accidents involving horses and trains were replaced in the twentieth century by car crashes.

The level of violence is almost unimaginable to us today. Self-preservation in the West called for defensive weapons; petty quarrels could have deadly outcomes. Justice was eye-for-an-eye, and a hanging often ended matters. Suicides were as common then as now, though the means might differ.

Why create connections between people dead for a century or more? Does anyone care? I believe they do. We all came from people who lived and died in the past. We are awakening to the meaning of our ancestors' lives. Some ended tragically. Others were barely noticed in the general hubbub of progress. Some lives were dismayingly short. But none were inconsequential.

Research leads to reconnection, and reconnection leads to . . . relevancy and empathy. Imagine a fascinating scene: a family reunion of ten generations or more. It will occur only on paper, online, or in some unknowable afterlife, but each dot connected to another in the procession of humanity ties us together in one big web—a knot, even. When we find our place in this web, we can see why we should not destroy it.

I began this work by collecting local, county, and state history material from libraries, museums and historical societies, and online. I combed these resources for names and cross-referenced them with Findagrave. com. I also examined every listing in the Colorado Cemetery Directory by Kay R. Merrill. When time and circumstances permitted, I traveled to the places and cemeteries covered in this book. Some that I saw are omitted. Others I have not seen are covered here.

I find that firsthand observations, more than online photographs, call me to explore a story. I tug a thread and unravel genealogical records and news reports. One story leads to another until a picture of a community in its early days emerges. Sometimes I find records for deaths and burials not on Find a Grave. Many cemeteries have no formal records. For any number of reasons, many deceased never received headstones. Or the monuments may have been destroyed or are too weathered to be read. I thank all the volunteers who submit memorials, photographs, obituaries, and other biographical information to this vast database. I sought to verify the information before adding it to my narrative. Though I know mistakes abound in news stories, if that is the only source available, I used the information. Even tombstones have errors engraved upon them. I made note of some here.

Though I combed through all of Colorado's sixty-four counties to uncover their history and their pioneers, it was impossible to include more than a sampling. What remains are those stories I found compelling for their variety, their rich illustration of a developing community, or for illuminating various aspects of nineteenth-century culture.

My goal is to present Colorado's settlement story without stressing the negative aspects of those days, but not overlooking them, either. As mining camps became ghost towns and pioneers developed government structures in real cities, much of the early violence began to fade. Coercive measures against Native Americans forced them onto reservations, mostly in other states, and reduced the cultural conflict between the two groups. Native American stories are an important facet of this work. Any Colorado history is incomplete without explaining how the United States came to possess the land that was once home only to indigenous people.

This book is divided into eight regions defined by the Colorado Tourism Board. I slightly modified the boundaries. The first areas permanently settled by non-native people were the south-central and southeastern portions of the state. From there I proceeded in a sideways S-shaped pattern through the state, approximating development, though the eastern plains were settled long after the gold rush period. Each region is covered in a geographic rather than chronological order, approximating driving routes.

In Colorado, the pioneer era is considered to be prior to February 26, 1861, when Colorado became a territory, formed from

Utah, Nebraska, Kansas, and New Mexico territories. The territorial era lasted until statehood on August 1, 1876. Therefore, the term "pioneer" is used rather loosely to describe the cemeteries and people covered in this volume. Here, a pioneer cemetery is one established prior to 1900, though not necessarily abandoned or forgotten. Many, in fact, are spacious and still in use today. Some are so small as to contain a single grave.

Sites were used as burial grounds, but for a variety of reasons, the bodies were exhumed and moved: the land had higher value as residential or agricultural property; a nicer cemetery became available; a road or reservoir obliterated the site. In some cases, not all the buried remains were removed, because no one would cover the cost. Pauper burials—unmarked graves—then became paved over or neglected until forgotten.

San Luis is the oldest permanent town in Colorado, established in 1851. A gold rush in 1859 brought the first big influx of Anglo miners and settlers to the foothills region. They created communities that would become Denver and other Front Range cities. Miners soon left the plains to find gold and silver lodes in the mountains. The eastern plains counties saw little settlement until after the Indian Wars concluded in the 1870s and railroads arrived in the 1880s, attracting homesteaders.

Utes retained control of western Colorado until after ratification of the Brunot Agreement in 1874 and their final removal in 1880–1881. This opened more land to occupation by Americans and immigrants. The southwestern section also developed due to mining interests. The far northwestern section developed last. As on the eastern plains, lack of water and competition for grazing land created conflict among various landholders there.

The earliest non-indigenous graves in Colorado belong to those who traveled with early Spanish explorers. American explorers and mountain men roamed the West in the early 1800s. Mexico issued land grants in the 1830s in an attempt to encourage settlement in southern Colorado, but Utes drove out most who tried. Those who died in these movements left no visible reminders. Even after the establishment of formal burial grounds, many graves had impermanent markers made of wood or soft stone. The crude monuments were soon obliterated by weather or vandalism. Thus, we have few recorded grave sites in Colorado prior to the 1860s.

Note: Names in **bold** are central to the narrative. Those with (dates) after their names are buried in the cemetery being discussed.

CHAPTER 1

MYSTIC SAN LUIS VALLEY

Nearly flat as a polished granite slab, the San Luis Valley spans a hundred miles north and south, and sixty-five miles east to west. It is one of the largest sub-alpine valleys in the world. Though in a desert climate, with irrigation it became an agricultural center. The alluvial topsoil, left over from a lake that existed 500,000 years ago, sits atop a fill of gravel, sand, silt, and clay as deep as 30,000 feet. On its eastern edge, Great Sand Dunes National Park boasts the tallest dunes in North America. Framed by the Sangre de Cristo range to the east, the Sawatch to the northwest, and the San Juans to the west, the valley has been a continental crossroads for centuries, with its numerous mountain passes accessing other parts of the state. The north branch of the Old Spanish Trail, through Cochetopa Pass, was used from 1829 to 1848. The Rio Grande, originating in the San Juan Mountains, crosses the south end of the valley, flowing into New Mexico.

The people who migrated from Mexico to northern New Mexico beginning in the late 1500s were of Spanish descent and known as Hispano. Isolated from the political and religious power centers in Spain and Mexico City, these settlers retained the culture and language of seventeenth-century Spain, up to the present day. Contact

Los Penitentes

The brotherhood of *Los Penitentes de Nuestro Padre Jesus Nazareno*, or Los Penitentes for short, like many fraternal organizations, has its secret rituals. Their sometimes-bloody penances, maligned and misunderstood, drove this group of devout Catholic men into hiding at times. Even a canyon on the west side of the San Luis Valley, near La Garita, is named Penitente Canyon, because they took refuge there.

The self-flagellation custom in the Catholic religion has its origins in Europe during the Middle Ages, particularly within the Franciscan Order. The Franciscans brought these customs to the Americas. Along with farmers and herders, the Order moved into the northern frontier provinces of Old Mexico, what became northern New Mexico and southern Colorado. The Church lacked trained priests to offer services to the remote settlements. This gave rise to Los Penitentes in the late eighteenth century. They held sway until Santa Fe became a bishopric under Jesuit John B. Lamy shortly after the Mexican War. Official disapproval of their penance practices drove the movement underground. Los Penitentes reached the pinnacle of their influence in the late nineteenth and early twentieth centuries, but they are still an active organization.

Their most important observation period is Holy Week prior to Easter. Their customs embrace flagellation with wet yucca whips, cross-carrying, and sometimes the tying of a Brother to a cross. They have been known to wrap their bodies in cacti or wear crowns of thorns. One initiation rite is carving crosses on a novice's back. These re-enactments of the Passions of Christ are considered a living embodiment of his suffering, relevant in the present, not just a dusty artefact.

The Brothers' devotion to Christ's teachings manifests in their services to the community. They show mercy to the suffering, aid the poor, provide funeral services, and offer religious instruction when no other is available. They gather in refuges, known as *moradas*, for prayers and penances. Many have been vandalized over the years, but some are still in use. The early Hispano settlers in the San Luis Valley and beyond would have found life much less bearable without the religious leadership, community-building, and devotion of Los Penitentes.

with Indians, French trappers, and Americans led to a dialect distinct from Latin American countries. The remoteness encouraged a Catholic offshoot, the secretive Brotherhood of Penitents, *Los Penitentes*. The valley's physical characteristics, with its hundred-mile views and other-worldly dunes, combined with its Old World cultural elements, infuses its mystic atmosphere.

Today, the valley retains its Hispano character, with many Catholic churches, Spanish place-names, and adobe construction. Colorado Territory's establishment in 1861, with its artificial straight-line borders, created a political disconnection between the residents of southern Colorado and their relations in New Mexico. In a state dominated by Anglo culture, the Hispanos faced discrimination and hardship.

Mineral wealth drove people to the mountains ringing the San Luis Valley but decades later than in other areas. Homesteaders arrived to supply miners with food and other goods. Many communities that sprung up are now ghost towns, though some, such as Crestone, live on as tourist centers or retreats.

San Luis

The earliest cemeteries in San Luis, Costilla County, were in the center of town, so the burials were removed to other locations. One older cemetery is the **San Luis Old Catholic Cemetery**. It is reached by driving east of town on Sixth Street and is just beyond the San Luis Cemetery at the top of the mesa, with prominent Blanca Peak visible in the distance to the north. Some influential San Luis founders and citizens are buried here.

Doña Genoveva Gallegos de Salazar (1860–1907) is one of nineteen women depicted on the Women's Gold Tapestry that hangs in the Colorado Capitol, because of her role as a businesswoman in Colorado's oldest settlement. Her parents, **Jose Desiderio "Dario" Gallegos** (1830–1883) and **Maria Eulogia Valdes** (1837–1912), helped found the town and established the general mercantile that remained in family hands for 165 years. Dario Gallegos sent a caravan as far as St. Louis to obtain merchandise for his store, an eleven-month round trip. On the second such trip, Indians stole the entire cargo, wagons, and oxen. Fire destroyed the retail building in 1895 and again in 1947, leaving only portions of the adobe walls. The last incarnation still stands and is now a co-op called The San Luis Peoples Market.

When Dario Gallegos and other early residents settled here, no nearby supply points existed. The people had to be self-sufficient, growing their food, raising sheep and cattle, and weaving woolen cloth. Crop production required developing local water resources. They constructed the first *acequia,* a communal irrigation project, in 1851 with nearly every man, woman, and child digging the trenches, which are maintained to this day. Family and community cooperation distinguished the Hispano settlements in southern Colorado from the wild and violent early mining towns in other parts of the state.

Genoveva Gallegos was born in San Luis and married **Antonio Arcadio Salazar** (1849–1926) when she was just fourteen. Salazar bought into his wife's family business to form Salazar & Gallegos and expanded its size. He purchased the entire operation from the

Doña Genoveva Gallegos de Salazar c. 1890, was an important businesswoman in the San Luis Valley. She is honored on the Women's Gold Tapestry in the State Capitol. PUBLIC DOMAIN.

Gallegos family in 1894, eleven years after his father-in-law died. Genoveva learned the healing arts, traveled the region as a *curandera*, and sold medicines in the family store. She reared eight surviving children. Thus, the Salazar clan became a solid and enduring presence in the San Luis Valley. Genoveva's daughter described her as "tiny in body, but great in spirit," a trait that helped her through the difficult time after the store burned in 1895.

Arcadio Salazar had a rough start in life. His father, **Juan Manuel Salazar**, who helped establish San Luis, was killed by Utes in

1854, when Arcadio was just three. He began supporting his mother at age eleven. At nineteen, Arcadio worked for retailer **Ferdinand "Ferd" Meyer**, who, along with the county recorder, taught him to read and write. Arcadio was a quick study. He went to work for Dario Gallegos at age twenty-six, leading to his future as Gallegos's son-in-law and business partner. The Salazar-Gallegos wedding followed the traditions of Old Spain, as these families had immigrated from that country in the early 1800s. Salazar was a Republican state senator in the 1880s and 1890s. The Salazars sent all their children to Catholic boarding schools in the Denver area. Their daughter **Maria Elisa Salazar** (1885–1914) had an exceptional academic record and wrote her thesis in Latin. She died at twenty-nine, after a lifetime of poor health.

 Louis Cohn (1837–1899) owned another early mercantile in San Luis. Like Salazar, he represented the region in the state legislature but as a Democrat. The two men co-owned the San Luis Flouring Mills. Born in Breslau, Prussia (today Wroclaw, Poland), Cohn immigrated to America in the early 1860s. He followed the Santa Fe Trail to its terminus in New Mexico where he and another Prussian traveler took jobs as bookkeepers. His parents and siblings remained in Prussia, and amazingly, he answered the emperor's call to participate in the Franco-Prussian War in 1869.

 When Cohn returned to America in 1872, he settled in San Luis and opened his store and other businesses. He accumulated two thousand acres, and owned the handsomest residence in town.

He purchased other investments, including the Colorado Hotel in Denver, which the legislature used as temporary quarters before the construction of the State Capitol. He partnered with a widow, **Juana Maria Ruperta Lucero**, and they had seven children, four surviving to adulthood. He adopted the culture and religion of his community, Catholicism, though he did not reject his Jewish heritage. He never married Juana, perhaps eschewing outright religious conversion, but he named her and their children in his will.

Dr. Joseph L. Kugler (1829–1889) and his New Mexican wife, **Simonita Vigil** (1855–1887), are found here too. Dr. Kugler was born in Württemberg, immigrated in 1851, and joined the US military in California the following year. He enlisted as a barber; in those days, barbers did minor surgical and dental procedures. It is likely that Kugler never had formal medical training. He mustered out at Fort Jones, California, in 1857, but soon re-enlisted, this time as a steward in the hospital unit. By 1866, he was a contract surgeon at Fort Garland, Colorado, under **Gen. Christopher "Kit" Carson**, a position he held until December 1867. He relocated sixteen miles south of the fort to San Luis, where he worked as a local physician.

Kugler fathered two children, Joseph Jr. and Helen, by two women: **Maria Candelaria Vigil** and her younger sister Simonita. The women were born in Taos County (probably in San Luis) in the days when southern Colorado was still part of Taos County, New Mexico. The babies' births were soon followed by their mothers'

Graves of Dr. Joseph Kugler (center) and Simonita Kugler (left) in the San Luis Old Catholic Cemetery. San Luis in the background.
AUTHOR'S COLLECTION

deaths from complications. Dr. Kugler lived two years longer than Simonita, leaving his two children orphaned at ages nineteen and two.

Maria and Simonita had another sister, **Manuela "Melita" Vigil**, who was the wife of Colorado's third Lieutenant Governor, **William H. Meyer.** Uncle William Meyer assumed legal guardianship of the Kugler children, applying for their father's military pension to support them. Meyer himself buried three young sons in this cemetery. Though they died years apart, they share a single headstone.

FROM SOVEREIGN TO SIDELINE: THE UTE TREATIES

The traditional Ute territory covered parts of what are now Utah, Colorado, Kansas, Arizona, New Mexico, Texas, and Oklahoma. The Colorado bands were the Yamparika, Parianuche, Tabeguache, Weenuche, Mouache, and Capote.

1670—Spain made their first treaty with the tribe (Mouache and Capote bands) for peace purposes.

1680—The Utes sided with Puebloans against the Spanish.

1700s—Additional Spanish–Ute treaties.

1848—**Col. Alexander Doniphan** signed a treaty with the Mouache and Capote bands in an effort to end raids. It was never ratified by Congress. The following year, headmen from these same two groups signed the Abiquiu Treaty, which did get ratified. These Utes agreed to US jurisdiction and allowed development of roads and forts in exchanged for gifts and supplies.

1863—Territorial Governor **John Evans** met with the Tabeguache to create a treaty that Congress ratified in 1864. It ceded traditional Mouache and Capote lands, though they were not parties in the treaty. The Tabeguache relinquished claims to lands east of the Continental Divide and Middle Park (now Grand County).

1868—All the Colorado bands signed a renegotiated version of the 1863 treaty creating the Consolidated Ute Reservation, which left them with roughly the western third of the state in perpetuity, cutting the tribe off from many traditional hunting areas in the mountain parks. The treaty provided annual payments in goods to the tribe and prohibited non-Ute settlement on the reservation. Both sides violated the terms.

1873—The Brunot Agreement (ratified in 1874) was called "Agreement" because in 1871 Congress declared the United States

(continued)

9

would no longer recognize tribal sovereignty. The Utes understood at first that they would only be selling access to current mines high in the southwestern mountains. They were unwilling to allow permanent settlement or cede the valleys. The government wanted full title to four million acres. Even Tabeguache **Chief Ouray**, a man known for his friendliness to whites, opposed the agreement at first. (Other Ute bands did not necessarily agree with Ouray's generous concessions over the years.) Finally, **Felix Brunot**, commissioner for the federal government, recruited **Otto Mears** to pressure the Utes. The government stipulated just $500,000 for the land (7.5 cents per acre), but would pay only the interest on this sum annually, rather than making an outright purchase.

1879—Violence at the White River Agency (see chapter 8, Meeker Incident sidebar) prompted outcries of "The Utes Must Go!" from American settlers.

1880—This deceptive Ute Agreement removed most of the tribe to reservations in Utah. The Mouache, Capote, and Weenuche bands received a narrow strip of land in the southwestern corner of the state.

1887—The Dawes Allotment Act led to a split in the Colorado reservation. The Ute Mountain Utes did not accept allotment, and their land is still held collectively by the tribe. Members of the Southern Ute Tribe received privately owned parcels (up to 160 acres) within the reservation boundary, and the remainder reverted to the government to be sold to homesteaders.

Conejos

Settlers from New Mexico came to live and farm along the San Antonio River in Conejos County in 1849. They called this area *Los Rincones*, "the corners," now a ghost town. **Anastacio Trujillo** of El

Rito, New Mexico, encouraged them to move north for more productive land. He befriended the Utes, who promised to protect them if they occupied the Conejos River portion of the San Luis Valley. He had difficulty persuading his neighbors, who knew of earlier pioneers whom the Utes terrorized and drove back south in the 1830s and early 1840s. Another group, from the Abiquiu region, established Guadalupe on the Conejos River. Leader **Jose Maria Jaquez** built the first home there in 1854. He also built the first gristmill and was the first *alcalde* (like a mayor and justice of the peace).

The Guadalupe pioneers included **Major Lafayette Head** (1825–1897). Married to a Hispano woman and politically connected, he had influence and created controversy. He became the state's first Lieutenant Governor in 1876. Guadalupe was superseded by the town of Conejos on the opposite, higher and drier bank of the river, which is where Head constructed his ranch home. *Conejos* is Spanish for rabbits, a reference to the thriving population of small mammals in the region. These settlements all occupied part of the Guadalupe land grant, also known as the Martinez or Conejos grant.

Lafayette Head's phallic granite pillar dominates the **Conejos Cemetery**. The cemetery is south of Conejos in a weedy field east of County Road 13. Missouri-born Head enlisted during the war with Mexico. He remained in New Mexico and wed **Maria Martinez** (1839–1886), a widow with one child. They had no children together, but "adopted" a number of *criados,* Indian servants purchased from Indian or Hispano captors. When Head moved to Conejos, he was the only Anglo among the settlers.

Head sat on the New Mexico territorial legislature and, after Conejos became part of Colorado, he joined its territorial legislature, helping to craft the state constitution. He was appointed US Marshall and also Indian Agent to the Utes. The 1863 Ute treaty conference called by Gov. John Evans (see chapter 4, Denver, Riverside Cemetery) took place at Head's *plazuela* (his large residence built in plaza style with an interior courtyard and defensive outer walls). Five thousand Utes congregated at his ranch in October, which angered the Hispano settlers. The San Luis Valley communities bemoaned being cut off from New Mexico upon the formation of Colorado Territory. The civil authorities resigned en masse, and the US Commissioner for Conejos and Costilla Counties requested military assistance to keep order.

The Conejos residents sent a petition in January 1864 to the US Attorney for Colorado asking to have Head removed from his position as Indian Agent. They accused him of being disloyal to the Union, responsible for garrisoned soldiers who allegedly killed three citizens, and for using government property to buy Indian children. Even if this final accusation were true, the practice had precedence. Early in the Spanish colonial days, Indians had been enslaved by other Indians and the Spanish. With an established market to supply, tribal raids for stealing children increased. When New Mexico Spaniards refused to purchase some Pawnee captives, the Navajo beheaded the luckless children, resulting in a policy to use Spain's royal funds to purchase them thereafter. Whether the Conejos petition caused Head's

Maj. Lafayette Head's monument in the Conejos Cemetery.
AUTHOR'S COLLECTION

removal as agent is unclear, but Governor Evans relocated the Ute's provision point from Conejos, closing the agency there.

In March 1897, Head visited the Capitol in Denver and sat in his former chair where, as Lt. Governor, he had presided over the senate. The same day, he suffered a stroke that led to his death three days later. He was laid to rest next to his wife, Maria, who preceded him in 1886.

The petition against Head was signed by the principal county officials and other prominent Hispano residents of Conejos County. Most of their gravesites remain unknown. One believed to be buried in the Conejos Cemetery is **Jose Seledon Valdez** (1814–1884), aka Seledonio or Celedonio. His property lay east of Conejos in an area called La Isla. His family was among those who petitioned the Mexican government for the Conejos land grant, which the US government never patented. Seledonio was a community leader and leading member of the Catholic Church. With his wife, **Guadalupe Valdez** (~1822–1873), he had five children. Guadalupe died at La Isla, but her burial site is also unknown. Son Cresencio Valdez carried on his father's work.

Antonito

Antonito is one of many Colorado towns established by the railroads. They often bypassed existing towns, in this case Conejos, causing considerable resentment. But they had a sound business rationale. Once rumors about the coming tracks circulated, land speculators drove up real estate prices in the presumed whistle-stops. It made sense for the railroads to buy cheaper land nearby. Today, tiny Antonito is known for its narrow-gauge railroad attraction, the Cumbres and Toltec Scenic Railroad, which chuffs along through remote landscapes from there to Chama, New Mexico.

The **Antonito Cemetery**, established in the early 1880s, occupies a scrubby nine-acre parcel adjacent to the Conejos Cemetery. It is no longer used due to a high water table. **Col. Charles Edward Broyles** (1826–1906) has the pointed-top, white-marble headstone found on Confederate graves. His marker (installed in 1940), and that of two Broyles children, lies inside a wrought-iron enclosure. His second wife, **Nellie Armstrong** (1860–1944), has a pink slab and headstone outside the enclosure. West of Antonito, near the Latter-Day Saints community of Fox Creek, is a landmark bridge across the Conejos River still bearing his name.

Born in South Carolina, Broyles farmed in Tennessee, then moved to Georgia to practice law. He had enslaved people to do manual labor on his property. Though he sat on the Georgia legislature and was personal aide to the governor before the Civil War, he did not favor independent state action. However, he did join the Confederate Army and fought in many major battles. With his first wife, Lucy, he had seven children. By 1875, like many Confederate veterans, he found life in the postwar South difficult and decided to go to Colorado, planning to bring his family out later. But Lucy died in Georgia in 1880. Of his children, Broyles wrote, "I am ashamed of none of them, yet might have been made to feel prouder." He may have been pondering his efforts to get his sons away from railroad work by setting them up in shopkeeping, at which they failed.

Broyles tried mining for a short time, without success, and turned to his legal profession, first in Del Norte, then Ouray. He floundered until he returned to the San Luis Valley and put up his shingle in Alamosa upon the railroad's arrival. He was also the uber-competent US land registrar at Del Norte. In 1887, he wrote a short autobiography after he suffered severe health complications, which he believed were the result of a deliberate attempt by land swindlers to kill him so they could proceed with their schemes. He homesteaded land west of the river crossing at the Broyles Bridge. He used it to raise horses, grow hay, and an enviable variety of vegetables such as turnips, cantaloupe, squash, potatoes, even sugar beets.

Graves of Nellie Armstrong Broyles, Charles Broyles, and children in the Antonito Cemetery.
AUTHOR'S COLLECTION

GENÍZAROS AND CRIADOS

It was customary for Spanish Mexican settlers in northern New Mexico—and later in southern Colorado—to buy Indian servants, frequently Navajo or Plains Indians, who may have first been enslaved by Utes or other dominant tribes. In Abiquiu, New Mexico, enslaved Indians were called the *genízaro*. The genízaro had their own pueblo at Abiquiu, though they were not Pueblo Indians. This community acted as a buffer between raiding tribes from the north and northwest (Utes, Comanches, and others), and the Spanish settlements to the south. Having been sold as children and been baptized in the Catholic Church, the genízaro suffered a disconnect from both the Indian culture of their birth and the Hispano culture they were forced into.

In southern Colorado, the term used for enslaved Indians was *criado*, or "servant." They received Hispano names and often familial titles, such as *Tia* ("aunt"), if they remained with the family into adulthood. Others left once they became teens or young adults. They married, had children, and lived independently, but sometimes still worked for those who had purchased them. Though technically a form of slavery, it bore little resemblance to the chattel enslavement of Blacks in the American South. Anglos who moved into southern Colorado's Hispano areas adopted this practice.

In the Mexican era, the local Prefect could remove an abused criado from the home and free him or her. Once a criado was baptized, it was against Church law to sell them, thus they were treated more like an extended family member, less like private property. Also, unlike enslaved Blacks, criados gained their freedom upon marriage (usually arranged by the head of household, known as their godfather). Abuses did occur, however. There are documented instances of physical and sexual abuse.

Having criados conferred status upon a community's well-to-do members. The Gallegos and Salazar families in San Luis each had one. Lafayette Head of Guadalupe/Conejos had several. **James B. Woodson** of Saguache had two well-known Navajo boys that "belonged" to him. Even Kit Carson's wife owned an Indian servant, known as **Juan Carson**. All these enslaved Indians achieved their freedom at the end of the Civil War, though many remained with their adoptive families.

He and Nellie lived in Alamosa for many years, moving permanently to their ranch in 1889. That same year, Broyles erected a fine residence in Antonito where he operated a law office. They have many descendants in Conejos County to this day. Broyles was a plain-spoken man who provided legal advice to his Hispano neighbors regardless of their ability to pay. After his death, Nellie continued to run the ranch, with the help of her sons. She moved around between Antonito, Denver, and the ranch, and finally to Alamosa, where she died in 1944.

SAGUACHE

Saguache, the town, became county seat when Otto Mears (see chapter 7, The San Juan Pathfinder sidebar) and **John Lawrence** persuaded the legislature to create Saguache County in 1866, despite the dearth of people living there. Even by 1880, fewer than two thousand resided in the county. Lawrence was a prominent citizen who kept a daily diary for many years. The diary reveals the need for a burial ground arose when an "old man" died while traveling north from Conejos to Saguache. **Edward R. Harris** (1824–1888), an important early settler, built a coffin for **Jose Antonio Borrego** (1810–1867) and they interred him at the base of the first prominent hill west of town. This became known as the *campo santo* or Spanish cemetery, initiated in March 1867. The St. Agnes Parish maintains the property, formally called **Chicago Cemetery**. It can be reached by driving west on Denver Road to County Road Z43. The drive passes hay fields and irrigation ditches lined with coyote willow. Borrego's grave no longer has a marker, if it ever did.

Entry gate to the Chicago Cemetery near Saguache.
AUTHOR'S COLLECTION

Harris was a seaman, born in Nantucket, Massachusetts, but he chose to spend much of his life in a land-locked state, arriving in Colorado with the rush of Fifty-Niners. He mined for a time in South Park, but then settled in what became Saguache County. He went into territorial politics and filled a number of roles in the community: county clerk and recorder, US assessor, postmaster, and census-taker. Because the dominant culture in the San Luis Valley was Hispano, he learned Spanish, and was hired as "Special Translator" for the negotiation and signing of the 1868 treaty with the Utes (Chief Ouray spoke Spanish but not much English).

Harris killed a man, **Peter Everett**, in 1869. Everett was a shoemaker who had recently arrived from Fairplay. After conducting some business with Harris at his office, Everett went to the house and made inappropriate advances on a teenaged servant. Harris ordered Everett to leave, but Everett belligerently threatened to kill Harris. Harris fired two shots in the air as a warning, but when Everett picked up a rock, Harris shot him. He and his wife cared for the injured man, but he died anyway. Some local women thought alcohol caused the altercation, so they went to the Gotthelf & Mears store, which had the only cask of whiskey in the county, and smashed it. A coroner's jury acquitted Harris.

Harris was buried in the Chicago Cemetery where he buried Borrego years earlier, but his grave has no marker today. The cemetery is laid out in orderly rows, but many early burials may have been placed randomly and without headstones. Harris's son-in-law, **Cresencio Samora** (1867–1925), does have a marker here with just his name, birth year, and death year crudely carved in a crumbling marble-like limestone.

Samora's father, **Manuel de Jesus Samora** (1821–1896), is probably buried here in an unmarked grave. His passing was noted in John Lawrence's diary:

13 Dec 1896. At about 2 o'clock today, old Manuel de Jesus Samora died. 14 Dec 1896. As the Adventists went and bothered the Samora wake with their prayers and preaching . . . So that it made the Catholic and the Penitent outfit mad, and no wake so that the Penitents could come and whip themselves was held. It was therefore agreed that the body should be held at the Chappel above tonight, and the body burried up above

tomorrow. And so, a big time is to be had tonight, and the Penitents be allowed and have a chance to whip theirselves all they want to.

A unique set of markers in Chicago Cemetery belongs to the Salazar/Abeyta (aka Aveita/Abeita) family. Made of red-colored concrete, family members' names were stamped by hand while the large slabs set. **Maria Filomena Salazar** (1854–1930) married **Jose Eugenio Abeyta** (1851–1917) in 1875. Eugenio (also known as Henry), farmed hay in Saguache, working his own land. Despite being a large family, they apparently kept a low profile in the Anglo community.

Headstones for the Salazar/Abeyta family in Chicago Cemetery.
AUTHOR'S COLLECTION

Two other unmarked burials likely in Chicago Cemetery are the Navajo criados from the Woodson household: Gabriel and Andres. Purchased from Utes in Conejos County and enumerated in 1865 by Lafayette Head, they grew up as adopted brothers in the fashion of the time. They both worked as farm/ranch labor for the family. **Gabriel Woodson** (~1848–1873), the slightly older of the two, got into a drunken fight with a white man named **Bob Morrison** on July 4, 1873. After Gabriel threatened to kill him, Morrison fired two shots at Gabriel, who ran off and died. Morrison was convicted of manslaughter and sentenced to three years. However, his white neighbors felt his actions were justified on grounds of self-defense. They petitioned the governor for a pardon, which he granted after Morrison had served about six months.

Andres Woodson (1850–1907), like Gabriel and other criados, was emancipated at the close of the Civil War. Andres and Gabriel may not have known their legal status when they moved from Conejos County to Saguache with the Woodson herd of cattle after the war. Andres seemed to adapt more readily to his new culture than Gabriel. Andres married a Hispano woman, **Senovia (aka Cenobia) Romero**, in 1874. Andres never learned to read or write, and spent his entire working life raising and herding sheep. He died of food poisoning at age fifty-six.

Andres and Gabriel's adoptive parents are buried in the pioneer **Hillside Cemetery**, southeast of Saguache, at the base of a treeless hill. James B. Woodson (1820–1894) spent his early life in Virginia, Kentucky, and Tennessee. He went to war against Mexico and later worked for the government as a guide/troubleshooter on the Santa Fe Trail. He ran the sutler's store at Fort Massachusetts, then Fort Garland, two early military posts in the San Luis Valley. While there, he met his wife, **Juliana Vigil** (1843–1901), a resident of San Luis. He also met his lifelong business partner, John Lawrence (1835–1908). Woodson had an early homestead in Saguache County. After his death, Juliana married Lawrence, age sixty, who had been a bachelor up to then. Juliana took in orphaned children and exhibited kindness and charity to all. Her simple gray headstone bears an epitaph: "A friend to the poor." She belonged to the Catholic Church, but her husbands were not religious. That may explain the utter absence of adornment on their headstones.

Both Woodson and Lawrence held office in the territorial government and at the county level. Lawrence, like his Anglo contemporaries in southern Colorado, endeavored to understand the Hispano and Native cultures that surrounded him. He was a mentor and facilitator between them, interceding on their behalf with county and state government. His interpretive skills aided the US government in making their treaties with the Utes. His long-term diary is an invaluable record of the early days in the county he founded.

Like most pioneer cemeteries, Hillside hosts its share of murder victims. The death of **Alice (Noland) Hallar** (1850–1883), killed by her husband, generated a fair amount of press. Many stories circulated about this beautiful, talented, and spirited young woman. Born in Independence, Missouri, to a family of Southern extraction, Alice entered her teens during the war years. She fell in love with a handsome rogue, **O. Johnson Hallar**, reputed to be a member of both Quantrill's Raiders and the Jesse James Gang. (Alice and Johnson named their first son Jesse James.) Both came from wealthy families, but money did not buy happiness. The couple separated many times during their stormy marriage.

Alice, an accomplished pianist, opened a millinery store in Saguache in 1877. Her father, **Jesse Noland** (1826–1884), had a mercantile establishment in town. In 1881, Alice procured the services of a dressmaker from the eastern states, allowing her to move and expand her business. They displayed their talents at a Washington's Birthday masquerade ball the following February.

Only Alice and Johnson's two sons seemed to keep the Hallars together. But Alice had a roving eye. She bolted for Denver where she opened a boarding house. She planned to marry her lover, **Samuel H. Morris**, once she could obtain a divorce. But Hallar came to the city with a loaded gun, intent on killing the interloper. Alice came between the men after Hallar fired the first shot, and she received a fatal wound. Hallar shot Morris again before a policeman on the beat pulled him away and arrested him. Morris lingered for weeks before dying. Hallar claimed the shot that killed Alice was an accident, and he was acquitted by a jury. Alice shares a headstone with her father. Her mother, **Nancy Ann Smallwood** (1827–1890), lies nearby.

Los Pinos Ranch

One of the most remote burial grounds in Saguache County is located on the privately owned **Los Pinos Ranch**, purchased by **John T.**

McDonough (1844–1906) in 1882. The ranch is located west of historic Cochetopa Pass and is reached by following CO 114 west from Saguache. The land previously belonged to the federal Los Pinos Ute Agency. McDonough and his youngest child, **Daisy McDonough** (1890–1893), are buried here.

John McDonough and his wife, **Narcissa Jane Kesselring** (buried in Gunnison), were both born in Pennsylvania. Of their nine children, only five survived childhood. They relocated to Colorado, first at Powderhorn, a small community in Gunnison County, then resided a short time in Saguache before moving to the ranch. "Big John" was a mountain of a man, something shy of four hundred pounds, and a blacksmith by trade. He raised cattle and thoroughbred horses. Narcissa had what it took to live in such a rough and remote place; she could drive the teams of horses and churn the butter that she sold in Gunnison. Their hospitality to all travelers, including Indians, going between Saguache and Gunnison was well known. Ute Chief Ouray gave John a gold watch that he had received as a gift from the federal government. John was so saddened by little toddler Daisy's death in 1893 that he requested to be buried by her side.

Villa Grove

Villa Grove, northeast of Saguache, supplied miners along Kerber Creek in the foothills to the west, and the farmers and ranchers in Homan's Park to the east, the narrow north end of the San Luis Valley. The Denver & Rio Grande Railroad used it as its southern terminus from 1881 to 1890. **Villa Grove Cemetery** is just north of the village, along CO 285, occupying two acres of sagebrush steppe. The earliest marked grave in the cemetery is the double burial of a young mother, **Mary J. Townsend** (1862–1882), and her newborn daughter, dying a day apart in October 1882. A couple illegible wooden markers suggest earlier burials.

Two diamond-shaped headstones, side by side, memorialize **Lottie May Whiteman** (1890–1894) and her baby brother, **Irvin Ross Whiteman** (1894–1894). Both died the same year, though Lottie May's headstone incorrectly gives her death year as 1890, the year she was born. They were the children of **Daniel Irvin Whiteman** (1858–1914), known to friends as "Pete," and **Ida Belle Ross**. Pete courted Ida, a servant in Saguache, beginning in 1888, and they married on December 18, 1889. Pete, a native of Ohio, ran a mercantile business in Villa Grove. Ida came to the San Luis Valley from Missouri with her parents, siblings, and an uncle.

Pete took Lottie May to Salida for tonsil surgery in early 1894, which apparently went well, but did not improve her health. The cause of baby Irvin's death is unknown. After his passing in 1894, Pete and Ida had one remaining child, daughter Emma. By 1901, they had three more daughters. The family began splitting their time between their home in Villa Grove and Cañon City, where Pete opened another store. By then, he had grown wealthy. In the early 1900s, he bought a Stoddard Dayton motorcar, which the family enjoyed taking on tours in the Pikes Peak region and beyond.

In late September 1914, the entire family was motoring through Gunnison County near Cebolla, a fishing resort that disappeared

Headstone on Lottie May Whiteman's grave in Villa Grove Cemetery.

under Blue Mesa Reservoir in the 1960s. After lunching in Gunnison, they headed west into a setting sun. They had a near miss when they encountered a slow wagon in a narrow stretch. Later, still a bit shaken, Pete said, "This driving is pure guess work." After swerving to miss a wayward stone chunk in the road, Pete likely hit another rock and the car tumbled sixty feet down the mountain. Pete and his youngest daughter, **Pearl Whiteman** (1901–1914), hurled onto rocky ground, suffered fatal wounds; the others sustained only minor injuries. Pete and Pearl are presumably buried in Villa Grove, where they were taken after their deaths, but they have no grave markers. The Whitemans were probably the first car-crash casualties to be buried in Saguache County.

Rito Alto

In the valley southeast of Villa Grove and east of Saguache, near the base of the mountains, are several pioneer cemeteries in a north-to-south line. Hispano families lived in the area, but there were also settlements of Germans, Americans, and other nationalities. One cemetery that remains from pioneer times is **Rito Alto Cemetery**. Rito Alto is one of numerous streams flowing west out of the Sangre de Cristos. Land along the creek, occupied by a church and cemetery, was homesteaded by the Wales family in the 1870s.

A Sunday school group picnicking along Rito Alto proposed the idyllic spot would make a fine location for a church. The enthusiastic gathering loved the idea and immediately raised over $600 toward the cost of building the tidy, plain, clapboard church. The patriarch of the

Church and graveyard at Rito Alto.

Wales clan, **Harrison Grey "H.G." Otis Wales** (1812–1889), and his sons agreed to donate ten to twenty acres of rocky land, dotted with cottonwood and juniper trees, for the church and cemetery in 1888. "Father" Wales focused on selecting the cemetery site, as he presciently stated that "he expected to be the first to occupy it." He passed away on Christmas Day 1889, certain to be the inaugural interment. (Earlier-dated memorials were moved from nearby Cotton Creek.)

H.G. Wales of Massachusetts, moved sometime in the 1830s to Illinois, where he married Elizabeth Snell in 1839. At age fifty, though married with a house full of children, he joined the Eighty-Ninth Illinois Infantry as a Sergeant for the duration of the war. His oldest son, **Otis A. Wales** (1840–1914) joined the Seventeenth Illinois Infantry from 1861 to 1864. Son **Edwin M. Wales**, though only seventeen, mustered into the same company as his older brother. After his discharge, Edwin signed up for another two years, leaving the military in May 1866 at Baton Rouge, Louisiana. He was wounded at the Battle of Shilo and took five months to recover.

H.G. Wales lost his wife Elizabeth in 1867. After burying her, he, along with Otis and Edwin, headed to Colorado to begin their cattle ranch in the San Luis Valley. The Wales family farm produced a premium-quality butter appreciated well beyond the valley, receiving top honors at agriculture fairs in the state. The family raised exceptional purebred Shorthorn cattle, including a notably large and fine bull, "Walnut Chief." The bull's name may hark back to the period when they lived in Walnut Grove, Illinois.

Edwin traveled home to Illinois to marry **Martha "Mattie" O. Abernathy** (1845–1901) in June 1870. Returning to Colorado, he involved himself in Republican politics as a Saguache County delegate. He spent time on the county commission, some years in conjunction with John Lawrence. He joined the Colorado Cattle Growers' Association in 1886. That same year, he served on the Cotton Creek School District Board as the board sought bids to construct a larger schoolhouse. By 1888, his herd reached 450 head.

Edwin and Mattie moved to Salida around 1899. Edwin was working on the ranch near Rito Alto when Mattie took suddenly ill with pneumonia and died of heart failure. Having no idea his wife was even ill, Edwin took the news of her death hard. Her body was returned to Rito Alto for burial. Edwin remarried two years later and began spending winters in Arkansas. He later moved back to Illinois. Though he died and was buried there, he has a memorial (cenotaph) on the same headstone as his brother, Otis A. Wales, in the Rito Alto Cemetery.

CENOTAPHS

Cenotaphs are monuments for people who are either buried else-where, cremated and scattered, or sometimes missing entirely. The word, derived from the Greek, *kenotaphion* translates to "empty tomb." A true cenotaph looks like a mausoleum or burial chamber. Frequently cenotaphs are constructed to honor war dead. The term has come to be applied to any memorial marker placed somewhere other than over a grave. It can also refer to a monument that remains after a body has been exhumed and moved to another location.

GREAT SAND DUNES

South of Rito Alto is the Great Sand Dunes National Park, straddling the Saguache-Alamosa County line. Just outside the park entrance, reached via CO 150, is a private campground that surrounds a tiny burial ground (request permission to visit). Three men were buried there in February 1899 (though the modern headstones say 1895). Formally known as **Bowerman-Nelson-Reimer Cemetery**, it is colloquially called **Bad Booze Cemetery**.

According to the *Denver Press*, **James "Jim" Bowerman** (1859–1899) purchased wood alcohol from a pharmacist in Hooper, twenty miles west of the Blanca mining camp where the men worked. The pharmacist stated he properly marked the bottle and explained its usage to Bowerman, who said he wanted it for "scientific experiments." Back at camp, Bowerman and his friends mixed the alcohol with water and rock candy and began drinking. At least six men fell ill and three died, including Bowerman. There were no doctors in the camp and the ones summoned from Hooper arrived too late to save them. Bowerman was divorced, but had three children who survived him. His brother, **John Bowerman**, was one of the poisoned men who survived. John moved to Delta County, where he took up farming and coal mining, living to the age of eighty-six.

Another who died was **John A. "Jack" Rimer** (1860–1899), born in Ohio. He was formerly employed as a railroad conductor. The third dead miner was reported to be **John Anderson** (?–1899). His name is so common that there was another John Anderson who died in a Colorado avalanche at nearly the same time. Oddly, about a week after the deaths of the miners made national news, a Swedish-language newspaper in Minneapolis published a retraction stating that John Anderson had recovered from drinking the toxic beverage and only his two companions had died. Nothing supports this assertion, but it does suggest that Anderson had a connection to the Swedish diaspora in Minnesota.

It remains a mystery why Jim Bowerman concocted his deadly cocktail.

Jim Bowerman's grave in the Bad Booze Cemetery in a private campground near Great Sand Dunes National Park.

CHAPTER 2

CANYONS AND PLAINS

Southeastern Colorado has always been sparsely populated. The climate is arid. At first glance, it may seem to be an unrelieved rolling plain. However, the western boundary is the Sangre de Christo Mountain range and the twin mounts known as the Spanish Peaks. The peaks' Indian name of *Wa-hah-toya* means "breasts of the earth," and they have long been a navigational aid. The plains themselves are not flat or simply rolling. Various Arkansas River tributaries cut through soil and rock creating canyons that dissect the landscape.

After the Mexican War, and with the arrival of prospectors in 1859, the United States began making treaties with the Plains tribes. For a few years, there was a Cheyenne Arapaho reservation covering parts of present-day Elbert, Lincoln, Crowley, Kiowa, Otero, and Bent Counties.

In the 1860s, cattlemen arrived from Texas to fatten their herds on the native grasses. In the 1870s and 1880s, the railroad companies promoted land to easterners. Many came from places such as Chicago, filed claims, put up shanties, and used the residency time as a vacation away from the big city. Few finalized their claims, especially after drought years in the 1880s illustrated the folly of farming here.

Coal mining vitalized the economy around Trinidad and Walsenburg by then. The railroads brought in ore from surrounding mines; smelters and steel factories added to the growing City of Pueblo. Miners working for large corporations had a rough life. Low pay, doled out in company scrip, could be used only in company stores. Unionizing efforts waxed and waned over the years, each effort driving violence on both sides. This culminated in the Ludlow Massacre, which occurred near Trinidad in 1914. It was the last bloody labor conflict but far from the first. The 1890s and early 1900s saw union-organizing efforts, with little reward for the workers, resulting in bloodshed throughout the state.

LA VETA

Huerfano County had early Hispano settlers from New Mexico. The Huerfano and Cucharas Rivers (sometimes just seasonal creeks) arise in Huerfano County and flow northeast to the Arkansas River. **Col. John Mays Francisco** (1820–1902) and a French Canadian, **Henry Daigre** (1832–1902), built a plaza in the Cucharas River Valley in 1862, after purchasing a portion of the Vigil and St. Vrain land grant (about 1,700 acres). Daigre farmed and ranched the land, while Francisco pursued his business and political interests.

A plaza was a fortress-like construction of logs and adobe with one or two entrances. The interior had adjacent rooms with all windows and doors facing a central courtyard where livestock could be penned at night. La Veta grew around Francisco Plaza (aka Francisco Fort), which still stands, the last survivor of Colorado's old adobe forts. It houses the principal county museum. La Veta, Spanish for "the vein," may refer to a mineral vein in the area that settlers used to whitewash their walls. Alternately, it could mean the dykes that radiate from the Spanish Peaks.

The **La Veta Cemetery** at the end of East Grand Street holds the remains of John Francisco (who never married), Henry Daigre, and other pioneers. Daigre has a simple granite stone, engraved with the Masonic square-and-compass symbol. His second wife, **Alice Collins** (1850–1929), and daughter, **Eva (Daigre) Brennan** (1887–1967) are also laid to rest here.

Coincidentally, Daigre and Francisco, the one-time business partners and co-founders of La Veta, died just ten days apart in March 1902. Daigre came to the United States as a child, first settling at New Orleans. He came west working as a freighter, and volunteered as a soldier in Utah, which later took him to Fort Garland, where he met Francisco. He filled civic offices as needed, including county treasurer, judge, and mayor of La Veta. Silver mines developed in the Spanish Peaks, about ten miles from La Veta, and he invested in one of these in 1879.

Francisco's ties to Colorado date to 1839, when he made his first supply trip from Missouri to Santa Fe. His second trip was delayed many years due to his father's death, forcing him to run the family's Virginia plantation. He spent a short time in Wisconsin before returning to teamster work out west about 1848. He counted Kit Carson among his close friends, and like Carson, he

John M. Francisco's headstone in the La Veta Cemetery.

was well-versed in the rougher aspects of western life. But he was known for his southern gentleman deportment, perhaps leading to his honorific title of Colonel.

Francisco worked as sutler for Fort Massachusetts and later Fort Garland in Costilla County, and built the first house at the latter fort. With Daigre at the helm of his Cucharas Valley ranch, Francisco headed to Pueblo, where he had a substantial two-story house. In 1861, he was elected to the first territorial council (equivalent to today's state senate). That same year, along with Lafayette Head, he obtained a permit for a ferry crossing on the Rio Grande. Francisco, once settled on the ranch for good, did not care much for the growth of La Veta, nor for the arrival of the railroad, but he learned to tolerate the disappearance of wild, open spaces. Unlike his contemporary Head, Francisco's headstone is every bit as modest as Daigre's.

Andrew L. Francisco (1821–1899), John's brother, is buried in La Veta, along with his wife, **Ann Reid Hamilton** (1849–1928), who went by "Reid." Reid inherited Francisco Plaza after John Francisco's death. Reid's brother, **James Gillespie Hamilton Jr.** (1847–1918) and his wife, **Elizabeth Anna Sager** (1847–1894), are here, he with a small, flat-topped granite slab, she with an elaborately carved niche featuring Christ laboring under the weight of the cross he carries. The words "Love," "Life," and "Truth" adorn the niche surround.

The Hamiltons, Reid and her siblings, are true pioneering stock. Their parents originated in Virginia but settled in Westport, Missouri, now a suburb of Kansas City. The father, James Hamilton Sr., had a mercantile and freighted goods over the Santa Fe Trail. James Jr. and his brother, **William B. Hamilton** (buried in Pueblo, where he was the first mayor), brought a thousand head of cattle to Colorado in 1867 and set up a 640-acre ranch north of La Veta, fully fenced.

In 1875, they survived the devastating plague of Rocky Mountain locusts (a species that mysteriously went extinct by 1902). In addition to cattle, they raised award-winning horses and even a bison for meat. The ranch, conveniently located on the main road leading west over La Veta Pass, served as a way-station for travelers, and William ran the comfortable inn there. James Jr. and Anna were instrumental in bringing the Presbyterian Church to La Veta in 1881.

Another member of the Francisco family in La Veta is John and Andrew's sister, **Mary Murray Francisco** (1829–1893), and her husband, **Robert Burch Willis** (1834–1900). Robert Willis was born in New York and trained as a machinist. Soon after arriving in Colorado in 1858, he formed the Quartz Creek Mining District with men such as **William N. Byers** (who founded the *Rocky Mountain News*) and **Richard Sopris** (a Denver mayor).

Willis developed the Huerfano County Stock-growers' and Wool-growers' Association in the early 1870s, with an eye toward ending hostilities between the two groups. He and Mary had two daughters, but the second died shortly after birth in October 1870 and was buried in the private **Willis Plateau Cemetery**. Willis died in San Francisco at the home of his surviving daughter, living just long enough to see the birth of his granddaughter.

The Maxwell Land Grant

Unlike pre-colonization Spanish and Mexican land grants issued in southern Colorado, the Beaubien and Miranda grant covered an extensive portion of New Mexico that already had settlers. New Mexico (Mexico) governor Manuel Armijo summarily granted **Carlos (Charles) Beaubien** and **Guadalupe Miranda**'s 1841 petition with little justification. The grant, spanning close to two million acres within a nebulous boundary, wound up in the hands of Beaubien's son-in-law, **Lucien Maxwell**, and was thereafter known as the Maxwell Land Grant.

Spanish and Mexican land grants did not pass fee-simple ownership to the grantee; ownership remained with the crown (in Spain) or the Mexican government. The grantee was directed to use the land for commons and offer smaller parcels to individuals who would settle and work the land. Holding such grants was always subject to political whim. Most Mexican grants gave each grantee permission to claim roughly 48,000 acres within a designated boundary.

Takeover by the United States in 1848 created a situation whereby a grantee could apply for a patent, though these could take years to get, if ever. Part of the trouble stemmed from the volume of claims that overwhelmed the bureaucracy and courts. The Americans' lack of understanding of Spanish land law also caused problems. In addition, the Departments of the Interior and Justice, and their leaders, issued conflicting rulings over time.

The Supreme Court sided with the Maxwell Grant claimants, deeming all others—tribes and settlers—to be squatters on the land. Those occupying the land, particularly the Hispanos, felt they had earned their claim to the property they had developed and that the bulk of the grant was public domain. The grant itself should have encompassed only 96,000 acres to the two original grantees, they thought. Instead, the United States authorized an essentially new grant encompassing an area of nearly 1.8 million acres. The survey came into dispute, particularly the northern border, which lay in Las Animas County, Colorado.

Lucien Maxwell sold the grant to a consortium created by a trio of heavyweights in Colorado history: **George M. Chilcott** (an early US Senator from Colorado), **Jerome Chaffee** (a founder of Denver, and US Senator from Colorado), and **Charles F. Holly** (Colorado Territorial legislator and Supreme Court Justice). Their funding came from England and the Netherlands. They named the enterprise The Maxwell Land Grant and Railway Company. For one year, another well-known Coloradoan, **William Jackson Palmer** (see chapter 5, Colorado Springs), headed the company. They planned to construct railroads and sell land along the routes to settlers. First, they had to collect from the people already living on the grant, or evict them. In 1873, the company began suing the settlers, which was a costly proposition. The backlash, called the anti-grant movement, was fierce. In the end, the company went bankrupt due to its inability to pay the taxes on its vast holdings, and the land was seized to become public domain.

STONEWALL GAP

South of La Veta, over Cuchara Pass and into Las Animas County, is Stonewall Gap. This inviting valley at the headwaters of the Purgatoire River attracted settlers in the 1860s, both Hispano and Anglo.

The legend behind the river's name harks to an unauthorized Spanish expedition into southern Colorado in 1594 led by **Antonio Gutierrez de Humaña** and **Francisco Leyva De Bonilla**. They allegedly had a train of forty burros carrying gold—a treasure for which Humaña killed Bonilla. Indians then found the group and slaughtered Humaña and the rest, except one who escaped and returned to bury the bodies along this stream, with no priest to offer last rites. For that, it earned the name *El Rio de Las Animas en*

Purgatorio (River of Lost Souls in Purgatory). Some old maps show it as Las Animas River, not to be confused with the Animas River in southwestern Colorado. French trappers renamed it the Purgatoire. Locals have corrupted it to Picketwire.

A small slice of Las Animas County, including the Stonewall Valley, made up the northernmost section of the enormous Maxwell Land Grant. The anti-grant movement accelerated with a series of murders in New Mexico in the 1870s and spilled over to the Stonewall Valley, where nine homesteaders had filed their final papers with the US government as early as 1876. The government stunned them in 1881, suspending their patents, pending resolution of the grant's northern boundary. Some key participants in the controversy are buried in the **Stonewall Cemetery**.

The cemetery occupies a graded field on a bench northeast of Stonewall Gap, overlooking the Stonewall and Purgatoire Valleys. A two-track dirt road through private land heads north from the Highway of Legends National Scenic Byway (CO 12), dead-ending at the publicly accessible cemetery. The land was set aside upon the death of **Martha Jane Chaplin** (1857–1873). It holds casualties of the Stonewall War of 1888. Two men were killed outright in the conflict. Another was broken by legal battles. **Richard D. Russell** (1839–1888), one of the two men shot, was buried in a family plot, now fenced. Lying near Russell, in an unmarked grave, is **Rev. Oscar P. McMains** (1840–1899), who established himself as the "Agent of the Settlers" in the anti-grant movement. Another of the hold-out

Graves of Marion, Richard D., and Chas Clifford Russell with fenced enclosure in the Stonewall Cemetery.
AUTHOR'S COLLECTION

homesteaders, and McMains's friend, **Frank B. Chaplin** (1829–1905), has a grave here. He was young Martha's father.

Oscar Patrick McMains was born in Ohio. He joined the Methodist Episcopal (M.E.) Church in 1858 and was a minister in Illinois until he was assigned to a post in Black Hawk, Colorado, in 1864. Two years later, he organized the first M.E. Church of Loveland. He held posts throughout eastern Colorado. He spent years in Colfax County, New Mexico, home to the larger portion of the Maxwell Grant. He was a newspaperman as well as a minister and used both "pulpits" to promote the anti-grant cause. As agent for the homesteaders, he made many trips to Washington, D.C., to make their case, all to no avail. He was himself evicted from grant land in Colfax County.

The Dutch investors in the Maxwell Company took it over, and **Martinus P. Pels** came to America to oversee the grant and attempt to turn it into a colossal cattle ranch. He offered deals to squatters to purchase their livestock and improvements. After the Supreme Court affirmed the Maxwell Company's rights to the land in 1887, Pels negotiated terms with Russell and some of the other Stonewall homesteaders. Chaplin refused to make a deal. Soon, agitation by McMains, and swelling resolve in the New Mexico anti-grant faction, convinced Russell to renew his opposition. The company retaliated by suing him for cutting timber. By 1888, both sides in the conflict hoped that federal troops would settle things once and for all.

In August, Pels hired a Pinkerton detective to infiltrate the Stonewall opposition. Six sheriff's deputies arrived at the Stonewall Hotel (aka Pooler's Hotel) on August 24. Word went out and anti-granters rode from all points on the compass to converge on the hotel on August 25. The lead deputy and McMains, just arrived from New Mexico, exchanged harsh words in front of the hotel. Someone among the settlers fired a shot, and a gun battle ensued. Russell, pressed up against the front of the hotel, was mortally wounded by someone firing from inside, presumed to be a lawman. Russell died two days later. In addition, twenty-year-old **Rafael Valerio** in the settlers' group was shot in the head.

McMains and Chaplin were indicted but not arrested. Much sympathy in the region remained with the settlers in Stonewall, especially with Russell's wife, **Marion (Sloan) Russell** (1845–1936), and her seven children. But the situation continued to be tense after the shootout and the burning of the hotel and a nearby barn. Eventually, those on the north side of the Purgatoire River kept their land, but the others had to sell out or lease/purchase the land from the Maxwell Company. The legal battles contributed to McMains's failing health. He was buried in Stonewall in 1899.

TRINIDAD

Hispanos founded Trinidad at the site of a former camp along the Santa Fe Trail in the Purgatoire River Valley. The **Gutierrez family** built the first homes in 1859. Trinidad became the county seat when Las Animas County was created from Huerfano in 1866. In the 1870s, two railroads arrived: the Denver & Rio Grande stopped in nearby El Moro; the Atchison, Topeka & Santa Fe came directly into Trinidad. The railroads brought more Anglo settlers.

North of town, situated atop a prominent butte, is a unique burial. A natural opening in the solid rock holds the remains of pioneer **George Semmes Simpson** (1818–1885). Long before his death, Simpson had eyed the cavity—shaded by a whispering evergreen—and declared his wish to be buried there. The butte soon became known as **Simpson's Rest**, and his wish was granted in 1885. His daughter, **Juana "Jennie" Simpson Camp** (1856–1886) was buried with him a year later. Vandals destroyed their monument by 1899 and it had to be reconstructed. The Simpson monument spire is visible from downtown.

Simpson was an early-day adventurer who made his way to Bent's Fort on the Santa Fe Trail to learn the Indian trading business (see Bent's Old Fort section later in this chapter). Mountain men and trappers fascinated him, but by the 1840s their heyday was over. Simpson came from St. Louis, Missouri, a doctor's son, trained in the law, but he never went into the profession. His father made sure he never lacked for funds. Simpson saw an opportunity to open a trading post further west than Bent's Fort, setting up in 1842 at the confluence of the Arkansas River at Fountain Creek (the site of present-day Pueblo). His partners included traders such as **Robert Fisher**, **Mathew Kinkead**, and **Joseph B. Doyle**.

Mathew Kinkead's wife had daughters from an earlier marriage who married Simpson and Doyle (see Doyle Ranch section). Simpson and his wife, **Juanita Marie Suaso**, had the first white child born in the Colorado Rockies, Isabel G. Simpson. Their marriage had initially been solemnized by a notary public at Bent's Fort in 1842, but they traveled to Taos in 1844 to be married by a priest and to have Isabel baptized. The Simpsons lived for a time at Mora, New Mexico, and later the family settled in the Trinidad area.

Simpson was the Huerfano County clerk and recorder in 1862. In 1867, he became county clerk in Las Animas County, without having to move. In business, he operated a newsstand. He and Juanita, who was much loved in Trinidad, had at least nine children. Simpson wrote poetry and prose, typically publishing under a pseudonym in

Colorado newspapers. One of his poems features his favored resting place. Published after his death, it begins:

Lay me to rest on yon towering height,
Where the silent cloud-shadows glide,
Where solitude holds its slumberous reign,
Far away from the human tide.

Trinidad has a substantial **Catholic Cemetery**. Many early Anglo settlers adopted Catholicism, taking Hispano wives (not always in a formal sense). The main entrance to the cemetery is off East Main (CO 350). The oldest sections are in the southern part of the cemetery with the fewest headstones. The magnificent view to the south encompasses the iconic Fisher's Peak, a common motif on Trinidad headstones. The cemetery contains a designated baby section and a charity section.

Two well-known pioneers buried in the Catholic Cemetery are **Richens L. "Uncle Dick" Wootton** (1816–1893) and **Casimiro Barela** (1847–1920). Wootton was a legendary frontiersman whose exploits may have largely been in his own mind. However, he had an early connection to Bent's Fort, worked as a trapper, and roamed the southwest region with other well-known mountain men until settling near Trinidad. He operated a toll road over Raton Pass from 1865 to 1878 before selling out to the Atchison, Topeka & Santa Fe Railroad. He testified in favor of the Maxwell Land Company regarding the Stonewall conflict. Wootton is buried with two wives (out of his five

Grave of Senator Casimiro Barela in Trinidad's Catholic Cemetery.

total): **Mary Paulina Lujan** (1855–1935) shares a granite headstone with him; **Maria Dolores "Flora" LeFevre** (1828–1855) has a small marble stone nearby.

Barela is one of sixteen men honored with a stained-glass portrait in the Capitol dome in Denver. This is a fitting tribute to a man elected to so many terms in the state senate that he became known as the "Perpetual Senator." He began his political career at twenty-two and did much to further the interests of the Spanish-speaking citizens of Colorado. His grave is marked with a large, white limestone monument, topped with a cross, and engraved in Spanish, giving the dates he served as senator as 1871 to 1918.

The **Masonic Cemetery** is located north of the city, abutting hills dotted with piñon and juniper trees. This large cemetery occupies gently undulating terrain, also with a view of Fisher's Peak. It contains the **Congregation Aaron** Jewish section. The main entrance is from West North Street.

Jacob G. Beard (1828–1916) arrived in Colorado in 1862 and ran a flour mill for Joseph B. Doyle, the territory's most successful pioneer entrepreneur. Beard opened his own mill in Trinidad and sold it in 1868. He was born in Virginia and learned the milling trade in St. Louis. He relocated to Mora, New Mexico, to run Ceran St. Vrain's flour mill. He accompanied Kit Carson and other scouts to California in 1853 and worked at freighting for a short time before he returned to New Mexico, resumed the milling business, and married Isabel Simpson (1844–1921), George and Juanita's daughter. After some business reversals in Trinidad, Beard wound up in real estate and held political

Damaged headstone of Ernest Beard in Trinidad's Masonic Cemetery. His parents share the lot but do not have markers.

office. He and Isabel had just one child, a son named **Ernest Beard** (1880–1898), who died at eighteen. Jacob, Isabel, and Ernest share a lot in the Masonic Cemetery, but only Ernest's grave has a marker.

The Congregation Aaron section is named for the father of three Jaffa brothers who came to Trinidad in the early 1870s. The Jaffas first settled in the Pittsburgh area. **Henry** and **Solomon "Sol" Jaffa** (1849–1941) migrated to Trinidad about 1871 to run a mercantile business for a friend. They started their own store, Jaffa Brothers Trading Company, and older brother **Samuel "Sam" Jaffa** (1842–1909) joined them, arriving with his family about 1873. Sam and **Amelia (Sommer) Jaffa** (1845–1921) had six children, two of them buried in the Masonic Cemetery: **Dr. Perry Jaffa** (1867–1915) and **Joseph S. Jaffa** (1870–1930).

When the city incorporated in 1876, Sam Jaffa was elected president of the town council. Sam and brother Sol started the Independent Order of Odd Fellows chapter in Trinidad. They constructed an opera house at the corner of Main and Commercial Streets in 1882. The lower floor held commercial enterprises, and the 700-seat opera theater occupied the second story. Many community groups, including Congregation Aaron, met for a time in the opera house. The sandstone structure, built in the High Victorian Italianate style, later became the Trinidad Opera House, but ceased to function as a theater after Sam's death in 1909. It is on the National Register of Historic Places.

Amelia Jaffa co-founded the Ladies' Aid Society, San Rafael Hospital, and the Pioneer Society of Southern Colorado. All her surviving children gathered at her bedside when she died in Denver in 1921.

Congregation Aaron built a synagogue, Temple Aaron, which is the oldest continually used synagogue west of the Mississippi. This historic structure, built in a Moorish Revival style, is also on the historic register and is a Trinidad landmark. The building was designed by **Isaac Hamilton Rapp** (1854–1933), who is buried in the Masonic Cemetery. He is known as the creator of "Santa Fe style" architecture. His firm designed many historic buildings in Trinidad, southern Colorado, and New Mexico. They include several churches and schools, the Las Animas County Courthouse, the New Mexico Museum of Art, La Fonda Hotel in Santa Fe (subsequently altered by John Gaw Meem and Mary E.J. Colter), and the Chaves County Courthouse and New Mexico Military Institute in Roswell, New Mexico.

DOYLE RANCH

Because some Hispano residents lived in what became Pueblo County before 1861, there are some old abandoned cemeteries that have been documented, but little is known of those interred. Homesteads hold some remains of the families who established them. There are two burial grounds located on the ranch owned by Joseph Bainbridge Doyle (1817–1864): **Doyle Cemetery** (aka **White House Cemetery**) and the **Plaza Cemetery** (aka **Terecita's** or **Dogtown**), located on Pueblo County Road 321.

Doyle purchased roughly two thousand acres of the Vigil and St. Vrain land grant, located on the Huerfano River east of Pueblo. This area contained the largest farms in early territorial history. He had six hundred acres of corn in the early 1860s, and he produced a large wheat crop. His trading ventures during the gold rush made him extremely wealthy in a short time.

Doyle married **Maria de la Cruz Suaso** (1831–1865), sister of George Simpson's wife. He sat on the territorial legislature in early 1864 and died suddenly in March that year. He was just forty-six. His body was brought back to his ranch, and his tall-spired memorial rises in the center of the Doyle Cemetery, where he is buried with other family members. All the monuments are weathered and broken. Maria died the very next year, leaving many Doyle orphans. Maria's mother, **Maria Teresa "Teresita" (Sandoval) Suaso** (1811–1894), a formidable Colorado pioneer, took responsibility for the children.

The Doyle family grave markers in the Doyle Ranch Cemetery. They are engraved in Spanish.
PHOTOGRAPH BY MYRON WOOD. COURTESY OF SPECIAL COLLECTIONS, PIKES PEAK LIBRARY DISTRICT, 002-2985.

The ranch had a Hispano community known as Dogtown with an adobe church. Teresita had permission to live on this land until her death. Hers is one of the few known burials in the cemetery about a mile east of the Doyle Cemetery. There are no headstones remaining; only a concrete fountain, lacking a pedestal, marks the area. Teresita first married Manuel Suaso of Taos in the 1820s. The Suasos were among the founders of Mora, New Mexico, in 1835.

A white trader in the new community, Matthew Kinkead, caught Teresita's eye and she left her husband to live with Kinkead and they removed to the vicinity of Pueblo around 1841, then went to Hardscrabble (in present-day Fremont County) with Joseph Doyle and George Simpson. Either there or possibly at Bent's Fort, Teresita met trader Alexander Barclay and he became her third "husband." She was an entrepreneur and an emissary between the Hispano and Anglo cultures in southeastern Colorado. A fierce-tempered, uninhibited, and attractive woman, Teresita was undaunted by the harsh conditions of living in a wild landscape.

PUEBLO

Though not credited as the earliest permanent settlement in Colorado, various immigrants built forts and trading posts near the confluence of the Arkansas River and Fountain Creek, near the site of present-day Pueblo. Even the Zebulon Pike expedition built a shelter at this location in 1806. The early communities, sometimes known as Pueblo, featured a cultural mix, frequently American men married to Mexican women. A group of Mormons had a temporary encampment near Fort Pueblo from 1846 to 1848 before moving on to Salt Lake City.

In summer 1854, the Mouache Utes contracted a devastating plague of smallpox that decimated the group and which they blamed on contaminated goods from the government. It may have been retaliation that prompted their Christmas Eve attack that wiped out the entire Pueblo settlement. Modern-day Pueblo started in 1858. In the 1870s, Pueblo became an industrial center, first smelting ore, then producing steel, aided by coal mining.

The oldest cemetery in Pueblo is the **Pioneer Cemetery**, which incorporates the Masonic, Odd Fellows, and B'nai Jacob cemeteries. The main entrance is at the corner of Montezuma Road and Masonic Cemetery Road. The Masons purchased the first parcel to be used by their members and sold a portion to the Odd Fellows lodge. The city purchased some of the land for public burials and sold a section to the Hebrew Benevolent Union. Grave markers are sparse and scattered, but historical plaques offer stories for some of those buried here.

Mountain View Cemetery, located in the southwestern part of the city at the intersection of Northern Avenue and Beulah Avenue, was used for burials in the 1870s before the cemetery was formally established in 1881. A portion was sold to the Catholic Church. A substantial number of graves were never marked, being occupied by the indigent and state hospital patients. The layout is compact and dense with monuments typical of the late nineteenth century to modern times.

Roselawn Cemetery, the largest of these three, opened in 1891 as Riverview. Both Mountain View and Roselawn are located on properties purchased from Colorado Coal and Iron Co., a major industrial force in the region. Roselawn is located in southeastern Pueblo on Roselawn Road. The city's wealthy citizens selected large lots and set them with impressive family markers: towering obelisks, altar-style tombs, and even staircases and benches on artificial mounds, indicative of their elevated social status. These include the **Orman, Thatcher**, and **Moore** families. The park-like setting, historic plaques, and ornate carvings make this a fascinating cemetery to stroll.

Because the lives of the following pioneers intertwined, and families are split among the three cemeteries, a letter has been added after their death date to indicate which cemetery they are buried in (P=Pioneer, M=Mountain View, R=Roselawn).

The first permanent Pueblo residents arrived in fall 1858; they were migrants from St. Louis, including **Josiah F. "Si" Smith** (1829–1904-P). Si spent a decade beforehand working around the western territory. The St. Louis group set themselves up on the eastern bank of Fountain Creek and called it Fountain City. Si was there to stay. He dug the first acequia the following spring. In early 1860, he traveled home to Ohio to marry his sweetheart, **Leah Anna Badgely** (1838–1920-P?). Their daughter, **Hattie Smith** (1860–1921-M), arrived in December, the first white girl born in Pueblo.

Si Smith's brother, **Stephen S. "Steve" Smith** (1833–1922-M) came from Missouri a year after Si. Both young men assisted in forming Pueblo County. Si was appointed justice of the peace by the

Pueblo's prominent and wealthy families have large lots with massive monuments in Roselawn Cemetery.

governor when the area was still part of Kansas Territory. He filled that role off and on for decades. Many a Pueblo pioneer had their nuptials performed by Judge Smith, whose face sprouted a magnificent horseshoe mustache that gave him a deceptively stern appearance. He was an early county sheriff and a police magistrate in the 1880s. Si's primary occupation was raising livestock, and he was known for his fine stable of horses.

Steve became the first county clerk, and a full-size portrait of him hangs in the Pueblo County Courthouse. He built the first county courthouse, a single-story adobe building at the corner of Third and Santa Fe. Steve was briefly postmaster, but soon tired of it. Washington refused to respond to his resignation, so he packed up all the government property into a barrel and left it in the street. Fortunately, **Peter K. Dotson** (1823–1898-R) came along needing some stamps, and took it upon himself to do the job for a time.

Both Si and Steve prospected in the summer months and had mining interests around southern Colorado and as far south as Santa Fe. Steve spent most of his time prospecting when not otherwise employed. In the 1880s, he worked as a guard at the State Penitentiary in Cañon City. (Si Smith founded Cañon City.) Steve always returned to Pueblo. He stayed single and spent his later years with his nephews, Frank and Prentiss. **Frank J. Smith** (1868–1961-M) was a fireman and veteran of the Spanish-American War. When **Prentiss Smith** (1871–1964-M) was in his teens, his foot was crushed between two rail cars. **Dr. Pembroke Thombs** (1839–1902-R) had to amputate.

JOSIAH "SI" SMITH

Josiah "Si" Smith, one of the first permanent residents of Pueblo, was living in the county when the first census was taken. Smith was born September 2, 1829, in Dayton, Ohio, and came west in 1846. For the next ten years he lived in Wyoming, California and Oregon. He returned to St. Louis, Missouri, in 1856. That same year he was with a party which located at the mouth of the Fountain where the old trail from Santa Fe to the Laramie plains crossed the Arkansas. The next spring they planted crops; a party of disillusioned Missourians came along and tried to seize the crops to feed cattle. A pitched battle ensued and several Missourians were killed. Smith served as sheriff 1864-66, was a deputy U. S. Marshal, was named Justice of the Peace in 1856 and served from time to time in the following years. He was police judge in 1881. His occupation was given as stockraiser. He died October 22, 1904, at his home at 609 East Fifth Street.

Josiah F. Smith's grave lacks an engraved marker, but there is a historical plaque marking his burial site in the Pioneer Cemetery.

AUTHOR'S COLLECTION

Si went to Cincinnati to get his son a prosthesis. Prentiss worked in mining and did odd jobs for a time.

A local charity that Si Smith supported was the Ladies' Benevolent Union (LBU). Led by **Joanna (Swayze) Sperry** (1835–1904-R), the women ran a hospital for the indigent and a shelter for the homeless in Pueblo. They also provided burials in a small section of Pioneer Cemetery for their charges. In 1857, Sperry married an older widower with five children in Illinois. Indicative of their compassionate hearts, the Sperrys' farm was a station on the Underground Railroad in the war years. The family arrived in Pueblo in the late 1870s and Sperry

Joanna Swayze Sperry did many good works for the people of Pueblo and beyond.
PUBLIC DOMAIN

became the reading room librarian. In 1881, she founded the LBU. In addition to caring for the sick and homeless, the LBU placed babies and young children in homes for foster care or adoption and helped women who were in trouble with the law.

Sperry held an important position with the state branch of the Women's Christian Temperance Union, and the governor appointed her to represent Colorado at the National Conference on Charities and Corrections. She worked for the Colorado Humane Society (regarding people as well as animals) and the Red Cross. She served with Red Cross founder Clara Barton in Cuba, and she helped relocate Filipinos in Los Angeles during the Spanish-American War.

The city matrons, who held Sperry in high regard, threw surprise parties for her and gave her a very expensive and handsome chiming clock that she kept at the LBU home. This petite, kindly woman left a lasting impact on Pueblo, the State of Colorado, and beyond. She rests under a modest, polished granite headstone.

Rather than digging for gold, silver, or coal, a young man who arrived in Pueblo in 1878 found his fortune in the mercantile business. **(Cullen) Paul Wilson** (1855–1922-R) and his partner at Wilson & Shepard were known as the "princes" of mercantile. By 1889, Paul had been elevated to the title of "Merchant King of Pueblo." His emporium filled a three-story building on Santa Fe Avenue. With the news media's characteristic nineteenth-century hyperbole, he was said to have a lock on the wholesale dry goods business in southern and western Colorado, plus New Mexico and Arizona. He made regular buying trips to the east coast and had a discerning eye and superior negotiating skills.

In his first few years in Pueblo, the local gossip columnist pronounced Paul to be one of the city's finest eligible bachelors—a man popular with men and women alike. It was not long before **Hattie A. Kearney**, daughter of Civil War veteran **Nathaniel Kearney** (1833–1903-P), had him at the Presbyterian Church altar.

By the year of his marriage, Paul's father, **Robert C. Wilson** (1820–1897-R), and brothers had joined him in Colorado. Paul began his career in Terre Haute, Indiana, at the tender age of twelve. His younger brothers, **J. Speed Wilson** (1857–1897-R) and **W. Rush Wilson** (all the brothers went by their middle names), lacked Paul's single-minded business focus. They both took a wide variety of jobs in town. Rush eventually moved to the western part of the state.

Paul suffered a double blow in 1897. In June, Speed's body was found stranded on a sandbar in the Arkansas River in the downtown area. He had recently quit his job as night clerk at the post office, saying he would rather be dead than stuck in that line of work. He moved out of his regular lodgings and took at room at the Elks club about a week before his death, which was ruled a suicide. In August, Robert Wilson died at age seventy-seven. Both are buried in Roselawn with simple headstones.

In the early twentieth century, Paul purchased land in Delta County and moved his family there for over a decade. He suffered a fall from a horse and returned to Pueblo, but never fully recovered. He passed on in 1922 and rests in Roselawn under a simple granite marker with his shortened name, dates, and the Masonic symbol.

The Colorado State Insane Asylum

In 1879, the state legislature created an institution to house the state's mentally ill residents. Colorado's first US senator, **George M. Chilcott** (1828–1891), buried in the Pioneer Cemetery, donated forty acres in Pueblo, thus assuring the location for the Colorado State Insane Asylum (now Colorado Mental Health Institute). The Chilcott home housed male patients and a new single-story dwelling accommodated the women. Dr. Pembroke Thombs, local physician and county coroner, took directorship of the asylum.

Of the roughly 2,000 admissions from October 1879 to January 1899, 513 people died while institutionalized. Families claimed some of the deceased. Others appear to have been buried in pauper graves in nearby cemeteries, with costs being covered by the county (or, if possible, by the patient's home county). Two locations at the hospital also became burial grounds. These cemeteries are listed in the 1985 Colorado Cemetery Directory, including their precise locations. For unknown reasons, employees at the institute forgot about them.

During a 1992 construction project, excavators dug up 135 bodies. They found twenty more in 2000. The bones are now the responsibility of the State Archaeologist and permanently curated at Colorado State University in Fort Collins. None have been identified, and they may never be.

Many asylum patients were immigrants. Some suffered from alcohol abuse (and were typically released once sober) or late-stage syphilis. Epileptics could be confined here, as well as older people suffering from dementia who had no family to care for them. Head injuries, leading to erratic or dangerous behavior, often resulted in institutionalization. The hospital's first patient, a carpenter named **Miles Madison Millsap** (1830–1880), became a danger to his family after such an injury caused violent outbursts.

Within months of opening, the facility needed to be enlarged. Previously, some patients, including Millsap, had been sent out of state; the relocations resumed. Due to crowding in 1881, many people were left languishing in county jails instead of being cared for at the hospital.

Insanity trials and transportation to the asylum often made the news, as well as patient deaths. A disturbing number of these

(continued)

were attributed to the vague causes of exhaustion, paralysis, or paresis (incomplete paralysis), sometimes occurring within days of admittance. An example is a young man from Wisconsin who lived in Greeley, working as a laborer. **George W. Huett** (1856–1881) was adjudged insane on August 18, 1881, and admitted to the Pueblo hospital on August 25. Records describe his condition as "acute delerious mania" stemming from exposure and ill health. He was dead of "exhaustion" on September 1. It is possible he was claimed by his family for burial—or he may be among those stored in a university vault along with 154 others.

This plaque commemorates asylum inmates who were buried anonymously on State Hospital grounds from 1879 to 1899.
<small>Courtesy of Richard Guenther</small>

BENT'S OLD FORT

After Mexican Independence in 1821, the new Mexican government reversed the Spanish prohibition against trade with Americans. Where before adventurous traders attempting the journey to Santa Fe had been arrested, they were now welcomed. As a consequence, the Santa Fe Trail developed between Missouri and Santa Fe. In Colorado, it originally followed the Arkansas and Purgatoire Rivers, turning south to cross the Raton Mountains. This became known as the mountain route after a shorter version of the trail took a more direct southwest turn from central Kansas.

Brothers **Charles and William Bent** and **Ceran St. Vrain** formed a partnership to build a trading post on the north bank (American side) of the Arkansas River that became known as Bent's Old Fort. Construction of the adobe citadel, completed by 1835, covered nearly an acre plus outbuildings and corrals. The walls were fourteen feet high, two feet thick, and had only one opening. Cannon turrets provided protection from two corners.

St. Vrain made his home in Taos, while Charles Bent ran supply caravans and William Bent managed the trading post. Though other posts sprang up along the Arkansas River, along the South Platte to the north, and in western Colorado, none achieved the dominance of Bent's during the 1830s and 1840s. It was the earliest American stronghold in what became Colorado. Business decline and a cholera epidemic in 1849 spelled the end of an era, and William Bent blew up the fort, relocated eastward, and built a new one. A few years later, he sold it to the US government and it became Fort Lyon.

Edward Dorris has the only marked grave at the site of Bent's Old Fort, though roughly a dozen people are believed to be buried here. The reconstructed fort is in the background.

A reconstruction of the original fort is now a National Historic Site east of La Junta, just south of CO 194. After Bent destroyed his first fort, the Barlow and Sanderson stage line used the site as a stop. The fort has an adjacent cemetery containing as many as thirteen graves, only one marked with a headstone: **Edward Dorris** (1834–1865). His red stone monument is peaked and bears the epitaph:

EDWARD Thou Hast Gone to Rest
In This Far Country of the West
Brothers and Friends Mourn and Weep
Thou in this Tomb Dost Sweetly Sleep

Dorris was born in New York and reared in Michigan. He learned the carpentry trade and relocated to east-central Kansas Territory, where he obtained a quarter-section of government land in Osage County and worked in his trade. According to a plaque at the cemetery, Dorris was driving the Barlow and Sanderson stagecoach when he suffered either a heart attack or heat stroke and died east of the station.

HIGBEE

South of La Junta off CO 109 is the tiny community of Higbee. Higbee Valley Road leads to the **Higbee Cemetery**. Around 1864, **Uriel Higbee** and **Samuel T. Smith** founded this settlement along the lower Purgatoire (Picketwire) River, formerly known as Nine Mile

Bottom. The river meanders through a grassy plain dotted with cottonwood and bounded by sandstone canyon walls sprouting scattered piñon and juniper trees. The Richards, Lujan, and Lopez families, late of Trinidad, but previously from New Mexico, joined Higbee and Smith. Various marriages connected the families.

Another Trinidad couple settled at Nine Mile in 1866: **Jesse Nelson** (1825–1923) and his wife, **Susan Carson** (1830–1917). Susan was a niece of legendary frontiersman Kit Carson. The son she named **Kit Nelson** (1869–1909) committed suicide in Bisbee, Arizona, after being kicked in the head by a mule, which caused mental disruption. They brought him home to Higbee for burial. They are not the only people linking Higbee Cemetery to Kit Carson. Another violent act sent **Manuelita (Lujan) Richards** (1850–1891) to her early grave.

Fifteen-year-old Manuelita Lujan married twenty-eight-year-old **William "Billy" G. Richards** (1838–1921) in an elaborate ceremony in Trinidad in 1866. She then sold her fancy wedding dress to outfit her husband's and father's freighting business. They all moved to Nine Mile in 1868. Manuelita and Billy Richards began rearing their large family, the oldest daughter being **Guadalupe "Lupe" Richards**. Billy Richards was a long-time friend of Kit Carson (see the Boggsville section later in this chapter), so it is not surprising that Lupe married Kit's son, **Cristobal "Kit" Carson II**, in May 1890. Kit Jr., orphaned at a young age, had a reputation as a hot-headed troublemaker. Throughout his early adulthood, he was accused of theft and attempted murder on more than one occasion.

Manuelita and William "Billy" Richards' headstone in the Higbee Cemetery.

Lupe and Kit Jr.'s marriage traveled a turbulent path. Their daughter, Josefine, was born in October 1891. Not long after, Kit decamped for New Mexico, perhaps intending to settle there. Lupe stayed with her parents, along with the baby. In early December, Kit unexpectedly showed up at the Richards's home and accused his in-laws of turning his wife against him. The argument escalated. Kit drew his gun and shot Billy through both hips. Manuelita, in self-defense, reached for a nearby ax. Kit killed her with a bullet to the head.

The case came to trial nearly a year later and the jury convicted him of attempting to murder his father-in-law but not for killing Manuelita. Though sentenced to fourteen years in the penitentiary, his attorney managed to secure his freedom. Lupe remained with her husband and they had a long marriage and many children. Manuelita, though, did not live to see her many grandchildren.

Shortly before the shootings at the Richards home, their daughter **Rebecca Richards** (1872–1963) wed **Elfido Lopez** (1869–1946). Elfido's father, **Damacio Lopez**, settled Nine Mile Bottom along with the Richards and Lujan families. Damacio enticed a traveling priest to minister the sparse, isolated community in exchange for a place to build a small church, which became known as the **Dolores Mission**. The stone/adobe chapel lies in ruins, but there are still four legible, decoratively carved sandstone markers in the tiny graveyard. The mission, graveyard, and remnants of the long-gone Hispano community are now within the Comanche National Grassland and can be reached by the trail into Picketwire Canyon from the Withers Canyon trailhead.

The Dolores Mission is a crumbled ruin in Comanche National Grassland, but four headstones carved in sandstone remain in good condition.

BOGGSVILLE

Boggsville State Historic Site, two miles south of Las Animas in Bent County on CO 101, was a ranching community on the Purgatoire founded by **Thomas Boggs**, or more precisely his wife, **Rumalda Luna**, who acquired land from her uncle, Cornelio Vigil, a Mexican land grant holder. Boggsville served as the supply point along the Santa Fe Trail after Bent sold his new fort to the government. The legendary Kit Carson (1809–1868) and his wife, **Josefa Jaramillo** (1828–1868) had their final home here, after Carson's brief stint as commander of Fort Garland in the San Luis Valley.

Carson had ranch land on the Purgatoire River near Boggsville, and at Nine Mile Bottom, but lived in a modest home belonging to Boggs. Boggs and Carson were close as brothers. In this home, Josefa passed away on April 23, 1868, from complications after a birth. As rising spring runoff threatened to swamp the tiny house, the ailing General Carson was taken to nearby Fort Lyon, where he died on May 23 of an aneurysm. Both were buried in Boggsville, but were later removed to a family burial ground in Taos, New Mexico. A cenotaph now marks their original burial site.

Carson left his home state of Missouri at fourteen, joining a supply caravan on the Santa Fe Trail. At sixteen, the mountains summoned him to live as a trapper and guide. A serendipitous meeting with explorer John C. Frémont on a riverboat led directly to national fame. Carson was the subject of many dime novels as a popular western action hero. In 1854, while living in New Mexico, the government hired him as a Ute Indian Agent. He remained in the government's service from that time on. He led New Mexicans during the Civil War.

In probably his most controversial act during the war, he used extreme measures to relocate the Navajo people to Bosque Redondo at Fort Sumner. The Long Walk and four years of harsh living conditions at the Bosque killed thousands of Navajo. Though illiterate, Carson spoke many languages and he was an interpreter and facilitator for the various cultures inhabiting the southwestern states. In early 1868, he accompanied Ute leaders to several eastern cities during the ratification process for a treaty that he had negotiated with the Utes.

Across the highway from Boggsville is the **Las Animas Cemetery** where pioneers from southeastern Colorado have found their permanent rest. William Wells Bent (1809–1869) has a relatively modest monument, given his legendary status. The cemetery is also called the **Bent County Cemetery**. His monument is crowned by a Grecian urn carved in stone, with heart-shaped and other geometric designs encircling it. Cremation was typical in Ancient Greece; thus, the urn is simply a symbol of death itself. He shares the tall headstone with his daughter, **Mary E. (Bent) Moore** (1839–1878), who was half-Cheyenne by her mother, **Owl Woman**. One of Mary Moore's dearest friends was **Amache (Ochinee) Prowers** (1846–1905), buried nearby.

Amache (aka Amy) was the daughter of **Ochinee** or **Lone Bear** (called "One-Eye" by whites), a Southern Cheyenne headman whom the Army murdered at Sand Creek. Though Amache accepted most Victorian American cultural ways (aside from wearing a corset), she did not entirely abandon her native culture. She learned English readily and used it at home, speaking Cheyenne only with her tribe. She also spoke fluent Spanish, though she could not read or write. She prepared native food treats for her children, and gathered prairie plants for medicinal purposes and food.

When her family visited on their migration route, they set up their tipis near the Prowers's house in Boggsville, and Amache donned her hand-beaded native apparel. Like many women of Native and Hispano origin in southern Colorado, Amache played a vital role in bridging the various cultures that worked together to provide livelihoods for all. She became a devoted member of the Order of the Eastern Star, a Masonic auxiliary. She probably would have little appreciated having the nearby Japanese incarceration camp from World War II named for her.

Amache is buried with her husband **John Wesley Prowers** (1837–1884), though she remarried after his death. John Prowers came to Colorado in 1854 in the employ of an Indian Agent. They made Bent's New Fort their distribution point and provided government rations to the Arapaho and Cheyenne. John accepted a position with William Bent and worked the trade route. On his visits to the fort, he courted Amache with gifts to her father—a process that took years. John and Amache acquired land along the Arkansas River and brought in cattle. Gradually their herd transitioned from Shorthorn to Herefords, better suited to the sometimes-harsh winter climate. They moved to Boggsville in 1867. Their large home reflected Anglo, Hispano, and Cheyenne design features.

John's popularity among the Indians helped protect white settlers in the Arkansas Valley during the years of unrest in the 1860s
and early 1870s. Boggsville waned after 1873 when the Kansas Pacific
Railroad arrived at the newly created town of West Las Animas (now
Las Animas—the original town eventually relocated). John went into
the commission business to distribute goods from the railway to surrounding areas, a line of work that became redundant as the railroad
expanded. Ranching remained his source of pleasure and profit.

Neither John nor Amache died on Colorado soil, but both were
brought home to Las Animas for burial. Their graves are marked by
a monument carved of red granite with architectural pillars on each
corner, gables, and a Grecian urn on top.

The Bent and Prowers monuments are near each other in the southeast section of
the Las Animas Cemetery by Boggsville.
AUTHOR'S COLLECTION

CITIES OF THE DEAD

Small cemeteries that grow organically, due to immediate needs, often have no set layout. Planned cemeteries are constructed a bit like a town: platted and subdivided. They are first divided into sections and/or blocks, designated by letter, number, or both, usually bordered by roads on at least one side. In some cases, the sections, blocks, and streets have names. The blocks are subdivided into lots, sometimes sold in entirety for family burials. Each lot consists of a variable number of plots, which are used for individual burial (though sometimes they hold multiple cremains).

When seeking a particular burial at a medium-sized or larger cemetery, there is typically an office where you can obtain a map and then a listing for the gravesite giving the block, lot, and plot information. This beats wandering around, especially since a cemetery really can be like a city. It is not unusual for a cemetery to have more "inhabitants" than the community it serves. For example, the Las Animas Cemetery has nearly 7,000 interments, while the population of the town in 2020 was just 2,300 and shrinking.

CHAPTER 3

PIONEERING PLAINS

Colorado's eastern plains saw little of Americans prior to the Pikes Peak gold rush. The area north of the Arkansas River nominally belonged to the United States as part of the 1803 Louisiana Purchase. The Treaty of Fort Laramie in 1851 affirmed Native sovereignty on the plains and granted the federal government permission to establish roads and forts in Indian Territory. It assured safe passage to migrants heading to Oregon and California. The government promised payments and supplies to the tribes, but rarely delivered.

In the far northeastern corner, where the South Platte River slouched into Nebraska, a French scoundrel by the name of **Jules Beni** set up a trading post, visited on occasion by travelers on the Oregon Trail. In 1859, Beni's post was called Julesburg and Beni became a stationmaster for the Leavenworth City & Pikes Peak Express. Julesburg had several incarnations, based on the location of Army forts and railroads. In 1865, Cheyenne Dog Soldiers burned it to the ground. The present-day town was incorporated in 1886.

During the Colorado gold rush, other trails crossed these gradually rising and sear plains, following the major rivers such as the South Platte, the Republican, and notoriously, the "Starvation Trail" along the Smoky Hill River—a stream bed that vanished when no water flowed. These migrants cut down the cottonwood groves and hunted the wildlife, destroying essential resources on tribal land. Upon the creation of Colorado Territory in 1861, the government signed the Treaty of Fort Wise, which created a reservation for the Cheyenne and Arapaho on the eastern plains.

As commonly occurred in other parts of the country, the government acknowledged tribal property rights, and settlers did their best to ignore and circumvent these agreements, intent on having the land for themselves. Cattlemen imported herds to feed the mountain mining communities, exacerbating conflict between Anglos and Indians. While the Civil War stormed, Colorado's plains became the scene of a different battle, one that engendered horrific slaughter. Tales of Indians killing settlers incited mass hysteria in Denver and other cities on the plains. The massacre of peaceful Indians at Sand Creek in November 1864 escalated the war that ultimately led to all the Plains tribes being expelled from the state, removed to Oklahoma Territory and other places.

More cattlemen arrived in the 1870s to take advantage of the prairie grasses. The aridity of these eastern counties retarded development in the nineteenth century. In the mountains, many a mining camp became a ghost town, but out on the plains, the number of vanished communities boggles the mind: at least forty-five in Elbert County alone. Many consisted solely of a general store and post office. The population remains low today, though irrigation water from the South Platte and the Ogallala Aquifer allows for some cultivation. The existing towns rarely have more than a thousand inhabitants.

THE SLAUGHTER OF SETTLERS

On June 14, 1864, **Isaac Van Wormer**'s neighbors found the grisly remains of **Ellen (Decker) Hungate** (1836–1864) and her two daughters—infant **Florence** and toddler **Laura**—by their burned-out home on the Van Wormer ranch along Running Creek (aka Box Elder Creek). Ellen's husband, **Nathan W. Hungate** (1835–1864), attempted an escape from the murderous Indians responsible, but his corpse was found a mile away the next day. All had been scalped and mutilated. Their bodies were taken to Denver, thirty miles away, and put on public display. A memorial to the Hungates sits on the Elbert County Courthouse lawn on Comanche Avenue in Kiowa. The blossoming civilization in Colorado Territory had drawn the Hungates westward from their Iowa home. Their dreams of rearing their family in the shadow of the Rocky Mountains were shattered in one bloody day (see chapter 4, Denver, Fairmount Cemetery).

The Hungate murders fueled an uproar in Denver and hysteria whenever someone announced a potential Indian raid on the city. None ever occurred. Gov. John Evans rebuffed negotiations with the Plains tribes. He ordered peaceful Indians to separate themselves from hostile factions and report to military forts where they would be safe. He tasked the newly formed Third Colorado Cavalry with removing those deemed troublemakers. These actions set in motion the events at Sand Creek later in the year.

The Hungate memorial also honors people killed by Indians in August 1868 near Kiowa: **Louis Alama** (?–1868), **Joseph Bledsoe** (?–1868), and **Henrietta Dietemann** (1837–1868) and her son **John Dietemann** (1863–1868). The Dietemanns, along with others from their farm, fled from Cheyenne and Arapaho who had been stealing horses. The group left Comanche Creek heading toward neighbors ten miles away on the Middle Kiowa. They made it about four miles before coming across Indians who fired on them. Henrietta could not keep up and was overtaken and shot in the chest with a pistol. John pulled away from the others and ran to her. The Indians peppered him with arrows, then broke his neck. Henrietta's husband was returning from a supply run to Denver when he heard about the deaths. He buried his loved ones in Mount Olivet Cemetery in Wheat Ridge. Though not named on the memorial, Indians killed others in the area in that period.

ERECTED BY
PIONEER WOMEN OF COLORADO
1939 A. D.
IN MEMORY OF PIONEERS
MASSACRED BY INDIANS
1864 A. D.
HUNGATE
NATHAN W. AND ELLEN
AND CHILDREN
LAURA V.
FLORENCE V.
1868 A. D.
DIETEMANN
HENRIETTA
AND SON
JOHN
LOUIS ALAMA
JOSEPH BLEDSOE

This memorial to settlers killed by Native Americans sits on the Elbert County courthouse lawn in Kiowa.

The counties closest to the Front Range, particularly Elbert, did have timber that was cut to supply lumber to the mushrooming City of Denver; little trace of it remains today. After the Indian Wars of the 1860s and 1870s, and railroad construction in the early 1880s, homesteaders finally claimed their 160 acres. As a result, few cemeteries existed before the 1880s, though there are an unknown number of unmarked burials along the gold rush routes.

BIJOU BASIN

Given its proximity to Denver, and its favorable location on the Palmer Divide (the division between the South Platte and Arkansas watersheds), Elbert County has fared well amongst the plains counties. The divide's higher elevation receives more rainfall and the county contains more streams than its eastern neighbors. The Big Sandy Creek arises on the south side of the divide in El Paso County and flows northeast through Elbert County before turning southeast to the Arkansas River in Prowers County just before the Arkansas flows out of the state. Three of the north divide creeks flow through Bijou Basin, an area that saw settlement as early as 1860. The streams did not supply irrigation water but were sufficient for livestock and domestic use.

The **Bijou Basin Cemetery**, on a private ranch, has about twenty remaining markers that are legible, and there are remnants of old wooden markers. The earliest marker dates to 1868, that of **William Griffith Matthew** (1841–1868). Though there is no legible marker, there is likely another grave nearby belonging to **William C. McLain** (1835–1868). Both young men's bodies were found on the divide after a severe winter storm. They became lost in a whiteout and succumbed to exposure, a common danger on the prairie.

The most recent burial is that of **Charles A. Mathews** (1857–1957). He ranched in the basin by 1874 and married **Mary Schillinger** in 1884. Mathews worked as the county surveyor at various times and as a land appraiser for the Union Pacific Railroad, always managing his ranch as well. When he died in San Diego, California, at the age of 100, his remains were shipped back to the basin to be buried with his children. His obituary touts his claim to witnessing Abraham Lincoln's funeral at age eight. He left many descendants in addition to his widow, Mary. She is buried in Colorado Springs. Many basin ranch families had residences there for the convenience of sending their children to school and for comfort in the winter months.

A nearly buried memorial stone honors **William Liptrap** (1813–1888), another Elbert County pioneer. Liptrap was born in Cabell County, (West) Virginia, where he married **Sarah Davis** in 1841. The couple migrated westward with stops in Illinois and Missouri before settling in Atchison County, Kansas, by 1855. William did some traveling as far as California and some freighting business before partnering in a ranch near Franktown (Douglas County). He and son Leander then purchased land in Elbert County along Comanche Creek, east of Kiowa. They expanded it into a large holding, primarily for cattle.

Years after the Cheyenne and Arapaho had been moved to Indian Territory (Oklahoma), about 150 Cheyenne roamed back to Colorado in 1873. After reaching Fort Lyon, the Army directed them to leave the state. They later circled around the fort and headed up toward Bijou Basin. The band was led by **Spotted Horse**, who gave conflicting stories about his purpose. He claimed to want revenge for the killing of his father at Sand Creek in 1864. In addition, he said they were preparing to have a confrontation with the Utes. The Cheyenne killed many cattle, sheep, and chickens, but did not threaten to kill any settlers.

Some of them arrived at the Liptrap ranch, and Sarah was obligated to spend the day and all their provisions cooking meals for Spotted Horse's men. When the Indians left, the Liptraps fled to a neighboring ranch. An alarm went out to Denver and Colorado Springs, and men began arriving to ward off any attacks. The assembly agreed to avoid bloodshed, but insisted the Indians must leave. Though the Indians were chased around the plains and hills, and occasionally the pursuers parleyed with their leaders, horse theft and livestock depredation continued for a day or two. Finally, the warriors were persuaded to leave and no human casualties occurred. Sarah and William returned to their ranch, where they resided until their deaths. Though William is buried in the Bijou Basin Cemetery, Sarah was buried on their property.

Caleb Charman (1829–1874), born in Worcestershire, England, immigrated to Philadelphia, where he married **Anna Critch**, also a native of England. Around 1866, Caleb moved out to Colorado without his family. He settled in Elbert County, where he worked at Gomer's sawmill, one of the earliest and most important businesses in the county. He also had a lumber company with a partner.

Family legend says his daughter Emma was sent out from Philadelphia to keep her from marrying a man her mother disapproved of. Caleb made arrangements for Anna and their other children to come to Colorado. Around that time, he took Emma and some friends on a three-week pleasure trip to the mountains. On their way back to Gomer's mill, two miles from home, a bolt of lightning struck and killed him. Many others in his party, including women and children were stunned by the strike, and Caleb's mule was killed. Emma lost her sight in one eye. Caleb's family followed through on their plans to move to Colorado, where they bid farewell by the fresh grave of the husband and father taken too soon.

ELBERT

The town of Elbert existed in some form as early as 1860 about eight miles southwest of its current location. It moved around until the railroad arrived in 1884. The **Elbert Cemetery** is located roughly a half mile north of town on the west side of Elbert Road. The site rolls over prairie hills.

After her father's death, **Emma Louis Charman** (1854–1932) fell in love with an employee at Gomer's mill, **Alexander "Alex" Brazelton** (1843–1938). They are buried together in this cemetery. Emma's widowed mother, Anna Critch Charman (1826–1913), later married Alexander's uncle, **Claborn Brazelton**, in Kiowa. They moved away to Iowa, but Anna returned to Elbert County to live with another daughter, **Clara V. (Charman) Hobbs** (1850–1916), after Claborn's death in 1906. Anna died in Elbert in 1913 and shares a headstone with Clara there.

Entrance to the Elbert Cemetery.

Alex Brazelton came to Colorado in the early 1860s, lured by gold, and driven by an abusive father. He was a tall, fair-haired man who attributed his longevity to his sobriety. He spent some time in the mining regions but became disenchanted and turned to ranching on the Palmer Divide. His brother **Jacob Brazelton** (1849–1916) joined him about 1879. They brought their suffering younger sister, **Anna Brazelton** (1857–1881), to Colorado, but her health had already been compromised and she was laid to rest in the local cemetery. Alex's descendants say that Indians loved to wrestle the big man and cheered when he threw his Indian competitor. Late in life, Alex and Emma went to live with daughter **Anna (Brazelton) Watts** (1875–1939) in Monument, where Emma died in 1932. Alex died at the home of daughter **Clara (Brazelton) Elsner** (1886–1986) in 1938. The ranch was sold after flooding in 1935, but the Brazelton home still stands and is occupied. All of Alex and Emma's children, except **Ida May (Brazelton) Epler**, are buried with them in Elbert. Ida's husband sold their Elbert burial plots, much to her dismay. She is buried in Boulder.

Also buried in Elbert is **Judge George C. Fahrion** (1836–1909), a native of Stuttgart, Germany, who immigrated at seventeen and came to Colorado in 1860. He spent thirty-seven years on the bench in Elbert County. Fahrion served in the First Colorado Volunteer Infantry from 1861 to 1864, mostly in New Mexico campaigns. He married **Elizabeth Swena** (1849–1921) in 1865. Judge Fahrion homesteaded about two miles north of Kiowa. He was among the party that found the Dietemanns' bodies and took them to Denver. The judge himself had been wounded by Indians the year before.

Elizabeth was born in Illinois and came to Colorado with her parents and many siblings. One of her sisters, **Minerva "Minnie" Swena** (1840–1876), published poetry in the *Rocky Mountain News* in 1860. She married another Elbert County pioneer, **George Aux** (1838–1893). Not to be outdone, another sister, **Helen (Swena) Thomas** published her poetry in the *News* in 1861. Some of these poems were memorials for friends or the children of friends.

Judge Fahrion was fair-minded and likely to arbitrate cases rather than involving lawyers and court costs. A Democrat in a Republican County, he always won re-election. Though a county judge, he had a statewide reputation. He and Elizabeth's memberships included the national organizations Grand Army of the Republic (GAR) and the

Woman's Relief Corps. Fahrion's health declined sharply in September 1909 and he died that December, when pneumonia set in, at age seventy-seven. Elizabeth continued to reside on the ranch with her youngest son, Paul, who was responsible for running the operation. She was buried beside her husband in November 1921.

George and Minnie Aux and their children have one of the larger monuments in the Elbert Cemetery. George Aux was of Pennsylvania German extraction, blond and attractive. He arrived in Colorado in May 1859. While soldiering in the First Colorado Volunteer Infantry in 1861, he married Minnie at Camp Weld. He and other family members obtained land north of Elbert on Kiowa Creek in 1868. That same year, his home became the refuge for the families fleeing the Indian raid in Bijou Basin on a late August night. "Soon after daylight the company were invited to a sumptuous breakfast, prepared by the generous Mr. Aux and his estimable wife."

As a cattleman, Aux belonged to the Douglas County Stock-Growers Association. He raised Hambletonian horses and had a livery stable in Colorado Springs. When Elbert County split from Douglas in 1874, he was appointed to the county commission. Both Auxes helped organize the Kiowa Grange in April 1874. Minnie taught in the Elbert school district. The lovely young poet suffered heartbreak when her first son, **Ora Aux** (1866–1873), died at seven. When she gave birth in January 1876, the labor led to her death at just thirty-five. The child she bore died a day or two later. Aux dug a third grave a few months later when son **Roy Aux** (1874–1876) died at age two. It took nearly two years before the grieving husband and father could bring himself to remarry.

George and Minerva Aux headstone in the Elbert Cemetery.

Infant Epitaphs

Though children's deaths were a common occurrence, each one tore the fabric of the family. The monuments erected on these tiny graves testify to the grief of those left behind. The following is a collection of epitaphs from some of those silent reminders of lives barely begun before they ended.

Tis a little grave, but oh! have a care,
for many hopes are buried there,
How much of light how much of pleasure,
is buried with our little treasure.

—Chester T. Auter, Aspen Grove Cemetery, Aspen, Pitkin

Budded on earth
To Bloom in Heaven

—Inf. Son of J.O. Davis, Cedar Hill Cemetery, Ouray

Our Darlings
Safe, safe at home

—Paul L., Catherine M., and Robert E. Sophy, Cedar Hill Cemetery, Ouray

Our darling one hath
gone before,
To greet us on the
Blissful shore.

—Ella Ruth Kettle, Dallas Park Cemetery, Ridgway, Ouray

Happy infant, early
blest,
Rest in peaceful
slumber, rest.

—Stella Kettle, Dallas Park Cemetery, Ridgway, Ouray

(continued)

She like the rose bloomed a few days.
But now lies silent in the grave.
She will not return to us.
But we may go to her.

—Ester Abakile Moore, Doyleville Cemetery #2, Gunnison

Tho lost to sight
To memory dear

—Thomas Fleming, Pioneer Cemetery, Pueblo

He shall gather the lambs
with His arms and carry
them in His bosom

—Nora Altman, Pioneer Cemetery, Pueblo

And they shall be Mine saith the
Lord of hosts . . .
in that day when I make up My jewells,

—Little Willie, Alvarado Cemetery, Georgetown

Her sun has gone down
while it is yet day

—Mabel Rainey, Greenwood Cemetery, Red Cliff

A daughter dear from us has gone
A voice we loved is stilled
A place is vacant in our home
Which never can be filled

—Bertha Johnson, Craig Cemetery, Craig

If God has raised thy tiny form,
That last year went to sleep:
Why should He not for raising too,
Our snowdrop baby keep.

—Reese Cadwalader, Dumont Cemetery, Dumont

You are not dead to us
But as a bright star unseen.
We hold that you are ever near
Though death intrudes between.

—John Coburn Hooley and Baby Hooley, Dumont Cemetery

Not now but in the coming years,
It maybe in the better land
We'll read the meaning of our tears
And there sometime we'll understand.

—Eugene Trantham, South Routt Cemetery, Yampa

O, cease dear parents, cease your weeping,
Adore the spot where I am sleeping.

—Catherine Nitchen, Swallows Cemetery, Pueblo

Weep not father and mother for me
For I am in glory waiting for thee

—Maggie A. Nitchen, Swallows Cemetery, Pueblo

Far upon the mountain side
We lay our darling, our little pride.
Dear, yes dearer to us was he
Than earth and all its wealth could be.

—Thomas Whistler Anderson, Leadville City Cemetery

SAND CREEK MASSACRE NATIONAL HISTORIC SITE

As Colorado stumbled toward statehood, Plains tribes in eastern Colorado were aggrieved by broken promises and lack of resources on the reservation. Younger warriors, such as the Cheyenne Dog Soldiers, attacked settlers and stole livestock. Gov. John Evans received permission from the federal government to recruit a 100-day regiment to deal with the disturbances. In the summer of 1864, he placed the regiment under the command of **Col. John M. Chivington**, the hero of Glorietta Pass, a key Civil War battle in New Mexico. Farmers, merchants, and tradesmen, eager to defend settlers from Indian attacks, joined the regiment. It can be argued that many of them, including Chivington himself, wished to exterminate Indians altogether.

Maj. Edwin Wynkoop, commander at Fort Lyon, took leaders from the peaceful Cheyenne and Arapaho bands to Denver to meet with Governor Evans, but the effort yielded nothing. Wynkoop assured these headmen they would be safe camping at Sand Creek, on the northeast edge of the reservation. A new post commander, sympathetic to the Third Colorado Regiment, abruptly replaced Wynkoop, who had changed his views toward Indians from negative to sympathetic.

Nearing the end of their brief enlistment, and the butt of taunts in the press calling them the "Bloodless Third," the soldiers itched for action. On the night of November 28–29, roughly seven hundred troops marched forty miles from Fort Lyon to Sand Creek. They planned a surprise attack at dawn.

First, the troops captured a herd of Indian ponies, witnessed by two men from the camp. Some ponies escaped and alerted the people arising from their slumber. The headmen waved white flags, and **Black Kettle** of the Cheyenne also raised an American flag he had received from President Lincoln to ward off attack by showing his loyalty to the country. But Chivington and most of the invading US troops ignored these signs of truce. Some of the First Colorado Cavalry from

Fort Lyon refused to participate in the attack and later testified about the ensuing massacre.

The Army slew as many as 230 Indians, many of them women and children, in a brutal manner and later mutilated their bodies. **White Antelope**, a headmen, stood his ground, arms crossed, holding his peace flag, and was an early casualty. Black Kettle survived, as did his wife, **Ar-no-ho-wok (Medicine Woman Later)**, though she received eight gunshot wounds.

Today, visitors can follow a trail along the low bluff from where the Army fired its howitzers into the sleepy camp below on that chilly November morning. Interpretive signs along the way describe the events as they unfolded, moving from south to north as the nearly defenseless Indians fled from the attackers hoping to reach the Dog Soldiers' camp on the Smoky Hill River. Many hid in sand pits along the stream bank. Some were found and shot. Others endured the six-hour siege, then waited until nightfall to begin the long trek to the northeast. The land within the historic site is still grassy prairie with a line of cottonwood trees along Sand Creek. The meadowlarks and mourning doves provide a subtle soundtrack that belies the violent history of this now-peaceful place.

Tribal members buried the repatriated remains of seven victims of the Sand Creek Massacre in a specially prepared area at the **Sand Creek National Historic Site** in 2008. Two short sections of log fencing designate one corner of the new burial ground. Colored cloth strips tied to the rails flap in the breeze, including small medicine pouches strung together and wrapped around the poles.

This section of fencing marks a corner of a new burial ground established to hold the repatriated remains of Native Americans murdered at Sand Creek in 1864.
<small>AUTHOR'S COLLECTION</small>

EADS

Kiowa County was home primarily to Plains tribes in the 1860s. Some ranchers fattened their cattle on the open range until the railroads arrived and ushered in a homestead era in the 1880s to the early 1900s. The county was established in 1889, and the first county seat was Sheridan Lake, founded in 1877, where the **Sheridan Lake Cemetery** holds about a hundred burials.

The Missouri Pacific Railroad steamed across the plains from Kansas. West of Sheridan Lake a series of rail worker camps sprouted in alphabetical order: Arden, Brandon, Chivington, Diston, Eads, on up through letter K. The first county courthouse burned in 1900. In 1902, the county seat moved to Eads. Pioneer **Byard Hickman** (1841–1918) was a commissioner who helped get the new courthouse built. He is buried in the **Eads Cemetery**, along with many family members. The cemetery property once belonged to the Hickmans.

Byard Hickman did not arrive in Colorado until 1886, but due to the late development on the plains, he is considered a founding father in that region. Like many other pioneers, this was not his first stop on the trail west, but the last. He was born in Wetzel County, Virginia (now West Virginia), the youngest of six children whose father died when Byard was a few months old. He left home to make his way in the world at sixteen. At nineteen, he married **Eleanor Jane Johnson** (1843–1928). They relocated to Illinois, and he enlisted in the Union Army near the end of the war. Afterward, the Hickmans ranched in Iowa, where they lived for many years and accumulated 560 acres. This they sold to come to Kiowa County, obtaining homestead land west of Chivington.

The Hickmans had nine children, and several of their sons were part of the cowboy culture that is endemic to Colorado. **Anderson C. Hickman** (1861–1927), **Thomas "Ed" Hickman** (1866–1941), and **Coral A. Hickman** (1879–1930), all homesteaded land north of Chivington and west of Sand Creek in the early 1900s. They herded cattle on the open range until grain production became prominent. Anderson and Ed both married late in life (at forty-eight and fifty-seven, respectively), and had no children. Coral, the youngest son, had a life that reads like a true Wild West tale, though much of it took place in the twentieth century.

Coral arrived in Colorado when he was eight. He lived on the family homestead and grew up in the cowboy lifestyle. In 1903,

President Teddy Roosevelt came to Hugo (north in Lincoln County) around the time of the annual cattle round-up. The cow-punchers, including the Hickman brothers, put on a chuck-wagon dinner for the President. The Hickmans all had a chance to shake hands with him.

Coral married in 1907 to **Mamie Johnson**, and they had three children. He joined the county sheriff's department as a deputy in the late 1920s. On March 14, 1930, three men robbed the Manter (Kansas) State Bank and fled in their Ford automobile toward Colorado. The Kiowa County sheriff's department received word to be on the lookout. That afternoon, Deputy Hickman and his companion **Bill Mosher** went southeast of Eads on patrol, spied the getaway car, and gave chase at speeds up to seventy miles per hour. Near Eads, the fleeing vehicle stopped, the men got out, and acted like they were inspecting the tires. Coral pulled up and the bandits opened fire, wounding Mosher and riddling Coral with bullets, leaving him for dead on the road.

Not long after the shooting, Ed Hickman drove east toward Chivington, where he came upon what he thought was an auto accident and found his brother lying face down. As Ed rolled him over, Coral gasped, shifted his eyes, and breathed his last. The fugitives headed to Cheyenne Wells (Cheyenne County), where they wounded two more lawmen, then turned back east to Kansas. They were finally caught after an extensive manhunt in Stanton County, Kansas. Because they would not have faced capital punishment there, they were put on trial in Colorado. The State executed all three by hanging at the state penitentiary in Cañon City the following January. This was no ordinary gallows, nor were the hangings a public spectacle. Each man was led into a room and a noose placed around his neck. The rope went over a pulley and down behind a partition to a 524-pound weight. An unseen executioner released the weight, jerking the convict up to the ceiling.

Nine hundred people from around eastern Colorado attended Coral Hickman's funeral. He was laid to rest in the Eads Cemetery with his parents.

Coral A. and Mamie Hickman in Eads.
PUBLIC DOMAIN.

BURLINGTON

The Kit Carson County seat of Burlington, created in anticipation of the arrival of the Rock Island Railroad in 1887, is the largest of the still-existing communities strung along the I-70/US 24 corridor. This area leads the state in wheat production. Previously supporting only grazing cattle after Indian removal, permanent settlements shot up with the arrival of homesteaders in the 1880s. A terrible blizzard in 1886 killed most of the livestock. A big prairie fire in 1889 scorched additional pain on pioneer psyches.

The county's largest cemetery is **Fairview Cemetery**. Situated on the north edge of Burlington, the access is from 15th Street near County Road West. The grounds are trimly laid out with trees planted in straight rows around the perimeter and dividing the sections. A large granite marker for the Pugh family is carved to look as if the stonemason was called away and neglected to return to his task. The Masonic symbol is chiseled in the "unfinished" portion.

John J. Pugh (1857–1913) and his wife, **Jane E. Richards** (1864–1961) were county pioneers. They arrived in 1886 and settled near the Tuttle post office. Tuttle is a ghost town, which faded upon the death of John Pugh. The post office and surrounding ranch, which Pugh purchased, had belonged to a former Union Army surgeon from Maine, **Dr. Herman B. Tuttle** (who is buried in Denver). Pugh was sometimes the postmaster in this important way station, which was used by the Pony Express in 1861. As no timber existed anywhere in the vicinity, even horse corrals had to be made of sod and mud.

The Pugh family marker with Masonic symbol in Fairview Cemetery in Burlington. COURTESY OF DOYLE BREWER

A Welshman, Pugh migrated to the United States in 1879, first settling in Iowa. He spent two years working on a New Mexico ranch before returning to Iowa to marry Jane, whose parents were also Welsh immigrants. The Pughs moved to Colorado, where all twelve of their children were born (four boys died in infancy). John took an avid interest in county development and was active in the stock growers association and many fraternal groups in addition to the Masons. About a year and a half before his death, he and his oldest daughter, **Leona (Pugh) Stapp** (1886–1977), made a trip to Wales so he could visit his aging mother and other family. Leona fell in love with the home country. They returned to the ranch in February 1912. John died of a stroke in April 1913. His widow, Jane, moved to Denver with her younger children. By 1935 she had returned to Kit Carson County, residing in Stratton. Jane lived to age ninety-seven before being laid to rest next to John in Fairview in 1961. Seven of her children mourned, along with her many other Colorado descendants. She was a true pioneer mother.

Three months before John Pugh's death, a fellow pioneer from Wales was laid to rest in Fairview. **Elias G. Davis** (1841–1913) was among the original county commissioners. He alternated with John Pugh as postmaster in Tuttle. Elias and his wife **Leah Glass** (1847–1935) started their family in Missouri. Elias took preemption and tree claims on the south fork of the Republican River, north of Bethune, where he built a sod house. A year later, his family arrived in wagons, along with a dozen cattle and some hogs. Leah's widowed father, **John Glass** (1812–1892), and a cousin of the family, **John J. Davis** (1857–1943), came with them.

Elias added to his holdings until he had at least 450 acres. At first, the land had no grass to support his cattle, because the open-range herds had grazed it to nothing. He fenced the land and soon could feed his animals and grow hay for neighboring farms.

According to a son, the Davis children attended school only three months of the year, traveling six miles to an abandoned house before a proper sod school building replaced it. They went to Sunday school in various homes, as there was no church. A visiting preacher came around only a couple times a year. In 1889, Leah had the pleasure of bringing a daughter, **Annie**, into the world, after a string of six sons. Annie grew up in Tuttle and opened a store in Stratton that she ran prior to her marriage in 1911. One son, **Elias Jr.**, was the Kit Carson County sheriff for a couple years. Rolling ahead with the times, Elias Sr. became a Ford dealer at Burlington in 1912.

After Elias's death in 1913, Leah continued to live on the ranch and she acquired additional homestead acreage in 1919 in her own name. She eventually moved to Stratton and her sons worked the land. She died in Kirk, Yuma County, in 1935.

AKRON

Akron began as a railroad stop, platted in 1882. Homesteaders arrived around 1886. The town incorporated and was chosen as county seat for newly formed Washington County in 1887. The town's first mayor, **Horace Greeley "H.G." Pickett** (1844–1939), is buried in the **Akron Cemetery**, established in 1886. It is a formally laid out burial ground, with a scattering of trees, on the plains west of town on County Road BB.

Horace G. Pickett was born in 1844 in Peoria, Illinois, son of Thomas J. Pickett of Kentucky and Louisa Bailey, who died when Horace was about ten. Thomas Pickett was a personal friend and

Carte de visite showing Horace Greeley Pickett as a young man.

promoter of Abraham Lincoln. In August 1861, H.G. enlisted with the Thirty-seventh Illinois Infantry and attained the rank of principal musician and drum major. He mustered out in 1866 while posted in Houston, Texas. Along with his three brothers, he learned typesetting from their father, a news editor. All four Pickett sons went into the newspaper business.

After the war, the Pickett family moved to Kentucky for a time. According to H.G.'s daughters, he held a variety of jobs, including postal clerk, railroad worker, tax collector, and clerk in the Illinois legislature. While working in Springfield, he lived in the Lincoln homestead and met the newly appointed governor to Colorado Territory, **Col. John Long Routt**. Along with his father and brother, he moved to Nebraska in 1876 and returned to newspaper work. They began in Nebraska City, but H.G. relocated to Lincoln. It was there he met **Margaret "Maggie" Hennessy** (1856–1928), born in Canada to Irish immigrants.

By 1871, Maggie lived in Omaha, Nebraska, with her widowed mother and four sisters. They worked as domestics. Perhaps due to anti-Irish sentiments, Maggie assumed the surname "Henderson" and told her employer, an Omaha banker, that she was from Scotland. Maggie and H.G. married in 1882 in Kirwin, Kansas, where he was the junior editor at the *Kirwin Chief*. In 1884, he worked for the *Ashland Gazette* in Nebraska.

A land promoter from Colorado convinced several dozen families from Ashland to relocate to Akron. H.G. filed on a homestead and moved his family in 1886. Once the purchase requirements were satisfied, the family moved into town. H.G. edited the weekly *Akron*

Pioneer Press—the first paper in Washington County—and he purchased the business in 1896. His paper printed the public records for homesteaders and was a tireless booster for the county.

H.G. Pickett helped develop Washington County as Akron mayor, as District Court clerk, postmaster, and commander of the Grand Army of the Republic (GAR) Post. He was active in Republican politics and the Masonic Lodge as well. His family belonged to the Presbyterian Church, the first to be established in Akron. Maggie was probably a suffragist. She was vice-chair for the Republican Party in Washington County in 1910. Her daughter, **Mildred Pickett** (1892–1983), was deputy county treasurer in the 1920s.

H.G., after selling his paper and retiring in 1912, went on to become police magistrate and justice of the peace. Maggie Pickett was known to be a fine cook and served meals to boarders at their large home on Golden Street (now Ash). Renting out rooms supplied the Picketts with a retirement income. They didn't need to list the address when they advertised rooms; everyone knew the Pickett home. The community referred to H.G. as "Uncle H.G. Pickett." Even into his nineties, he kept up with the news and loved to follow sports.

The Picketts, all except the eldest daughter, Harriet, are buried together with a family monument and individual headstones, all in gray granite. They played large roles in the early history of Washington County and remained dedicated to their Colorado home for life.

Another pioneer interred at Akron is **George Ian Tuttle** (1847–1904), "The Cattle King of Eastern Colorado," a fellow Republican well-known to H.G. Pickett. Tuttle began ranching with a claim near

Akron in 1866, a time of open range. His son, **Frank Tuttle** (1868–1955), homesteaded land northeast of Akron. Knowing that the open range would come to an end, George bought up additional grazing land whenever he could. This wealthy cattle baron was president of the Stockman's Association of Colorado for two years. George was appointed and then elected to be the first Washington County sheriff when the county was formed from Weld in 1887. Frank assisted him as the under-sheriff during that time.

The Tuttle family had a close affiliation with another local pioneer family, the Irwins. Two Tuttle siblings married Irwin offspring. **Perry Tuttle** married **Alta Irwin**, and **Pearl Tuttle** (1882–1967) married **John H. Irwin** (1877–1902). The fencing of the open range, though George planned for it, did not ease conflicts between various livestock producers, exacerbated by falling cattle prices around the turn of the century. A range feud arose between the Tuttle-Irwin families and the Meenan ranch family. On December 27, 1902, John H. Irwin met **Joseph I. Meenan** on the highway from Akron that led to their ranches. A quarrel ensued and both opened fire. Both men suffered serious injuries, but Meenan sought medical help and survived. John Irwin lingered a few days before dying of his wounds. Meenan was acquitted by a coroner's jury, but he was a marked man as far as the Tuttle-Irwin men were concerned.

When Meenan dropped his guard one evening in early April 1903, he never made it home. His bullet-riddled body was found just a quarter-mile from his place the next day. Six men were held on inquiry into Meenan's death and later put on trial: George Tuttle,

Perry Tuttle, Elmer Shanks (George's nephew), David Irwin, Frank Irwin, and ranch hand Clinton Dansdill. The coroner's jury gave an equivocal verdict, and recommended the men ought to prove their innocence, contrary to constitutional law.

Almost exactly a year after the murder, George Tuttle, Perry Tuttle, and Elmer Shanks were convicted of first-degree murder after a thirty-day trial and sentenced to life in prison. George was released on bond pending appeal, but the younger men remained in custody. The Tuttle family steadily maintained George's innocence. However, many witnesses testified the three men had made death threats.

In September, George Tuttle was found dead in his ranch house under unusual circumstances. He had been deceased about two days. Initial news reports blamed asthma for his death; he was known to suffer violent attacks. Some suspected murder, however, and the coroner concluded the cause of death was a blow to the head. The jury agreed the injury to George's left temple resulted in his death, but they could not determine if it was intentionally inflicted or accidental. However, they unanimously stated that no evidence presented suggested murder or foul play.

The State Supreme Court remanded the Tuttle-Shanks murder case for retrial, but it appears the lower court did not pursue the matter, resulting in the release of Perry and Elmer. The feud and murders caused a deep rift in Washington County, as people sided with one faction or the other.

The Meenans buried Joseph (1866–1903) in the small **Curtis (Lutheran) Cemetery** about a mile north of his homestead land.

The family immigrated from Ireland in 1885, settled at Chicago, and worked in the meat-packing industry. Joseph and siblings drove a wagon west, lured by promotional literature about Washington County. Their mother, **Margaret (McMullen) Meenan** (1821–1907) joined them later, and she is buried near Joseph. All applied for homestead land. A few years before Joseph's murder, three of brother Richard's seven children died of diphtheria and were buried in the Curtis Cemetery. The children—**Joe** (1887–1900), **Frankie** (1896–1900), and **Etta Meenan** (1891–1900)—lie in unmarked graves. A recently installed marker indicates there are many other infant burials in the cemetery dating from its establishment in 1894 to 1919.

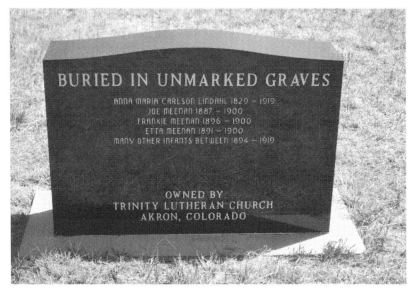

This marker memorializes the Meenan children and other children buried in the Curtis Cemetery.

Summit Springs

South of Sterling, at the east end of Logan County Road 2, is a locked gate and dirt road leading to the site of the **Battle of Summit Springs**, and the grave of **Susanna (Zigler) Daily Alderdice** (~1845–1869). This July 11, 1869, attack on **Tall Bull's** Cheyenne Dog Soldiers by **Maj. Gen. Eugene Carr's** Fifth US Cavalry marked the end of the Indian Wars in Colorado Territory after five years of conflict resulting from the Sand Creek Massacre. **William F. "Buffalo Bill" Cody**, who was a scout during this action, later glorified his role, and the battle itself, as the finale of his Wild West Show.

Cheyenne raids on white homesteads in Kansas led to Carr's action. In one raid, pregnant Susanna Alderdice, her infant daughter, and **Maria Weichel** were taken captive on May 30. The Indians killed nine settlers, including two of Susanna's children and Maria's husband. Almost miraculously, Susanna's son, **Willis Daily**, found four days later, survived with five arrows in his back, one lodged in his sternum. The captives eventually wound up at the Cheyenne village at Summit Springs, near the rain-swollen South Platte River. There, the Cheyenne strangled baby **Alice Alderdice** (1868–1869).

The day Carr's troops attacked the Summit Springs encampment, the US forces went undetected by the Cheyenne as they moved into three strategic positions within a half mile of the village. As the battle began, Tall Bull struck Susanna in the face with a tomahawk, killing her. Someone shot Marie Weichel, but she survived. The troops included fifty Pawnee scouts who played a central role in the battle against Tall Bull's warriors. Leader of the scouts, **Maj. Frank North**, killed Tall Bull. Of the nearly four hundred people in the village, fifty-two died. The US soldiers seized the Cheyenne's food and supplies. The warriors who escaped scattered into various bands, going north and south. The following day, Major North found Susanna's body. The troops buried her in the middle of the village. The actual burial site is unknown, but probably within a mile of the memorial erected in her memory. There are also memorials to the Cheyenne killed.

Generations later, **William Tallbull**, a descendant of Tall Bull, attempted to have artifacts that were taken from the battle site returned to the tribe, without success. His efforts, though, stimulated two important pieces of legislation: the National Museum of the American Indian Act (1989) and the Native Graves Protection and Repatriation Act (1990).

RESTORATIVE JUSTICE

Before the passage of the Native American Graves Protection and Repatriation Act (NAGPRA), indigenous burials had no protection. Archaeological teams routinely looted or excavated sacred sites. In the early days of this country, some eastern colonists placed their own dead in Native grave sites, asserting ownership over them. Even with this law, the possession of Native American remains and grave goods in university collections and museums creates tension between tribes and the archaeological community, though many bridges have been built and new cultural understanding developed. The law applies only to federal and tribal lands, and to organizations that accept federal funding. It requires any institution receiving federal funds to inventory their collections for indigenous remains, funerary objects, and related items and to work with tribal entities requesting repatriation for proper reburial.

At Mesa Verde National Park, for example, the process took countless hours of inventory preparation and consultation with eighteen tribes. Items had been excavated in the region for roughly a hundred years. In 2006, the Hopi of Arizona reburied a collection of five thousand physical remains and other objects in an undisclosed location, accompanied by traditional ceremonies.

Though NAGPRA does not pertain to foreign countries, the US government supports tribal requests for repatriation of ancestral remains and cultural items from foreign governments and institutions. In 2020, the Trump administration completed an agreement with Finland and the National Museum of Finland for the return of the remains of twenty individuals and twenty-eight grave objects taken from Mesa Verde by scholar **Gustaf Nordenskiöld** in 1891 and shipped to Stockholm, Sweden. Four southwestern tribes accepted the items and reinterred them in their ancestral homeland.

CHAPTER 4

DENVER AND CITIES OF THE ROCKIES

The nucleus that became the City of Denver was a pair of communities on opposite banks of Cherry Creek: Auraria and St. Charles. The founders of St. Charles lost their claim to **Gen. William Larimer**, who brought a governing delegation with him from Kansas and named the community for Kansas governor **James W. Denver**. Auraria and Denver officially merged in 1861, when Colorado became a territory. Denver grew to absorb many other communities lying east of the Rockies (now called the "Front Range"). Some early cemeteries no longer exist due to urban expansion.

The cities that hug the Front Range hold the bulk of the state's population, and thus the largest cemeteries. Some date to pioneer times. Many communities began as gold mining camps or supply points for the miners. The region climbs from less than 5,000 feet on the plains, west to the Mile-High City, then rises sharply to lofty Long's Peak at 14,255 feet elevation.

EVANS

The earliest Euro-American establishments in Weld County were trading forts built in the 1830s. The last of these, Fort St. Vrain (built by the Bent brothers and Ceran St. Vrain, and run by St. Vrain's younger brother, Marcellin), was the first county seat. That duty transferred to Latham in 1868. Latham was a stage stop on the Denver-Overland Trail, originally known as Cherokee City. Nothing remains of it today but a commemorative marker on private property east of the current county seat, Greeley.

Weld County is one of the original seventeen. Evans, created by the Denver Pacific Railroad in the late 1860s, was named for former Gov. John Evans who was instrumental in the railroad's founding. Evans was the county seat in 1870 and wrangled with Greeley over the position until it moved permanently to Greeley in 1877. Evans had another distinction in Weld County: it was the one "wet" town where people could buy alcohol.

The **Evans Cemetery** is situated just off US 34 at 11th Avenue, a square plot of eight acres with many mature trees. The most famous interment here is **Sgt. Charles H. Welch** (1845–1915), a Medal of Honor recipient for his heroism in the Indian Wars of 1876. His citation indicates he brought water to wounded men at the Battle of Little Big Horn. Welch has a military headstone and a family marker he shares with his wife, **Carrie Godfrey** (1864–1943).

Carrie was the daughter of pioneers **Holon Godfrey** (1812–1899) and **Matilda Richmond** (1823–1879). Holon Godfrey was a tall, bearded man of slender build and known as an eccentric who indulged his proficiency in picturesque profanity. He went to California during the gold rush, leaving his family in Grafton, Wisconsin. The Colorado rush sent him west again; he began his adventure near

Julesburg before settling a ranch northeast of Fort Morgan. He twice defended his stage stop when attacked by Indians, leading to his naming it Fort Wicked.

By 1863, Godfrey sent for his family, and Carrie was born at Fort Wicked the following year. Around 1869, Godfrey resettled his family in Weld County, in an area between La Salle and Evans then known as "Godfrey Bottoms." He participated in the economic and agricultural development of the county. He helped form the South Platte Ditch Co. and served as its president for a decade.

The last Godfrey child born was **Nettie Godfrey** (1866–1875), who lived less than nine years. She has a stone marker in the family plot at Evans Cemetery. Matilda was the next to be buried in 1879. Godfrey lived to the seasoned age of eighty-six before joining his wife and young daughter. The *Rocky Mountain News* published a sensational account of his life (giving an incorrect location for Fort Wicked) on February 19, 1899 with the subtitle, "Escaped from a stage coach when all others were killed by the savages—Siege of 'Fort Wicked' near Greeley by the Indians."

Margaret Louisa Wilson (1828–1873), an esteemed member of the community drew a large funeral procession upon her death in Evans in 1873. Her husband, **Andrew Calvin Todd,** joined the clergy of the Reformed Presbyterian Church, and Margaret was a devoted preacher's wife and mother. Todd formed the St. Louis Western Colony to attract pioneers from Illinois and western Missouri to settle in eastern Colorado. The first group arrived in Denver in early 1871 and soon relocated to Evans. The Todds established a church, a normal school, and the *Evans Journal* newspaper and had a civilizing effect on the rowdy young town. Just two years later, though, Margaret succumbed to an unspecified long-term ailment. Her son, **Thomas M. Todd**, later became mayor of Grand Junction.

A rural family cemetery is located east of Evans on a private ranch. Buried here is **Elbridge Gerry** (1818–1875), the county's first Anglo settler. The gravesite is about two miles north of Kuner near County Road 61. Gerry left his home in Massachusetts to explore the West in the 1830s as a trapper and trader. Sporting a ship tattoo, the 180-pound, stocky man may have been in the Navy or Merchant Marines in early life. He settled in Colorado along the South Platte and set up a ranch/trading post.

Elbridge Gerry and members of his family are interred in this small burial ground on a private ranch.
COURTESY OF MIKE WORTH

All Gerry's many wives were Indian women, some of them sisters. His facility with native tongues suited him to be an interpreter for Governor Evans when dealing with Arapaho and Cheyenne. In the summer of 1864, two Cheyenne informed Gerry of a planned raid on Denver and he rode off to warn the citizens in the middle of the night. In retaliation for thwarting the raid, this "Paul Revere of Colorado" suffered property loss to the Indians. Gerry built a large public house in Evans and one in Greeley, though he remained on his ranch. He died at age fifty-seven of an illness and was buried on his ranch along Crow Creek.

GREELEY

Weld County's oldest pioneer cemetery was that of the stage stop, **Latham** (sometimes called Fort Latham). The nine people buried there had to be moved due to construction of US 34 in 1926. After the demise of Julesburg, Latham became an important stop on the Overland Trail, being a good place to cross the South Platte. The cemetery was in use until 1873. The first burial appears to have been Swiss immigrant **Magdalena Simon** (1809–1861). Two of her grandchildren, infants by the surname **Plowhead** who died of unknown causes, were also buried at Latham. The Plowheads had a farm near the station, and several of the family's children were born there. The Latham burials now rest in an enclosure at Greeley's **Linn Grove Cemetery**, where they were re-interred in 2003.

Linn Grove, on Cedar Avenue, is a spacious cemetery established in 1874 that has close to two thousand burials dating prior to

1900. Two Colorado governors are buried here: **Benjamin Harrison Eaton** (1833–1904) and **George Alfred Carlson** (1876–1926). **Lt. Gov. Jared L. Brush** (1837–1918) has a modest marker, though both his wives, **Ada M. Maltbie** (1849–1877) and **Mary D. Sterling** (1848–1901) have tall, elaborate monuments.

Greeley founder **Nathan C. Meeker** (1817–1879) has a sizeable pink granite stone, shared with his wife, **Arvilla Delight Smith** (1815–1905). Meeker enlisted the endorsement and backing of his friend and employer, **Horace Greeley**, founder of the *New York Tribune*, to create a religious colony in Colorado. Along with **Robert A. Cameron** and **H.T. West**, Meeker formed the Union Colony Association in December 1869, drawing subscribers primarily from New York. They used the money to purchase land from the Denver Pacific Railroad along the Cache la Poudre River. They founded the Union Colony near the river's mouth in 1870, and named it for benefactor Greeley. Unlike Evans, Greeley permitted no saloons or liquor stores.

Meeker edited the *Greeley Tribune* and was president of the Union Colony until his death. He was fifty-three when he moved to Colorado. He began writing for newspapers at an early age, primarily poems and stories. He married Arvilla in Ohio in 1844. The couple ventured into commune living for several years, which did not last. Meeker turned to shopkeeping in Cleveland. While there, Meeker wrote for the *Cleveland Plain Dealer,* which attracted the notice of Greeley, who hired him to be a war correspondent and later the agricultural editor. Greeley helped Meeker promote the Colorado colony, which garnered three thousand responses. Meeker accepted seven hundred, though more than 10 percent dropped out. Many did not take well to the religious bent, and others did not favor temperance. Greeley remained dry until the 1970s.

In Colorado, Meeker took interest in the Indians' plight, though he knew nothing of their culture, and accepted the post of Indian Agent at the White River Agency in Rio Blanco County. He met his death there at the hands of Utes in 1879 (see chapter 8, Meeker Incident sidebar). Arvilla and her youngest daughter, **Josephine Meeker** (1857–1882), were taken captive and later released. Josephine

Nathan Meeker, founder of Greeley.
PUBLIC DOMAIN VIA WIKIMEDIA COMMONS

published her account of the incident that same year. Just a few years later, she died of pneumonia at age twenty-five. After Nathan Meeker's death, Arvilla remained in Greeley until shortly before her death in White Plains, New York. She was buried by her husband's side.

FORT COLLINS

Fort Collins grew along the Cache la Poudre River, starting out in 1864 as an Army camp called Camp Collins. Home to Colorado's first land-grant college, Colorado State University, it developed into a northern Colorado hub and is today the fourth-largest city in the state.

The **Grandview Cemetery** at Fort Collins holds the remains of many Larimer County pioneers. This is the third city cemetery; the first two no longer exist. About ten people were buried first at Camp Collins. The City of Fort Collins opened **Mountain Home Cemetery** in 1873 on a tract southeast of town. Municipal expansion put an end to using this cemetery around 1888, and bodies were gradually removed to Grandview, with final notice given to descendants in 1907. Whether any burials remained is unknown. For a time, the land was used as a playground.

The new cemetery occupied half of an eighty-acre parcel the city purchased from **Thomas Connolly** in 1887. Once a rural area west of town, it is now surrounded by urban growth and bounded on the south by a city park. The cemetery expanded to forty-five acres due to the 1918 flu epidemic. The main entrance is at the west end of West Mountain Avenue, a tree-lined boulevard. In the center of the cemetery, graves form a ring of concentric circles. Other sections are laid out in various geometric patterns around this core group. The grounds are verdant with mature trees and elegant landscaping.

The first civilian home built at Camp Collins belonged to **Lewis Stone** (1791–1866) and his legendary wife, **Elizabeth Hickok** (1801–1895), known as "**Auntie Stone**." Before their marriage in 1857, both were widowed with children, most grown by that time. The couple migrated from Minnesota in 1862 after Indian conflicts in that region, arriving in Denver in a wagon pulled by two cows, rather

Elizabeth Hickok "Auntie" Stone was the founding mother of Fort Collins.
FORT COLLINS MUSEUM OF DISCOVERY, H03002.

than oxen. They bought twelve lots, built a boarding house, and left it in the charge of one of Lewis's sons.

Lewis went into a mining concern with **Dr. T.M. Smith** who recommended them to Camp Collins. They arrived at the fort to run the officers' mess hall in the downstairs portion of their two-story house. Lewis died in 1866 and was laid to rest in the fort cemetery, which was about a half mile southwest of the post. A year after his death, the fort was decommissioned. The soldiers and others buried at the fort, likely including Lewis, were exhumed in 1874 and transferred to Mountain Home Cemetery. The bodies moved again to Grandview.

Widowed again at age sixty-four, Auntie Stone forged ahead as a pioneer businesswoman, becoming the "founding mother" of Fort Collins. She could be called a serial pioneer, having established homes and businesses alongside her husbands in several states. With the fort closed and dismantled, her boarding house, formerly the officer's mess, became the foundational building/business for the city to come. She formed a partnership with **Henry Clay Peterson**, and they opened a gristmill and brickyard, vital services for new communities. She brought her niece to live with her to start a school.

Stone was known for her positive attitude and generosity, as well as her boundless energy. Firmly in the temperance camp, she bribed young men to stay away from saloons by offering them a fine supper if they abstained for two months. A fixture at social occasions, even into her waning years, she could be found dominating the dance floor, toeing a waltz or quadrille. A grateful community threw her a lavish surprise party for her eighty-seventh birthday. She was also a suffragist and gleefully cast her first general election ballot the year before her death at ninety-four.

Stone's cabin has been preserved and can be visited at the Fort Collins Museum of Discovery. She shares a grave monument with her granddaughter, **Mary T. (Van Brunt) Havener** (1872–1891), who died of typhoid fever less than a year after her marriage to **John E. Havener**. Mary was a vivacious and popular young woman, mourned by many at her passing.

Among the Stones's neighbors near the fort, across the river and about a mile east, were **John G. Coy** (1834–1912) and his wife **Emily Adams** (1838–1921). John was from New York, born of English parents who died by the time he was ten. He went to live with an uncle in Illinois at age thirteen. Emily immigrated from England and grew up in Illinois. They married in Iowa and came out to Colorado on their wedding trip. John filed a homestead claim shortly after their arrival in August 1862.

At a pioneers' banquet in 1909, Emily related the journey she and John took to Colorado. The ongoing war caused them concern until they reached Kansas, since they traveled alone most of the way. The Indians they passed were peaceable, but bushwhackers held them up and stole their shotgun. Though their initial destination was California (John had gone west to the coast during the gold rush), they overwintered on the Cache la Poudre and found it to their liking. They settled on their farm and remained as Fort Collins pioneers. John filled two terms as county commissioner.

Their graves have a large family stone and individual headstones for them and some of their children. They had six children who survived childhood. The eldest, **Elizabeth Coy** (1865–1944), was in the first class to graduate from the university. She married a professor, **James W. Lawrence** (1858–1933). All but one of the Coy children are buried in Grandview.

LONGMONT

Southwest of Longmont on North 63rd Street between Nelson Road and Prospect Road is the Ryssby Swedish Lutheran Church and its graveyard, the **Ryssby Cemetery. Sven Johan Johnson** (1833–1905) was the leader of the first group to settle Ryssby in 1869, named for the community they came from in Sweden. They were drawn to America for the free land promised by the Homestead Act. For the first decade, though, they struggled to develop essential irrigation and lost crops to grasshoppers. Due to the difficulties in cultivating their farms, the men who came prior to bringing their families worked at other jobs. Some went to the mines at Black Hawk.

These religious immigrants formed a congregation early on, meeting first at the home of Sven and **Anna (Stina) Johnson** (1834–1896). Johnson had the only frame-built house in the early days, having a better financial cushion than his neighbors. **Hugo Anderson** donated three acres for the church and cemetery. **August Olander** donated sandstone from his homestead toward the construction of the church, which is listed on the National Register of Historic Places and is modeled on their church in Sweden.

The church no longer holds regular services, but the First Lutheran Church of Longmont maintains the building and uses it for weddings and two longstanding annual services: Midsummer Day and "Julatta" or Early Yule before Christmas. Parishioners dedicated the church and cemetery in 1882. Some earlier-dated burials were moved from family farms to the cemetery at that time.

Johnson worked as an agent for the White Star Line, a ship company that brought many Swedish immigrants to America. At his office in Longmont, he collected third-class fare from Swedish farmers and businessmen to bring young people over from Ryssby, Sweden, to help grow the community. He wrote them, "Tell your women-folk I will give them enough calico for a dress when they arrive in our midst." Girls worked as domestics and boys took jobs as laborers around the region.

The Johnsons are buried together with a lectern-style monument. The base gives a Biblical reference to 2 Timothy 4:7–8, which reads in part, "I have fought the good fight, I have finished the race, I have kept the faith. Now there is in store for me the crown of righteousness, which the Lord, the righteous Judge, will award to me on that day."

Another early settler here was **August Nelson** (1841–1915), who had a unique story about acquiring his farm from **C.J. Hoover** in 1873. Nelson quit the mines and moved to Ryssby. As he approached the Hoover farm, he noticed a crowd of men and assumed a farm sale was in progress. Rather, the men were vigilantes planning to hang Hoover's son for burning down a schoolhouse. The boy had set fire to the place after the headmaster horsewhipped him for something he had not done. The crowd agreed to release the teen if the family would leave within twenty-four hours. Nelson took the opportunity to buy Hoover out on the spot, an offer gratefully accepted. The property lies on the north side of what is now Nelson Road. He acquired another eighty acres on the adjoining south side of the road and developed it all into a productive and attractive ranch.

Nelson arrived in America in 1866. He wed **Clara Soderberg** (1849–1920) in Denver in 1877. They reared two daughters and four sons, who all continued to live and work in the area. The Nelsons erected a brick residence in 1883, said to be one of the finest homes in Boulder County. Befitting their social standing, the Nelsons have a large vault-style family monument. August and Clara rest side by side with individual markers, their graves outlined in concrete and planted with irises.

The August Nelson family of the Ryssby community at their large brick home on Nelson Road near Longmont.
PHOTOGRAPH COURTESY OF LONGMONT MUSEUM, 2014.014.002

BURIAL AND CREMATION

Laws regarding the disposition of your earthly remains in Colorado are not onerous. Within twenty-four hours of death, a body may either be embalmed or simply refrigerated. You do not need to buy a casket or vault, unless your chosen cemetery requires them. It is okay to build your own casket or purchase one online, if you wish. Some rural cemeteries permit natural burials, allowing a body to decompose into the earth, recycling the organic components. You can be buried on your private property, as long as your survivors register the site with the county within thirty days.

Colorado was the second state in the nation to legalize human composting, aka "natural reduction," in 2021. Commercial operators reduce your remains to soil, which can be used for planting (though not for human food), or donated to conservation efforts, such as for planting trees to revegetate riparian or burned areas. Using only natural means, the composting process can take three to four months. However, some operators may opt for using mechanical means to hasten the breakdown.

The term "cremation" no longer refers only to reducing a body to ash. Since 2011, it is legal in Colorado to use the process of alkaline hydrolysis to render a corpse to liquefied soft tissue and bone. The liquified portion (water, salts, and amino acids) is simply drained into the sewer system, and the pulverized bones are placed in a small container for the next of kin to bury. This process uses less energy and is considered more environmentally friendly than flame cremation. The process was patented by a farmer in 1888 to use dead livestock as fertilizer. It was first used on humans in 1993.

If your body is burned, though, your remains may be scattered nearly anywhere, though getting a permit for federal land, especially in National Parks, is a good idea. The ashes are not considered hazardous, though some people may think them unsightly if spread in certain places. Use good judgment and do not distribute them on private property without permission. If you wish to be scattered at sea, federal laws apply; it must be done beyond three nautical miles from shore and the EPA needs to be notified within thirty days. Inland waters may require a state permit. Do not improperly discard any non-compostable containers.

Denver

Not long after the 1858 gold strike on Cherry Creek, the need for a burial ground arose. Denver founder General Larimer set aside 320 acres for this purpose. Denver's first cemetery has gone by many names, partly because sections were leased to particular groups, notably the Hebrew section and the Catholic section, but also to fraternal groups, such as the Masons, and for veterans. The general public section was called **Mount Prospect** or **Prospect Hill**, and the first interment occurred in 1859. The federal government determined in 1872 that the cemetery squatted on federal land and sold it to the city. Denver renamed it **Denver City Cemetery** in 1873, but people continued to call it Prospect.

As other cemeteries opened in outlying areas, Prospect found itself the repository of the city's indigent population, and some lessees quit maintaining their sections. The city petitioned the US Congress to convert the land to a park, which was granted in 1890. Burials from Mount Prospect were removed to Riverside Cemetery to the north. However, some two thousand bodies remain under what is now Cheesman Park. The archdiocese purchased the Catholic section, called Calvary or **Mount Calvary**, using it until 1908. The bodies were gradually removed to Mount Olivet Cemetery in Wheat Ridge, a process completed by 1950. That land is now the Denver Botanical Gardens. The **Hebrew Burial Ground**, just east of Calvary, was returned to the city in 1923 and the bodies removed. It is now part of Congress Park.

Situated on the east bank of the South Platte, **Riverside Cemetery** is the oldest still-operating cemetery in Denver. Established in 1876, when Colorado became a state with Denver crowned the capital, the city's elite found the cottonwood riparian setting an idyllic resting spot for deceased loved ones. This cemetery is just northeast of the I-25 and I-70 interchange, near Commerce City in Adams County, and holds over sixty-seven thousand interments. Among them are many founders of the city and state. There are other pioneers among its multitudes, and in fact, this is also called **Pioneer Cemetery**. Riverside fell out of favor when Burlington Northern trains began rumbling by. The grounds and financial assets were transferred to the Fairmount Cemetery Association in 1900. Recently, the cemetery lost its hand-shake water rights, so it is no longer irrigated.

Denver founder and mayor Richard Sopris (1813–1893) lies here, along with fellow mayors **Richard Green Buckingham** (1816–1889), **Charles A. Cook** (?–1878), **Dr. William H. Sharpley** (1854–1928), **Amos Steck** (1822–1908), and **Baxter Stiles** (1825–1889). Four of Colorado's governors from territorial and early statehood days are **Samuel Hitt Elbert** (1833–1899), **Alexander Cameron Hunt** (1825–1894), and John Long Routt (1826–1907).

Colorado's second territorial governor, **John Evans** (1814–1897), left the state a mixed legacy. Born in Ohio, Evans received a medical degree at Cincinnati College. He developed a successful medical practice in Illinois, where he founded a hospital and Northwestern University. Active in establishing the Republican Party in that state, his friend Abraham Lincoln appointed him territorial governor in 1862, which brought him out west. Evans enhanced Denver by bringing in railroads from several directions. He founded Denver University. His political career ended abruptly three and a half years later, when the true nature of the Sand Creek Massacre became known.

Though a foe of slavery, Evans envisioned Native Americans confined to reservations, and killed if they left them. The arrival of miners and settlers during the gold rush made it clear that treaties had little value in preserving Native claims to territory. Denver's citizens expected retaliation by the Indians, and murders in rural areas stoked those fears. At first, they cheered Colonel Chivington's slaughter of Indians at Sand Creek. Recoloring this rosy shade of the event came about due to the testimony of another person interred at Riverside.

Capt. Silas S. Soule (1838–1865) commanded Company D of the First Colorado Cavalry at Sand Creek. His farm-fresh, freckled face belied the toughened soldier and idealist within. He participated with Major Wynkoop in the Smoky Hill peace talks, where he became acquainted with Black Kettle and other Cheyenne and Arapaho leaders. When he saw them flying the Union colors at Sand Creek as a sign of peace, he and his Lieutenant, **Joseph Cramer**, ordered their men not to participate in the massacre. He later testified against Colonel Chivington, knowing he might be signing his own death warrant.

Soule was born to an abolitionist couple in Maine. In the 1850s, the Soules were among the founding families of Lawrence, Kansas, and worked with John Brown to free enslaved people from Missouri. After Brown's capture at Harper's Ferry, Silas Soule attempted to free

Capt. Silas S. Soule wedding portrait
from April 1865.
Public domain via Wikimedia Commons

two of Brown's associates, feigning public drunkenness to get placed inside the jail.

In 1860, he and a brother headed to Colorado. He joined the First Colorado Regiment (later Cavalry) in 1862 and participated in the successful Union rout at Glorietta Pass in New Mexico. On April 1, 1865, twenty-six-year-old Soule married **Hersa A. Coberly** (1845–1879) in Denver. Three weeks later, assassins gunned him down outside his home. The killer(s) were never brought to justice. He was originally interred in Mount Prospect, and citizens erected a thirteen-foot monument over his grave. The monument did not migrate to Riverside with his remains, which are now marked with a veteran headstone. Hersa remarried to a miner, **Alfred E. Lea**, and she died at age thirty-four. She is also buried in Riverside.

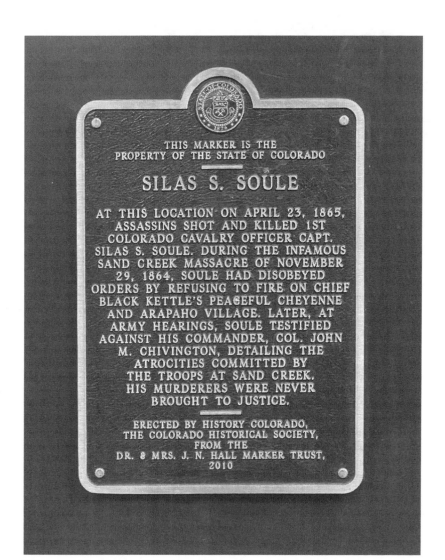

THIS MARKER IS THE
PROPERTY OF THE STATE OF COLORADO

SILAS S. SOULE

AT THIS LOCATION ON APRIL 23, 1865,
ASSASSINS SHOT AND KILLED 1ST
COLORADO CAVALRY OFFICER CAPT.
SILAS S. SOULE. DURING THE INFAMOUS
SAND CREEK MASSACRE OF NOVEMBER
29, 1864, SOULE HAD DISOBEYED
ORDERS BY REFUSING TO FIRE ON CHIEF
BLACK KETTLE'S PEACEFUL CHEYENNE
AND ARAPAHO VILLAGE. LATER, AT
ARMY HEARINGS, SOULE TESTIFIED
AGAINST HIS COMMANDER, COL. JOHN
M. CHIVINGTON, DETAILING THE
ATROCITIES COMMITTED BY
THE TROOPS AT SAND CREEK.
HIS MURDERERS WERE NEVER
BROUGHT TO JUSTICE.

ERECTED BY HISTORY COLORADO,
THE COLORADO HISTORICAL SOCIETY,
FROM THE
DR. & MRS. J. N. HALL MARKER TRUST,
2010

This memorial marker for Capt. Silas S. Soule is located near the scene of his death in downtown Denver close to the intersection of 15th Street and Arapahoe Street.
AUTHOR'S COLLECTION

Some Blacks who were early residents and successful entrepreneurs found their final rest here. They used their accumulated wealth and influence to help other Blacks rise from poverty by providing basic means for survival and education, or by setting an example. They settled a new territory where Blacks were ignored, at best, and greatly discriminated against. For most, the only business opportunities open to them were laundries, restaurants, or barber shops. Otherwise, they found work as low-wage laborers.

"Aunt" Clara Brown (1803–1885), born into slavery in Tennessee, grew up in Kentucky. She married and had at least five children, but that cruel institution tore the family apart. Upon gaining her freedom, she moved to Kansas, on a mission to locate members of her family. Hearing that a daughter might be in Colorado, she became a cook in a gold train heading for Pikes Peak. She opened a laundry in Central City and her home served as hotel, hospital, and church. She helped all who came to her, and still managed to accumulate ten thousand dollars in savings by 1865. In 1879, she contributed money and labor to the Great Migration of Blacks from the South after the end of Reconstruction. She brought many formerly enslaved people to Colorado from her trips east to find her family. She finally located a daughter in 1882, three years before her own death in 1885.

One person Clara assisted in 1860 was **Barney Ford** (1822–1902). Ford also began life enslaved, but he escaped after his owner rented him out as a waiter on a steamboat. He made his way to Chicago, where he met **Henry O. Wagoner** (1816–1901), a Frederick Douglass protégé, working at Douglass's newspaper. They became friends and business partners for life. Ford married Wagoner's sister-in-law, **Julia Lyons** (1827–1899). Going to Colorado, Ford could not get a ride on a stagecoach, so he joined a wagon train as barber. Once in the territory, he was denied a hotel room and turned to Clara Brown.

Ford and Wagoner opened many successful businesses in Denver and Cheyenne, Wyoming, notably two Inter-Ocean Hotels. In Colorado's first attempt to achieve statehood, the state constitution barred Black men from voting. Ford lobbied in Washington against the provision. A group of Blacks led by another Denver barber, **William Hardin**, greatly aided the cause. Hardin, son of a white man and a free Black woman, had a reputation as a firebrand orator. The statehood attempt failed, but Hardin is credited with ensuring the Colorado Constitution included suffrage for Blacks. Denver's whites ran Hardin out of town after he married a white woman; his burial site is unknown.

Ford and Wagoner used their profits to open adult education centers in the city. Ford, self-taught to read and write, knew the importance of these skills to his success in a white-dominated world. Both men, along with Hardin and others, were mentors and inspiration to **Lewis Price** (1849–1913), who arrived in Denver in 1870, after losing his laundry and real estate investments in Cheyenne. Formerly enslaved by Confederate General Sterling Price, Lewis Price hated his name and the way whites treated Blacks such as himself. Barely able to write, he used profits from a laundry business to found the *Denver Star,* the first Black newspaper west of the Mississippi. He hired literate Blacks to share his views on civil rights. The paper failed, and Price started over once more.

He turned again to real estate and used strategic maneuvers designed to intimidate whites—such as spreading rumors about putting a Black church in a white neighborhood—to leverage his money. He amassed a fortune to rival any white in the city, built a mansion on the edge of the Capitol Hill neighborhood, and hired white servants. Then he lost it all in the Silver Crash of 1893 and died a pauper. He had plenty of company. A well-known figure who lost it all in the crash was **Horace A.W. Tabor**, whose his ex-wife, **Augusta Pierce Tabor** (1833–1895), remained solvent. She, too, rests in Riverside.

Another Black woman buried in Riverside, in an unmarked grave in Section 10, is **Mary (Jackson) Randolph** (?–1901) of New York. In 1863, Mary married **William C. Randolph** (1827–1908) in Denver. It was not a happy union and they soon separated. Mrs. Mary Randolph, as she was ever after known, earned enough money to buy a number of lots in East Denver, which she later sold at a nice profit. Mary was a washerwoman living with her mother in Denver in the summer of 1870, but by December she had opened a boarding house/ catering business. In the early 1870s she opened a restaurant in Idaho Springs and then Georgetown, and bought mining claims in Clear Creek and Summit Counties.

Mary had a reputation as a large woman; the newspapers claimed she tipped the scales at three hundred pounds. There is no doubt of her stellar reputation in the food business—in 1874 she won the bid for the largest refreshment concession at the Denver Fair. In the 1880s, Mary moved to Montezuma, a town in Summit County, where she opened a restaurant and purchased a mine with an old friend, **Alexander Johnson**. By 1900, she had dementia and resided at the Arapahoe County poor farm. She died in the county hospital in the summer of 1901. Johnson saw to it that she was decently interred, though it took many years for him to be repaid from her scanty estate.

Suffragist **Elizabeth Piper Ensley** (1847–1919) did much to advance women's rights. The daughter of formerly enslaved parents, she grew up in Massachusetts among abolitionists and those fighting for equal rights for women and Blacks. She received advanced education in Europe for two years, became a teacher, and was active in political causes. She married **Newell Houston Ensley** (1852–1888). They moved for a time to Mississippi, where Newell contracted tuberculosis. They relocated to Denver in hopes of improving his health. Unfortunately, Newell was soon interred in a family lot in Riverside. Elizabeth became treasurer in the Non-Partisan Equal Suffrage Association, which pushed the legislature to put women's suffrage on the ballot in 1893. When the measure passed, Colorado became the first state to pass women's suffrage by popular vote. Elizabeth remained active in organizations geared toward integration and civil rights for Blacks, and political campaigns. She died shortly before the Nineteenth Amendment gave universal suffrage to women in the United States.

Chinese immigrants suffered extreme discrimination, perhaps worse than free Blacks. **Chin Lin Sou** (?–1915) fared better than most for a number of reasons: he was six-feet tall, spoke English, and wore western-style apparel. He immigrated to California in 1859 and mined gold for several years. He became a supervisor on the Central

Pacific Railroad construction project, helping bring additional "overseas Chinese" to America to work. Chin also worked for the Union Pacific, bringing their tracks up to federal standards (Chinese workers achieved better results). Working for the Denver Pacific, he helped construct the feeder to Denver from Cheyenne.

He lived for a time in Black Hawk, where Chinese could not file new mining claims and were forced to work abandoned claims. Despite these poor prospects, he amassed sixty thousand dollars. He brought his wife over from China, and their daughter **Lily**, born in Black Hawk in 1873, is believed to be the first Chinese American born in Colorado.

On Halloween night in 1880, Denver residents lynched an innocent Chinese man and torched much of Chinatown, located on Wazee between 14th and 17th Streets. How this impacted Chin is unknown, but he owned businesses in Denver and did much to aid this community. The riot, coupled with laws preventing Chinese from obtaining citizenship, no doubt led to the dramatic decrease in Denver's Chinese population.

Located on South Quebec Street, Denver's **Fairmount Cemetery** has over 175,000 interments in a park-like 285 acres. Many famous Colorado politicians, Medal of Honor recipients, and business tycoons are buried here. The latter group includes *Rocky Mountain News* founder William N. Byers (1831–1903) and **David Moffat** (1839–1911), railroad builder, mining magnate, department store owner (with Woolworth), and co-founder of Denver University with John Evans.

Chapel at Denver's Fairmount Cemetery.

Among the soldiers is Col. John M. Chivington (1821–1894) of Glorietta Pass fame and Sand Creek Massacre infamy. His granite headstone gives his military service and notes he was the first Grand Master of the Masons in Colorado in 1861. The Hungate family, whose murders at the hands of Arapaho in 1864 precipitated revenge on the Indians, were reburied here in Block 6 of the military section after Mount Calvary was decommissioned. The single-pillar monument lists all four family members: Nathan, Ellen, Laura, and Florence (see chapter 3, the Slaughter of Settlers sidebar).

One controversial political figure is **Joseph Henry Stuart** (1854–1910), the first Black man elected to the Colorado General Assembly in the 1890s, not long after he came to Colorado for health reasons. He was born in Barbados and educated there and in the eastern United States. He opened a law office in Topeka, Kansas, in 1879. One of his cases involved school desegregation, a model for the later *Brown v. Board of Education* decision. He spent a year practicing law in San Diego, but the city's Black population was too small (under three hundred) to satisfy his ambitions. He headed to Denver, where he was admitted to the bar in December 1891. He was soon assigned to defend criminal suspects in the Denver courts.

When Stuart was placed on the Republican ticket in 1894, a couple Black citizens published letters in the *Rocky Mountain News* accusing him of being in the American Protective Association, an anti-Catholic secret society, and possibly not a legal citizen. Supported by the Women's Republican Club, which applauded his advocacy for women's rights and racial equality, Stuart won. It was the first statewide election where women voted.

During his term, Stuart introduced and passed a key anti-discrimination bill. He also fought against an anti-miscegenation law, and lost. He was nominated again in 1906, but did not win. Two years later, a Black newspaper claimed he had worked against his race in the election and had allowed his anti-discrimination bill to be watered down. The law did lead to a couple successful lawsuits prior to his death, but it was not widely enforced until after the civil rights movement in the 1960s. His headstone incorporates the Masonic symbol. Like other fraternal organizations at the time, the lodges were segregated.

Lying in an unmarked grave in Block 33 is **Caroline Westcott Romney** (1840–1916), a globe-trotting, pioneer newspaperwoman

Caroline Westcott Romney as a young woman.

and inventor. Romney was born in New York and grew up in Ohio. She began her journalism career with the *Chicago Tribune*. One of few women admitted into the reporter's gallery, she covered three congressional sessions in Washington, D.C. In 1876 she fabricated a marriage to "John Romney" in Denver, Colorado, and became a "widow" three months later. As a widow, she had much greater freedom than she would have had as a spinster.

In 1880, after working as a correspondent in Leadville, she headed to the new town of Durango, in southwestern Colorado. The railroad had not been completed, so she traveled from Cumbres via mule team and bobsled along with a pair of miners. The route required nearly fifty river crossings, sometimes over the ice, sometimes breaking through. Romney kept up a cheery banter with the men, singing "One More River to Cross." Arriving in the community of a few log cabins, she set up her own newspaper, the *Daily Record,* pitching a tent in two feet of snow to run her press. She distributed it widely, making Durango a household name. The fast-growing periodical was a smashing financial success. In addition, she used her bully pulpit to help run the gangs out of the fledgling city.

A few years later, she started a paper in Trinidad, Colorado. She moved on to Texas, then New Mexico, and in 1888 resettled in Chicago. There, she entered fourteen of her inventions at the 1893 World's Fair in the White City, the most of any female inventor. They were machines such as a milk cooler, a foot heater for cars, a water filter, and a warming closet. She owned and edited industrial trade journals, and she planned to start a paper in Alaska during the Klondike gold rush, though the plan petered out. Not surprisingly, Romney championed women's rights, stating, "The best way for women to pursue, in business enterprises at least, is not to wait for men to accord them their rights, but to go ahead and take them." She died in Denver at the home of her sister, **Anna W. (Westcott) Goddard** (1850–1930), wife of **Justice Luther M. Goddard** (1839–1917) of the Supreme Court of Colorado.

Another single woman who made her mark on Colorado history is **Emily K. Griffith** (1868–1947), an educator who founded the Emily Griffith Technical College in Denver (formerly the Emily Griffith Opportunity School). Her stained-glass portrait hangs in the State Capitol. Griffith was born in Cincinnati. Her parents struggled to make a living and moved west to farm in Nebraska. Emily made it

Emily K. Griffith is honored in the State Capitol with this stained-glass likeness.

through the eighth grade before she had to work to help support the family. She began teaching at age sixteen.

In 1894, she came to Denver, where she continued her teaching career, living in the multi-ethnic Five Points neighborhood. When she realized her students' parents often could not read or write, possibly not even speak English, she decried the lack of educational opportunities for adults and immigrants. She held statewide office in the educational system from 1904 to 1912. By 1916, she created the educational center that now bears her name. By then she had learned to navigate the political system and formed alliances with large businesses to give her students access to practical job skills and opportunities. Her teaching philosophy and methods garnered national attention.

Griffith retired at sixty-five and went to live in a cabin in Pinecliffe, Boulder County, to care for her invalid younger sister, **Florence Griffith** (1870–1947). The sisters dined in the evenings with their neighbor, **Fred Wright Lundy**, whom they relied on for assistance at times. Lundy had formerly been a carpentry teacher at Griffith's school, and he built the cabin for the sisters. He and Griffith had a close relationship. In the early 1930s, Fred located a gold seam near his own cabin and planned to use the accumulated funds to take Griffith on a trip.

The deaths of all three in the summer of 1947 remains an unsolved case. The sisters died in their home, shot execution-style in the back of the head. Many suspected Lundy, offering a motive of mercy for the aging women, supported by the fact there was no sign of a struggle nor anything missing. But those who knew them all well did not believe Lundy was the killer. He left an apparent suicide note and $555 in his abandoned car, found shortly after the Griffith murders. His body came to light downriver from their house two months later. Per his request, he was buried in Roscoe, Illinois.

After finding Lundy's body, the Denver police concluded their investigation. Emily Griffith's legacy lives on at the oldest institution in the country dedicated to adult vocational and technical education.

WHEAT RIDGE

Mount Olivet Catholic Cemetery in Wheat Ridge, on West 44th Avenue, is just a small part of the enormous pioneer legacy of Colorado's first bishop, **Joseph P. Machebeuf** (1812–1889), whose remains are interred here within a vault in the Gallagher Memorial Chapel. The cemetery is large and formal, established in 1892 on land that was part of the bishop's farm.

Machebeuf was born in France and ordained a Jesuit priest in 1836. He came to America as a missionary in 1839. After the Mexican War, he was sent to Santa Fe, New Mexico, joining his life-long friend, Bishop Jean Baptiste Lamy. Lamy sent Machebeuf throughout the southwest territory—an area larger than their homeland of France—to minister to Catholics. The gold rush brought him to the Pikes Peak region. Machebouf was a short, slender, plain-faced man. He wore wire-rimmed spectacles and had a pleasing personality. His New Mexico years are chronicled in Willa Cather's novel *Death Comes for the Archbishop* in which Machebeuf's fictional name is Father Joseph Vaillant.

Bishop Joseph P. Machebeuf arrived in Colorado in 1859 and became the first bishop in Colorado. He performed many Catholic wedding ceremonies in pioneer times.
PUBLIC DOMAIN VIA WIKIMEDIA COMMONS

During the 1877 campaign for suffrage, Machebeuf was a formidable foe for women's rights. In their multi-volume history of the suffrage movement, Elizabeth Cady Stanton, Susan B. Anthony, and Matilda Joslyn Gage printed excerpts of a speech he gave in Denver that year. Naturally, he drew on the Christian principle that women were intended to be men's helpmates, not equals. He said, "The class of women wanting suffrage are battalions of old maids disappointed in love—women separated from their husbands or divorced by men from their sacred obligations—women who, though married, wish to hold the reins of the family government, for there never was a woman happy in her home who wished for female suffrage."

In 1884, Machebeuf invited the Las Vegas College in New Mexico to relocate to Morrison, Colorado. Renamed the College of the Sacred Heart, it became the only Jesuit college in the Rocky Mountain region. Prominent Catholics, such as Sen. A.A. Salazar of San Luis, sent their sons there to be educated. In 1885, Senator Salazar said, "The interior of the college is fitted up with an elegance and comfort that I have never seen in any other boarding-school . . . The class work was admirable, as is to be expected from Jesuits . . . but I was struck with one class that is not a common feature in colleges—the class of gymnastics." He went on to praise additional features of the school and the high esteem the students held for the college president. The college moved to Denver and expanded to become today's Regis University.

When Pope Leo XIII created the Diocese of Denver, Machebeuf became its first bishop in 1887. At the time of his death, the diocese had 112 churches and chapels, nine hospitals, nine academies, and the college, all under the care of sixty-four priests.

Machebeuf contemporary and first territorial governor **William Gilpin** (1813–1894) is buried here in Section 9 with a simple marble headstone and footstone. Gilpin graduated from West Point in 1836, the same year Machebeuf was ordained. He was governor from

1861–1862. He acquired an enormous portion of the Sangre de Cristo land grant. While this grant did not precipitate the level of violence of the Maxwell land grant (see chapter 2, Stonewall Gap), it did set up perpetual legal battles over land in the San Luis Valley. Gilpin died when a horse and carriage ran over him on the streets of Denver.

Two people who titillated Denver society, becoming legendary in Colorado history, are Horace A.W. Tabor (1830–1899) and his second wife, the famed beauty, **Elizabeth "Baby Doe" (McCourt) Tabor** (1854–1935). They share a large granite headstone in Section 18.

Horace A.W. Tabor made his riches in the Leadville silver mining boom and lost it in the 1893 silver crash. He is buried with his second wife, Elizabeth "Baby Doe" McCourt, in Mount Olivet Cemetery.
BRADY-HANDY PHOTOGRAPH COLLECTION, LIBRARY OF CONGRESS, PRINTS & PHOTOGRAPHS DIVISION, LC-DIG-CWPBH-03711

Monuments Men

The earliest commercial monument carvers in Colorado lived in the Denver area and sold headstones to the entire state. **George Morrison**, a Canadian immigrant, had his stone business in Mt. Vernon (now a ghost town, part of the Matthews/Winters Park). Like many other monument men, he produced building material as his primary product line. This included stone blocks, as well as decorative mantles, steps, and other adornments. Morrison built a historic home in Mount Vernon, and founded the town of Morrison.

His major competition in the 1860s was **Edward Gaffney**, who located his shop in downtown Denver. Unlike Morrison, Gaffney made grave markers his principal occupation. He created large, carved monuments, including the one for Silas Soule's original burial site. Rather than marble, Gaffney used a marble-like limestone that did not age well. He retired around 1866, and **Eli Daugherty** took over his shop near the Larimer Street Bridge. He renamed the business Denver Marble Works, and later Denver Marble and Granite, as granite became popular.

The southern part of the state obtained a monument source in 1881 with the opening of a branch of the Greenlee Co. called Pueblo Marble Co. **William C. Greenlee** and **George Drake** opened their business in Boulder in 1873 and moved to Denver the following year. They remained in business well into the twentieth century. In Pueblo, the chief carver was **Donald Harold Sr.** and later his son, **James Hedley Harold**. Their work can be found at least as far west as the Animas City Cemetery in Durango.

The M. Rauh company began as the Pioneer Marble Works of Denver, founded by **Adolph Rauh** and partners in the early 1870s. By 1880 it was known as M. Rauh Marble Works, and their claim to fame was high-end figurative monuments. These ranged from allegorical female figures to the elaborate Lester H. Drake log cabin monument in Denver's Riverside Cemetery.

The limestone log cabin memorial carved for Lester Drake's grave in Denver's Riverside Cemetery is the work of the M. Rauh Marble Works.

COURTESY OF CAROLE TAYLOR

CHAPTER 5

PIKES PEAK WONDERS

The Pikes Peak region encompasses the City of Colorado Springs plus the mountains to the west and the basin known as South Park. The last buffalo in Colorado was killed in South Park in 1897. But long before that, many historic events were set in motion by the Euro-American influx. French trappers roamed the forests and streams in the early 1700s, more than a century before American trappers. They called South Park *Bayou Salade* or salt marsh. Gold miners combed the Pikes Peak region along with other mountains in the state, but the placers were tapped out quickly and hard rock mining became the norm.

Though the upper reaches of the South Platte and Arkansas Rivers flow through South Park, much of this region is too high and dry for farming; ranching dominates instead. Railroads helped miners by hauling ore to smelters in places like Pueblo. The train cars also brought tourists into the mountains where they eagerly picked the periwinkle-shaded columbines in such quantities that a law had to be passed to keep the flowers from disappearing.

The number of ghost towns surrounding South Park and Pikes Peak far outnumber the existing communities, but the present-day population of Colorado Springs and its exurbs exponentially outweighs the number of nineteenth-century inhabitants.

MONUMENT AND SPRING VALLEY

Homesteaders arrived in the vicinity of Monument, El Paso County, by 1865. Not until Gen. William Jackson Palmer's Denver & Rio Grande narrow gauge railroad arrived in 1872 did a town develop. Incorporated as Henry's Station in 1879, after settler **Henry Limbach**, the name changed to Monument a few years later. The railroad helped Monument thrive while other towns struggled. A number of villages dotted the area in and around the present-day city. They included Greenland, Gwillimville, Table Rock, and Spring Valley. Some were located in Douglas County, others in El Paso County. The surrounding residents farmed, raised cattle and milk cows, and sold eggs and butter to supply Colorado Springs. Both Gwillimville and Monument boasted cheese-making factories, and **G.R. Gwillim** had a large cheese exporting trade. Each village had a general store, post office, blacksmith, and other products and services needed by the farmers. In pioneer days, Monument became known for its potato crop.

Monument Cemetery is located just off I-25 at the north edge of town along Beacon Lite Road. **Spring Valley Cemetery** lies east of I-25 at the County Line Road exit, then north on South Spring Valley Road. The need for these cemeteries partially arose from the various epidemics—scarlet fever, diphtheria, and smallpox—that swept through the pioneer communities, typically killing young children. The family of **David McShane** (1830–1907) is believed

Entrance to the Monument Cemetery.
COURTESY OF MARGARET N.L. THOMPSON

to be the first to homestead in the Monument area. Two McShane children, **Charles** (1875–1880) and **Effie Pearl** (1877–1880), died of diphtheria in January 1880. They have matching side-by-side marble headstones in the Monument Cemetery.

McShane came to Colorado in the gold rush, mining in Summit County, a vocation he did not prosper at but kept his hand in over the course of his life. He returned home to Iowa, thinking his Colorado campsite would be desirable pastureland, so he brought his family out to stay. McShane built a stone house with walls two feet thick, narrow doors, and recessed windows for protection. Nearby he built a stone-walled fort that was used from 1865 to 1868 during conflicts with the

Plains Indians. A tunnel connected the two structures. He operated a construction firm in addition to his ranch. He helped build railroads and a total of ten reservoirs in the county. He was a multi-term county commissioner, early postmaster, and helped erect several schools in Monument. His wife **Catherine (Willyard) McShane** (1836–1898) spent years managing the family home in Iowa while David roamed Colorado. She had the pluck to be a pioneer. They had seven children in addition to the two who died in 1880. David and Catherine have a chunky granite headstone engraved with the Masonic emblem.

Along with the McShanes, Henry and **Caroline H. (Lindner) Limbach** (1842–1894) were co-founders of Monument. Henry and another man filed the town plat in 1874. (Henry is buried in Denver.) Caroline, a sturdy, Germanic woman, known for her sewing skills, ran a millinery and fine dressmaking shop on Front Street, the main road through town that paralleled the railroad tracks. In the early 1890s, she was secretary of the school board.

Henry, round-faced and mustached, immigrated in 1863 and fought in the war. Caroline, who knew Henry from childhood and spoke no English, arrived in 1872 in St. Louis, where they married, per prior arrangement, and went home to Colorado. Caroline's mother, **Maria Lindner** (1819–1899), lived with the Limbachs and is also buried here. She and Henry partnered to buy up much of the land in and around Monument.

Henry had a store in town and was postmaster in the 1870s. His shop was the site of a murder in October 1876 when **Daniel Davidson**, who had a longstanding quarrel with **Francis M. Brown**

(1839–1876) over a cattle issue, shot Brown twice. Brown's marble headstone reads "F.M. Brown—Who was killed."

Nine children of the extended **Gwillin family**, from Wales, were buried in the Spring Valley Cemetery between 1879 and 1883. Though the Gwillim brothers (Gwillim, Richard, and Thomas) were instrumental in developing the area east of Monument, had a large mercantile in that town, and cheese factories, neither they nor their wives are buried at Spring Valley with the children. It is a sad fact of many pioneer cemeteries that children who died young remained behind while their parents and surviving siblings moved on.

Smallpox, sometimes called the Black Plague, struck Spring Valley in January 1885. **Lorenzo Leppert** (1854–1885) drove the stage between there and Denver, bringing supplies and mail for the **Jacob Geiger** store/post office. He lived in the back of the store and worked on the Geiger farm. Leppert, afflicted by the disease, was about to be married to **Louisa Jane "Janey" Richey** (1867–1885), who nursed him and caught it, too. She remained in Leppert's apartment at Geiger's store and her grandmother came to tend her in her illness. She had nearly recovered when she caught a cold and died about a month after Leppert.

Her family put her in her wedding dress for the funeral and burial. Geiger built the simple coffins with local lumber, and his wife, **Anna (Nelson) Geiger** (1833–1904), lined them with muslin. The two sweethearts were interred among the tall, butterscotch-scented ponderosa pines in the Spring Valley Cemetery. Their headstones, created many years later, have erroneous information. After Leppert and Richey's deaths, the Geigers moved to the farm in order to reno-vate and disinfect the store and post office, but it soon burned to the ground amid rumors.

Simple headstones and a family marker adorn the graves of long-lived pioneer **Samuel Brown** (1832–1927) and his second wife, **Jane Keene** (1832–1913). Jane had been widowed three times before mar-rying Brown in 1891. At last, she had a husband who outlived her. She was the grandmother who nursed Janey Richey in her final days. Brown was born in Kentucky, married and had children in Kansas. When his first wife died, he brought his children to Colorado for the first time in 1868. Indian issues at the sawmill where he worked pushed him back east for a time, but then he began purchasing land to make Colorado his permanent home. He held a number of positions in local govern-ment over the years. In addition to his wife Jane, Brown's daughter, son-in-law, and five grandchildren are buried in Spring Valley.

COLORADO SPRINGS

Unlike Denver and many communities dating from Colorado's terri-torial days, Colorado Springs was a planned community, first called the Fountain Colony. **Gen. William Jackson Palmer** (1836–1909), founder of the Denver & Rio Grande Railroad, envisioned the city. He visited Colorado City at the base of Pikes Peak and fell in love with the colorful rock formations (now Garden of the Gods), Foun-tain Creek, and the peak itself. Palmer created the Colorado Springs Company in October 1870. Income from property sales helped fund the railroad; another large chunk went toward developing infrastructure. Though not a gated community, it was intended to be exclusive for the well-to-do.

Colorado Springs is now the state's second-largest city with a population of roughly half a million. Over seventy thousand former residents now inhabit **Evergreen Cemetery**, the city's largest and oldest continuously used cemetery, including Palmer. Evergreen, with an entrance on Hancock Expressway, was established in 1871 and deeded to the city in 1875. It replaced the large **El Paso County Cemetery** situated near the railroad depot—not a welcome sight for disembarking passengers.

Evergreen is a luxuriant garden in an urban setting. Families planted many rose trellises in the early twentieth century, adding to the park-like feel. William Jackson Palmer's grave is remarkable for its lack of an ostentatious monument, in keeping with his Quaker faith. He was a staunch abolitionist from the Philadelphia region and a lifelong supporter of education for Blacks and rights for Native Americans. His cemetery lot features four small boulders resting on a raised grassy bed and includes his military service plaque, much as you would find on any other soldier's grave. He rose to the rank of Brevet Brigadier General in the Civil War with the Fifteenth Pennsylvania Cavalry and received a Congressional Medal of Honor in 1894. His wife **Mary L. "Queen" (Mellen) Palmer** (1850–1894) has her own boulder with inset metal lettering. Though Palmer's burial site is modest, he is also memorialized with a statue in a prominent intersection in downtown Colorado Springs. It depicts the General wearing a civilian suit, astride his favorite horse, Diablo, facing Pikes Peak.

Gen. William Jackson Palmer and Mary L. "Queen" Palmer have a modest gravesite in Evergreen Cemetery. Palmer is best known as the founder of Colorado Springs and builder of the Denver & Rio Grande Railroad.

Palmer had entrepreneurial vision and developed a variety of businesses. He is famous for building 1,500 miles of railroad, a career pursued from his teen years on. Though he tended to lose controlling interest in his many enterprises, this modest and generous man amassed a fortune and gave much of it to community improvements. He left a number of legacies for the state, including the Colorado School for the Deaf and Blind, Colorado College, the City of Manitou Springs, and Colorado Springs itself.

Queen Palmer, at age twenty-one, opened the first public school in town, holding classes in a rented house. Her health required a move

Gen. William Jackson Palmer received the Congressional Medal of Honor in 1894 for his Civil War service.

to England, where she lived for many years. The General visited his family whenever possible but lived in Colorado. The Palmers had three daughters and numerous pets; dogs often surround Palmer in photographic portraits.

Evergreen contains other historic Colorado figures. Two whose claims to fame are closely tied with the gold mines of Cripple Creek are **Winfield Scott Stratton** (1848–1902) and **Robert "Bob" Womack** (1844–1909). Womack is known for starting the Cripple Creek gold rush, though his earlier finds, dating back to the 1870s, were considered to be humbugs (that is, worthless). But his discovery in 1890 led to the last great rush in Colorado. Womack did not become wealthy, though. The reason for that is murky. Stratton, on the other hand, became a multi-millionaire from his Cripple Creek mines. He never married and was legendary for his generosity and philanthropy, even helping down-on-his-luck Womack.

Helen (Fiske) Hunt Jackson (1830–1885), a fierce advocate for Indian rights, took a roundabout route to Evergreen. The author of the novel *Ramona* and the nonfiction work *A Century of Dishonor* died and was buried in San Francisco, but her body was later moved to a private gravesite on Cheyenne Peak, not far from Colorado Springs. Fears of vandalism prompted a final removal to Evergreen, where she rests under a massive slab of granite.

Boston

Author Helen Hunt Jackson was reburied in Evergreen after previously being buried on Cheyenne Peak.

Others in the creative arts resting in Evergreen include author **Andy Adams** (1859–1935), writer of western novels; **Francis Henry "Frank" Maynard** (1853–1926), a poet remembered for "Streets of Laredo," which became the lyrics for a popular song; and **Artus Van Briggle** (1869–1904), award-winning founder of the Van Briggle Art Pottery studio in Colorado Springs. Van Briggle rediscovered the Ming Dynasty formula for satin matte glazes. His grave laid unmarked until an anonymous donor installed a red granite headstone inscribed, "Whosoever loveth the labor of his work, the Gods have called."

Robert Williamson Steele (1820–1901) has more of a trivial or footnote place in state history. Originally from Ohio, he moved to Nebraska and sat in the territorial legislature. After the gold strike on Cherry Creek, near the base of the Rockies, he followed the mines. He was elected to be governor in the provisional government of Jefferson Territory from 1860 to 1861 when the federal government denied it status and created Colorado Territory instead. He is sometimes referred to as Colorado's first governor.

William Augustus Conant (1816–1909) was buried with his family in a triangular lot in Evergreen Cemetery, but he lacks a marker. He is probably between his wife, **Maria Louisa Weed** (1819–1902) and his son, **William L. Conant** (1844–1900), a Union veteran. Conant spent his early adulthood in New York City, where he married and had three children: William, Fred, and Florence. The family relocated to Long Island, where Conant sold clothing.

He had an extraordinary baritone voice and performed under the auspices of P.T. Barnum. In late 1871, Conant dissolved his

THE SOLID MULDOON

In the summer of 1877, prominent Colorado Springs resident **William A. Conant** took a sudden interest in paleontology. He targeted a conical hill southwest of Pueblo, near the road to Beulah. In August, he found a petrified fish that he sent to his former home, Suffolk County, New York, to be exhibited in their county fair.

A month later, back at the dig site, he noticed an unusual rock protruding from the soil. Using his pick-ax to dig through the dense clay and cut through a tree root, a stone human foot emerged. Astonishing! He continued his excavation and uncovered a petrified male form, seven-and-a-half feet long, in a pose clearly not meant to be a sculpture. The man's arms were unusually long, and he had a four-inch tail, exciting speculation that this could be Darwin's "missing link." Conant had his find hauled to a Pueblo livery stable. Before exhibiting it, he reattached the head he had accidentally broken off in the move.

Speculation ran rampant. So did skepticism. Some recalled the Cardiff Giant hoax in New York just seven years earlier. People lined up to view the marvelous figure and observed minute pores in his petrified skin. Conant offered his find to **Phineas T. Barnum**, who happened to be in Colorado Springs on a lecture tour. Barnum offered twenty thousand dollars for the stone man, who had been dubbed "Muldoon" after a popular boxer who was known as "The Solid Man." Conant declined the offer, figuring Muldoon to be worth at least five thousand dollars more.

Letter-to-the-editor writers and journalists argued over Muldoon's authenticity. The *Rocky Mountain News* hired **F.S. Dellenbaugh** to examine the exhibit. Dellenbaugh was an artist and explorer who had worked closely with the geologist on John Wesley Powell's trip down the Grand Canyon in 1869. His findings were logical and unequivocal. Fossils tend to be found in limestone, not clay. If an ancient people had lived in that area, there would be other artifacts, but none had been found. He proceeded to knock the giant down to size, inch by column-inch.

In January 1878, an exposé revealed that **George Hull**, perpetrator of the Cardiff Giant hoax, had created the Solid Muldoon. The latest giant man had even been funded by Barnum, who had been Conant's employer before Conant relocated to Colorado in 1872. Cardiff had been carved from stone, but Muldoon was sculpted from a variety of materials, including bone and ground crystals, and fired in a kiln in Pennsylvania. The men secretly transported it west, where Conant would pretend to discover it five years later. Whatever money the men hoped to reap by displaying the giant man never materialized. Oh, and Conant's fossilized fish was phony, too.

The name Solid Muldoon stuck around a lot longer than the fake missing link. **David Day**, newspaperman of Ouray, and later Durango, named his paper *The Solid Muldoon*. For many years, Durango also had a bar by that name.

business and announced his move west. He operated a store in Black Hawk, Colorado, in 1872. He relocated to Colorado Springs and obtained employment as an agent for the Atchison, Topeka & Santa Fe Railroad (AT&SF). After the Denver & Rio Grande repossessed part of the AT&SF line, Conant, with his wife and daughter, removed to Santa Fe, New Mexico (and for a while, Winslow, Arizona), working for the railroad, and later as a real estate agent. The Conants returned to Colorado Springs in 1888.

Conant went to the convention in 1856 that established the national Republican Party and forwarded John C. Frémont as a presidential candidate. He remained dedicated to the Republican party for life. Conant relished his connections in high places, having his correspondence with celebrities such as Theodore Roosevelt published in the papers. Conant was on the welcoming committee when Gen. Ulysses S. Grant visited Santa Fe in 1885. Many news reports indicate he earned high esteem wherever he went. The Conants hobnobbed with the highest society in each place they lived.

Conan helped found the Universalist Church in Colorado Springs and by all accounts had a sterling character. It is a mystery why he risked his reputation to go along with Barnum and Hull when they hatched the plan to build a better petrified man. He wrote vociferous defenses of the giant in the papers, and never retracted them. Perhaps he considered it a harmless practical joke. But many people never forgot his involvement in the affair, which may be why his grave is unmarked.

Daughter **Florence Conant** (1849–1921) is not buried with her family, but cemetery records place her in a plot next to **Alice C. Palmer** (1875–1921). The Catholic Church performed her funeral service. Florence never married, but chose a career instead. She worked in the El Paso County clerk's office. Like her father, she belonged to the Republican party and worked as an election judge. Later she sold insurance. She even served on the board of directors of the Union Gold Mining Co. in 1900. She lived to the age of seventy-three.

Son **Frederick H. Conant** (1847–1884) preceded his family to Colorado, coming shortly after the war. He tried his hand at mining in Gilpin County, opened a store in Black Hawk (to be joined by his father), and engaged in a failing business in Denver. He took up journalism and worked for newspapers in Colorado Springs and Leadville, becoming part-owner of the *Leadville Herald,* covering the mining news. He also helped publicize his father's petrified-man discovery. When Fred died suddenly in Pueblo, just thirty-six years old, it was big news. He was so widely known and respected that former **Gov. Frederick Pitkin** traveled from Pueblo, and the Denver & Rio Grande Railroad offered a special low fare to Denverites wanting to attend the funeral in Colorado Springs.

MANITOU SPRINGS

Manitou Springs sits at the base of Pikes Peak and features cold-water mineral drinking springs, sacred to the Utes and Plains tribes that wintered here. The first American to find the springs was **Dr. Edwin James**, the botanist in the Long Expedition of 1820. Like Colorado Springs, Manitou's 1872 founding began with Gen. William Jackson Palmer and **Dr. William Abraham Bell**, an English physician best known as a photographer of the American West. From the beginning, they planned it as a resort, partially to help convalescing tuberculosis sufferers. To some extent, Colorado's altitude and clean, dry air may have alleviated symptoms for people from polluted eastern cities.

The **Crystal Valley Cemetery** is the only burial ground in Manitou Springs, some of the interments having been moved from an earlier cemetery on Pawnee Avenue. It is listed on the National Register of Historic Places because of the architecture, landscaping, and locally important people buried here. The cemetery nestles in a valley between two ridges south of town and follows the curving geography at the base of the western ridge. It became the target of wanton vandalism in 2021, when at least fifty monuments were damaged.

For the past few decades, a woman who died at Manitou of tuberculosis has been annually resurrected, so to speak, in a new role to promote the community. **Emma L. Crawford** (1863–1891) was born in Massachusetts and came to the mountains for her health. In Boston, she was a concert pianist, taught by her mother. She was engaged to marry, but her death intervened. Her wish to be buried on top of Red Mountain was granted. Years later, erosion exposed her coffin, and legend has that it slid down the mountain. She was re-interred at Crystal Valley in an unmarked grave but later given a memorial stone. Around Halloween each year, the Emma Crawford Coffin Races and Festival takes place, drawing locals and tourists alike for a day of costumes, creative coffins pushed uphill by pallbearers, a "Best Emma" contest, and spooky mayhem.

After her death from tuberculosis, Emma L. Crawford was buried on Red Mountain per her wishes.

Many graves in Colorado are unmarked, but some veterans have multiple headstones. **Gen. Charles Adams** (1844–1895), born Carl Heinrich Albert Schwanbeck and changed to Charles Adams by special act of the territorial legislature, is among them. He has a granite pillar and a marble veteran's stone. Born in Germany, he arrived in New York in 1863 and immediately enlisted in the war effort. He came to Colorado afterward and joined the Third Colorado Cavalry. He was appointed Indian agent at the Los Pinos Ute Agency, where he took control of the notorious Colorado cannibal **Alferd Packer** after his capture. Adams is particularly known for negotiating the release of the women and children taken hostage during the Meeker Incident (see chapter 8, Meeker Incident sidebar). He went with Chief Ouray, **Chipeta**, **Chief Ignacio**, and **Woretsiz** of the Utes to Washington in 1880 to meet with Secretary of the Interior Carl Shurz and was photographed with them.

He married divorcee **Margaret (Thompson) Phelps** around 1871, while living with Margaret's brother-in-law, territorial governor **Edward M. McCook**. Under President Chester Arthur, Adams served as minister to Bolivia. The family home between Manitou and Colorado Springs held a museum's worth of artifacts from Colorado's indigenous people and those of South America. He owned land at Monument and platted the town along with Henry Limbach (see Monument section).

Denver's Grumly Hotel had a boiler explosion in 1895, setting fire to the building and killing twenty people, including General Adams. Margaret lived to 1917 and is buried in **Crown Hill Cemetery** in Wheat Ridge.

FLORISSANT

While the development of Florissant, thirty-five miles west of Colorado Springs, dates only to the mid-1860s, history is found in the very rocks. Early travelers spied enormous petrified tree stumps, many of which went away in pieces as souvenirs. Later, the local shale deposits yielded exquisitely detailed fossils, attracting even more tourists (and scientists) to the area with the help of the Colorado Midland Railroad, which arrived in 1887. These features are preserved in Florissant Fossil Beds National Monument.

First known as a mining camp called Twin Creek, the town site lay at the intersection of two important Ute trails. What is now US 24 is roughly the Ute Pass Trail. Running north-south was the East Oil Creek Trail (now Teller County Road 1). The town became Florissant after **James** (1814–1878) and **Catherine (Hughes) Castello** (1819–1898)—formerly of Florissant, Missouri—arrived from Fairplay to build a home and the Ute Trading Post in 1870. By 1872, they expanded to include a hostelry, post office, and general store. The Castellos befriended the Ute chiefs Ouray and **Colorow**, and the chiefs bestowed a nickname on Catherine, "Heap Big Rocky Mountain Biscuit."

After mining for gold in Central City from 1860 to 1863, James, a robust and kindly man, moved to Fairplay in Park County and sent for his family in Missouri. Catherine, with the aid of two men James hired, packed up the ox-drawn wagon and five children, and made the sixty-day crossing. At Fairplay, she endured the isolation and shouldered the pioneer workload. Soon, though, they entertained travelers at their Castello House. Altogether, James and Catherine had nine children, with six surviving to adulthood. Many of them were born in Florissant, Missouri, and died in Florissant, Colorado.

The Castellos are buried in the **Florissant Cemetery** south of town on Teller County Road 421 (Upper Twin Rock Road). The cemetery has monuments dating to at least 1877, though the first cemetery organization began in 1888, formed by James and Catherine's son, **Frank Castello**, and his neighbor, **John C. Wilson** (1831–1914). Early burials among the fluttery-leaved aspens and pines had only wooden markers that have long since vanished, consigning some burials to permanent obscurity.

John Wilson married **Mary Jane Bates** (1832–1904) in Missouri in 1853. John, who did his share of prospecting, missed out on the big Cripple Creek gold strike. In 1891, he and his son **Calas Wilson** (1857–1896) went up to Pisgah, as Cripple Creek was known at the time, and staked out claims on the hillsides seeking lode seams, but they did not find any good leads. Prospector Bob Womack had opened a gold mine the year before, but the richest lodes did not spur a rush until 1893. John became a partner in the Florissant Gold Mining Company in 1896, but whether he succeeded in finding riches is unknown. His modest granite headstone suggests not.

South of Florissant, at the national monument, is the house that belonged to homesteader **Adeline (Warfield) Harker Hornbek Sticksel** (1833–1905). She is buried about a mile south in the **Four**

The entrance to Four Mile Cemetery.

Mile Cemetery along Teller County Road 12. Along with Florissant pioneers, a number of Cripple Creek residents were interred in this small burial ground. The cemetery, established in 1875, is in a woodland setting with native vegetation.

Adeline Warfield grew up in Massachusetts and headed west in the 1850s with her brother and sister-in-law. They settled in Indian Territory (Oklahoma), where her brother became a trader. She married his business partner, **Simon Harker**, and moved to Colorado Territory during the war. They acquired a small ranch in the Denver area, which suffered devastating floods in 1864. Simon died soon after of tuberculosis, leaving Adeline with three young children. She had a fourth child after marrying ranch hand **Elliot Hornbek**. But he proved a fickle partner and abandoned her. In 1876, Adeline moved to the Florissant Valley, where the high-altitude vegetation was ideal for cattle grazing. She was one of the first women to file a homestead claim in Colorado. She developed her ranch, filed for a brand, and built her herd.

Adeline helped establish the area's first school. In addition to ranching, she supported the community through social events, aiding other homesteaders, and working at a general store. She also employed several ranch hands. She died of a stroke at age seventy-one, having married a third time at sixty-six to **Fred Sticksel**. Her homestead and original 1878 house are now part of the national monument.

George A. Welty (1847–1896) and his sister, **Anna (Welty) Faulkner** (1857–1932) are buried at Four Mile, along with their spouses. Their parents, **Levi and Catherine Welty**, settled on the "Divide" in 1861, when George and Anna were children. (The Divide, in El Paso County, runs from Palmer Lake in the west to near Peyton in the east, dividing the South Platte from the Arkansas watershed, Denver from Colorado Springs. It is also called the Arkansas Divide and the Palmer Divide.) As population increased, they moved west of Pikes Peak to give their cattle room to roam, squatting on the land in 1872.

The creek in their new Pisgah Valley home was a mere trickle, but after suffering a series of mishaps, the Weltys christened it Cripple Creek. The injuries began when a yearling calf broke its leg in a prairie dog hole. **Alonzo Welty** nearly severed a big toe with an ax. George was shingling a roof and slid off, injuring his back. A ranch hand was thrown and injured by his horse, which spooked at the smell of a packet of bear meat attached to the saddle. Two years after naming the creek, Levi Welty crippled one of his hands by accidentally discharging his revolver.

George Welty moved to the Four Mile Valley northwest of Cripple Creek and had a ranch, which later became known as the Half Way House, being half way between Cripple Creek and Florissant. He married **Julia Marcott** (1845–1905), originally of Quebec, in 1873. George and Julia moved to Rio Blanco County, where her parents lived. George was a commissioner and filled other county offices. He returned to the Cripple Creek district about 1892 and died there of typhoid fever at age fifty. He was laid to rest at Four Mile Cemetery where his infant son, **Charles Raphael Welty**, was buried in 1881. The following year, the Woodmen of the World erected his tree-trunk style monument, the trunk signifying a life cut short. Julia, with the help of her son, Frank, continued to manage the Half Way ranch until her death in 1905.

Anna Welty's husband was **Simon P. Faulkner** (1849–1894). They had a stock-growing operation near her parents' ranch. They had two surviving children. Four Faulkner children are buried with Anna and Simon, all their names engraved on a single monument. Three— **Etta Eva**, **Freddie**, and **Oscher**—died as infants. **Mabel Ester Faulkner** (1878–1892) was nearly fourteen when she died. After her husband's death, Anna lived with a daughter in Colorado Springs.

The Welty Half Way ranch was halfway between Cripple Creek and Florissant.
Courtesy of Special Collections, Pikes Peak Library District, 001-5100

Possibly the wealthiest man buried in Four Mile was **William Henry Grose** (1842–1910). He died a bachelor, so his siblings, nieces, and nephews divided his sizable estate. They provided him a substantial granite marker, engraved with the Odd Fellows three-link chain symbol and a lengthy but unoriginal epitaph. The three links represent Friendship, Love, and Truth. He was a Cornish miner, son of a Cornish miner, **Henry Berwetherick Grose** (1819–1895), who is also buried here, along with William's brother, **Thomas Grose** (1851–1929) and his wife **Louisa Jane Tremayne** (1857–1926).

William built the first house in Alma, near Fairplay in Park County, settling there in 1866. Thomas had a ranch in southeastern Park County, west of Four Mile. William also set up a ranch there that straddled the Teller-Park County line. He had mining interests in both counties, many in Sacramento Gulch. He even found some rare uranium, being about the only miner around familiar with that particular mineral. In 1884, a report of gold at Four Mile caused a minor sensation but proved to be unfounded. Thomas quickly put out the fire of enthusiasm, unhappy to have prospectors swarming around the ranch.

The entire Grose clan in America gathered for a family reunion at Alma in 1885. Henry had sixteen grandchildren present. William semi-retired from his mines around then and went to live on his Four Mile ranch. August and September 1888 brought terrible grief to the Grose clan. Two of Thomas and Louisa's daughters died of whooping cough about two weeks apart. On top of that, a freak hailstorm dumped three feet of ice on the ranch, destroying grain and hay crops.

The family patriarch, Henry, passed away in 1895 at Four Mile. He had mined in his younger days in Cornwall, Scotland, Sweden, and Norway. Upon arriving in Colorado, Henry offered his extensive mining expertise as an assayer and ore processing consultant. He opened an assay office at Alma. He mined at Alma and in Pitkin County. He did the first assays from the Cripple Creek district and made a substantial fortune from that camp before his retirement. The Grose name was legendary in mining circles of the Pikes Peak region for decades.

WETMORE

Just north of Wetmore and the Custer County line on Fremont County Road 19 is the **New Hope Cemetery**, established in 1870. New Hope Church stands at the entrance to the graveyard, with a commanding view of the Wet Mountain range to the west. It is the second oldest Baptist church in Colorado and was constructed with wooden pegs, using no nails. The grounds are fenced with river-rock stanchions and pipe rails. **Ira Ryan Porter** (1838–1921) donated the land for the church and cemetery.

Porter wed **Sarah Catherine Kelley** (1844–1901) in 1862 in Iowa, where their first daughter was born the following year. In May 1864, all the men of Shoal Creek Baptist Church in Appanoose County, with one exception, packed up their families into a wagon train and made a more than three-month trek to Cañon City, Colorado. The Porters settled a homestead on Hardscrabble Creek, where they had another daughter and five sons, one boy dying in infancy. The second-youngest boy, Clyde, at about age five, caused the family grief when he chased some mice into a haystack and set it aflame to roust the rodents. The brand-new barn, a granary, some smaller outbuildings, and several tons of hay went up in smoke.

Sarah's father, **James M. Kelley** (1820–1889), came to live nearby in the 1880s and was buried in the New Hope Cemetery upon his death. Sarah was known as a neighborly woman who tended the sick. She was fifty-six when she suffered a fatal heart attack at 3 a.m. on February 15, 1901. Ira never remarried, and they are buried together with a variegated marble pillar headstone.

Friends of the Porters and fellow pioneers were **Jacob A. Betts** (1830–1909) and his wife **Sarah Parker** (1847–1911). Jacob Betts came to Colorado as a Fifty-Niner and engaged in mining for a time at Central City with long-time mining partner, **Hugh H. Melrose**. Jacob had a combined grocery, liquor store, and billiard saloon in Pueblo for several years called "El Progresso." He was Pueblo County sheriff for a couple years before marrying Sarah in 1866. In 1873, they moved to Wetmore, a township named by and for **William "Billy" Wetmore**. There Jacob opened a two-story saloon and dance hall. He and Sarah had a ranch east of the Porters and owned properties scattered around the state.

The Betts family were known for their large cattle and horse herds and were among the wealthiest people in Fremont County. "Uncle Jake" was a generous money lender, sometimes to his detriment. Jacob and Sarah's son, **Willie Betts** (1867–1883), was the victim of a shooting at a store in Huerfano County where he and a friend had been camping. Some speculated that one of the shooters, named Espinosa, was related to the murderers of 1863 and had a grudge against Jacob Betts. However, that theory was quickly dismissed. Sixteen-year-old Willie was just in the wrong place at the wrong time.

One person buried at New Hope was indeed a victim of the Espinosas. In the midst of the Civil War, a murder spree terrorized the people of Colorado. The perpetrators were two brothers and a nephew: **Felipe, Vivian, and Jose Espinosa**. They seemed to have a vendetta against the whites who had overrun the territory in such a short time. Mountain man **Tom Tobin** hunted down and killed them after they murdered an estimated thirty random victims. In Fremont County, the Espinosas killed **Franklin William Bruce**, first in the string of victims. He was buried where he died near Cañon City.

His widow was **Ruth Calistia Bacon** (1808–1891). Women have dealt with such heartbreaks from time immemorial. But her resilience and gumption garnered her recognition during her long life-time. Born in Vermont, she moved with her family to New York, then Ohio. She married her first husband and they traveled the Midwest until his death seven years later.

Ruth married Franklin Bruce and continued her westward migration. They came to Colorado in 1860, stayed a short time near

Gravesite of Ruth Calistia Bruce in New Hope Cemetery. She became a homesteader after the Espinosas murdered her second husband, Franklin Bruce.
COURTESY OF ROSS BREWER

present-day Leadville, then settled on Hardscrabble Creek. After Bruce's death, Ruth lived in Cañon City, then moved to the ranch. Once surveys had been completed, she filed on her homestead, receiving the patent in 1878. She purchased the adjoining 160 acres a few years later. She reared eight children by her two husbands.

New Hope Cemetery contains a cryptic character who spent his final days in Wetmore: **James W. Sears** (1847–1931). His grave is marked by a metal mortuary plaque. Local lore says his real identity was the outlaw Jesse James. Sears reportedly kept to himself, never removed his gloves (Jesse James had a partially missing finger), and made remarks that intensified the suspicion he might be the long-believed-dead criminal. Sears's background is indeed an enigma. He arrived in Florence, Fremont County, in 1895 and he appears in census records from 1900 to 1930, but prior to that his whereabouts are unknown. There is no doubt, though, he was not Jesse James, whose remains in Kearney, Missouri, were exhumed and DNA tested in 1995.

SILVER CLIFF

Between the Sangre de Cristo Mountains and Wet Mountains lies the Wet Mountain Valley, actually quite dry. Settlers set down roots here in 1869. Brothers Si and Steve Smith of Pueblo came to the area as early as 1863 but didn't stay. A colony of Germans from Chicago arrived in early 1870, led by **Carl Wulsten**. The first mining boom occurred at Rosita, where Wulsten is buried. Later, an exposed mineral cliff found to be 75 percent silver gave rise to a mine and the town of Silver Cliff. This influx led to the creation of Custer County (named for Gen. George Armstrong Custer) from Fremont County (named for explorer John C. Frémont). The Denver & Rio Grande Railroad arrived in 1881—at their own new community called Westcliffe. In 1880, Silver Cliff was the third largest city in Colorado, after Denver and Leadville.

The **Silver Cliff Cemetery** is on the open prairie about a mile south of town on Mill Street. Burials date to the late 1870s. The cemetery itself has its own claim to fame: baffling blue lights about the size

Entrance to the Silver Cliff Cemetery, which is known for mysterious blue lights that appear on moonless nights.
PLAZAK ON WIKIMEDIA COMMONS CREATIVE COMMONS ATTRIBUTION-SHARE ALIKE 3.0 UNPORTED, CREATIVECOMMONS.ORG/LICENSES/BY-SA/3.0/DEED.EN

of a silver dollar that float above the graves. They appear on overcast, moonless nights, and so far, have defied explanation. Even *National Geographic* tried to discover their origin in the 1960s.

Like all pioneer cemeteries, Silver Cliff has a large number of infant and child burials. Two young brothers—**Herman W. Hanssen** (1890–1899) and **Otto Hanssen** (1894–1899) died a day apart of "membranous croup." They share a gabled-pillar headstone in the cemetery section reserved to the Ancient Order of United Workmen (AOUW). Another child buried here, daughter of an AOUW member, is **Laura Olive Stanfield** (1881–1888). She died of pneumonia at age six. Her family had homes in Pueblo (where Laura died) and in Silver Cliff, where her father, **Samuel B. "Squire" Stanfield**, had mining interests and a side business as both a house painter/paper hanger and landscape painter. Stanfield made several substantial mineral finds during his time in Silver Cliff, both silver and gold. Laura's grave location is unknown.

Two brothers in the cemetery, both bachelors, were part of the original German colony. **Anton John Schopp** (1842–1893) died of pneumonia at fifty, on a cold December day. His obituary claimed he had no enemies—save one man who defrauded him of several hundred dollars—but even of him, Schopp spoke kindly. Anton and **Arnold Schopp** (1840–1909) had adjoining homesteads on the west edge of the valley, at the foot of the Sangre de Cristos.

Eight of the ten men killed in the Bull Domingo Mine fire on November 13, 1885, are buried and memorialized here. One victim was sent out of state and another buried in the **Catholic Cemetery**.

The fire followed a blast in the boiler room attributed to actions by the mine superintendent, **H.W. Foss**, who was nearly lynched as a result. The coroner declared him to be criminally negligent. The building blaze spread to the shaft house and hoist, then to the mine timbers, trapping the men below. The men appeared to have suffocated. Two of them managed to pen goodbye letters to family. The following are the men buried in the Silver Cliff Cemetery:

- **B. Baptiste** (1856–1885), born in Italy, married, two daughters
- **William H. Strong** (185?–1885), born in New York, divorced, one son
- **Conn Nourse** (185?–1885), born in England, single
- **Elmer E. Heister** (1863–1885), born in Pennsylvania, single, lived with his parents, many siblings, and other relatives in Silver Cliff
- **David William Patton** (1845–1885), born in Indiana, married, two sons (has two headstones, one for military service in the Civil War—Union)
- **P. Hiram Westfall** (1856–1885), born in Illinois, probably single, left a note designating a sister and two orphaned nieces as his AOUW beneficiaries
- **John Laube (aka Lanbe, Lobby)** (1855–1885), born in England, single
- **M. La Point** or **Simon Baptiste**. Lists of the dead include either of these names, but no further information has been found for them

CLEORA

Settlers arrived in the South Arkansas Valley soon after the gold rush began. Many came looking for mining opportunities, and others took advantage of the fruits of the soil.

Cleora Cemetery is a true boot-hill-type burial ground. It has no planned layout, and the terrain remains in its natural state: a slightly hilly site, riven by gullies and covered in native vegetation such as sagebrush, prickly-pear cactus, and juniper trees. The burials may have begun around 1875, and the cemetery is acknowledged as the first one in the South Arkansas Valley. The cemetery takes its name from a short-lived town created by the Atchison, Topeka & Santa Fe Railroad, before they had to relinquish the route through the Royal Gorge at Cañon City to the Denver & Rio Grande (D&RG). The US Supreme Court settled the rival railroads' bitter battle in 1879. The town took its name from a stage stop owned by **William Bale**, whose daughter was named Cleora.

The D&RG created their own town, Salida (originally South Arkansas), about two miles northwest of Cleora and offered free town sites to residents and businesses (except saloons) that wished to move their buildings. Many took them up on the offer, dooming the earlier settlement. Salida had no cemetery until 1883, so valley residents continued to be buried at Cleora from as far away as Monarch. Most of the interments date prior to 1920; the cemetery closed to burials in 1948. It is located along US 50 and has a convenient parking area.

Four members of the Hawkins family are believed to be interred together at Cleora. **William A. Hawkins** (1812–1888) was Cleora's first mayor, but he soon moved to Salida where he held a number of offices: first police magistrate, second mayor, and justice of the peace. He ran the Grand View Hotel in Salida, owned by **Alexander Hunt**, and remained active in local politics until his death. The family monument is badly crumbled, probably made of concrete. Hawkins was born in New York and wound up in Milwaukee, Wisconsin, where he married Jane Catherine Parks and, after her death, her sister **Deshia Parks** (1818–1889).

William's youngest son, **James William Hawkins** (1859–1878), died before there were any newspapers in the valley to record his death. Two years later, the youngest daughter, **Mattie Louise Hawkins** (1858–1880), age twenty-two, passed away. The news report gave no cause, only an epitaph:

> Gone from this world, its care and its strife,
> Gone from the dear ones beloved during life;
> Gone to the home of the ransomed above,
> Gone to the Savior whose fulness [*sic*] is love.

Deshia, the mother of these two, arrived home to Salida on the train after visiting friends in Park County. Feeling ill upon disembarkation, she passed away an hour later. Living into their seventies, Judge Hawkins and his wife were deemed to have reached a ripe old age. The family marker has only the children's names, but the engravings have crumbled almost entirely.

This crumbling marker probably memorializes four members of the Hawkins family buried in Cleora Cemetery.

Even miners sometimes reached a "ripe" age. Fortunately, in pioneer communities an old widower could count on his neighbors. **Joseph Edwin "J.E." Gorrell** (1819–1892) came from New Hampshire for gold. He prospected, mined, ranched, and farmed. After spending time in California Gulch, Del Norte, and other places, he called Chaffee County home. He owned a mine in the Monarch District and patented 160 acres between Salida and Cleora, just north of the cemetery. In April 1892, Gorrell apparently had a stroke and fell into his fireplace. A friend named **L.H. Brown** found the seventy-two-year-old and took him home to care for him in his final six weeks. His grave has no marker.

Though there has been some vandalism in Cleora, many markers remain in good shape. Even a few wood ones remain partially legible. One big insult to those interred here was a prospector digging in the cemetery for gold in 1894 with plans to start mining it forthwith.

SALIDA

One of Salida's pioneer cemeteries lies south of town on a north-facing slope covered with sagebrush and piñon. Burials began about 1883 (though some markers have earlier dates) and the cemetery was incorporated in 1889 as **Woodland Cemetery** (aka **Woodlawn**). Though there is a larger, manicured cemetery in town, Woodland is still in use. It is accessed by County Road 107.

Four members of the Beck family are buried side by side. The parents are **Melvin Beck** (1861–1903) and **Hattie L. Wolfe** (1861–1929), who share a headstone, though they were divorced at the time of Melvin's murder in 1903. The Becks married in 1886 and had three children, two of whom died young: **Myrtle M. Beck** (1889–1892) and **Jesse E. Beck** (1893–1899). The Becks lived for a time at Monarch where Melvin was shift boss at the Madonna mine in its prosperous days. They moved to Victor and he worked as a shift boss for the Vindicator Mine. Hattie ran a confection shop in nearby Cripple Creek.

On November 22, 1903, Melvin and the mine superintendent, **Charles H. McCormick**, were killed by a massive dynamite blast in the shaft. The dynamite had been booby-trapped to explode as the men exited the hoist car. The Cripple Creek Mine Owners and Operators quickly blamed the murders on the Western Federation of Miners (WFM) union and offered a five thousand dollar reward for capturing the culprits. The union men also condemned the murders and planned their own reward. This event sparked the Victor Labor War of 1903–1904.

A second sabotage event in January 1904 killed fifteen miners. At the trial of WFM leader **William "Big Bill" Hayward** in 1907 for killing the Idaho governor, a state's witness claimed responsibility for the incident at the Vindicator Mine. **Albert Horsely** (aka **Harry Orchard**), said he had been paid by Hayward and a local union organizer to commit the crimes. Some people thought Orchard lied and that the Mine Owners had actually been the ones to hire him. The violence forced the Colorado governor to proclaim martial law in Teller County in December 1903.

Two of the largest monuments in Woodland belong to the Lewis family of Pennsylvania. The were living in Colorado as early as 1880, residing at Breckenridge and Saguache before coming to Salida.

David H. Lewis (1847–1921) was an engineer at a coal chute and owned a restaurant in town for many years. He also had a ranch west of Salida at Tomichi in Gunnison County. He and wife **Mary J. Lewis** (1850–1916) had four children.

Mary had two surgeries in 1916 for goiter and throat cancer. Though the surgeries appeared to be successful, the cancer had spread to her brain, and her family laid her to rest in Woodland. After his wife's death, David relocated to Salt Creek, Wyoming, where he worked as a pumper in the oil fields though already in his seventies. After his death from infection resulting from a fall and kidney disease, he was returned to Salida for burial with his wife.

Daughter **Maggie Lewis** (1877–1883) shares a large granite marker with her brother **James M. Lewis** (1871–1892). James, known to be a jovial fellow, worked for the railroad as a fireman (one who fuels the boiler). A train wreck near Browns Canyon crushed him under the engine, instantly snuffing his life.

Another young man at Woodland came to an untimely end due to a railroad wreck in the same area as James Lewis died the previous year. **John B. Myers** (1863–1893) worked as a repairman for the railroad and was riding in the engine compartment as a passenger. The engine derailed due to a large rock and Myers was thrown into the Arkansas River where he drowned. His grave is marked by a variegated marble headstone on a sandstone plinth.

A fine example of a zinc monument stands in the forested, upper portion of the cemetery. It marks the resting place of **Wesley Frederick Stroud** (1859–1890) and **Catharine Jane "Jennie" (Pennington) Stroud** (1862–1894). Though a panel is missing, the rest of

This fine example of a zinc grave marker is for Wesley and Jennie Stroud in the Woodland Cemetery in Salida.

the ornate marker remains intact. Frederick, a sober and industrious young man, worked for the D&RG as a clerk and bookkeeper in the bridge and building department. He married Jennie in May 1890, and a few months later he took ill. The exact nature of his fatal affliction is unknown but said to have affected his brain and been a result of overwork. Jennie was inconsolable with grief. She returned home to Gunnison to live with her parents. Four years later, Jennie suffered from a "brain fever" herself, but recovered. However, it seemed she never recovered from the shock of losing her husband. In August 1894, suffering "paralysis of the stomach," she died and was buried by Frederick's side. A panel on the south side of the monument reads, "Not lost, but gone before" and "No pain, no grief, no anxious fear, can reach the peaceful sleeper here."

CEMETERIES ON HILLS

Many of Colorado's cemeteries and burial grounds are found on hill-tops. Pioneer cemeteries were often known as "Boot Hill," because the young adults buried in them "died with their boots on" meaning in the prime of life (often dying of a gunshot or by hanging). There were practical reasons for placing graves on hills. Settlers prized level ground for building homes and towns, and for cultivating crops. Most corpses were not embalmed and were buried in simple wood coffins. Decomposition odors could carry if the graves were shallow. The need for drainage is a good reason to place burials on high ground. Sentimentality also plays a role. Sometimes people are buried at a favorite site with a particular view in mind, usually from elevated ground. And Christians considered hilltops to be "nearer to God."

ALMA

Buckskin Joe was one of many mining camps surrounding the area near Fairplay that eventually became ghost towns. The closest community today is Alma, and the **Buckskin Cemetery** is located on a hill just west of town on County Road 8. William H. Grose, founder of Alma, donated part of the cemetery land (see Florissant section). Though the burials date to 1860, the cemetery was incorporated as the **Alma Cemetery** in 1902.

Some unmarked graves belong to victims of a smallpox epidemic. A beautiful dance hall girl, known as **Silver Heels** for the shoes she wore, took it upon herself to nurse the sick miners and their families. No one knew her real name for certain. She contracted the disease herself and became disfigured by the scars. When town representatives went to her little cabin across the creek to reward her for her caring service to the sick, they found it abandoned. She had slipped away, never to be seen again. They named the lone peak to the north of town Mount Silverheels in her honor. People claimed to see a shadowy veiled woman visiting a grave in the cemetery. *Could it be Silver Heels?* they wondered.

An old-timer buried here who is believed to have lived in Buckskin Joe since its inception is **Giles Ilett** (1817–1888), who perished from pneumonia. He arrived in the camp by 1864. That same year Ilett joined the Third Colorado Cavalry under Colonel Chivington. In Buckskin, he sometimes worked at mining. He owned a claim called the American Flag, but it did not yield riches to fill his purse.

Ilett began life in Curry Mallet, Somerset, England. He married and had a large family; what induced him to leave them and sail to America is unknown. In his last decade of life, he married a woman named **Jennie McDowell**. Jennie inherited his mining claims and military pension. She married again, shortly before her death in 1908, and is buried in Denver. She died on the same day of the year as Ilett, exactly twenty years later.

This enclosure holds the remains of early Buckskin Joe pioneer, Giles Ilett, of England. COURTESY OF STEVEN VEATCH

CHAPTER 6

ROCKIES PLAYGROUND

This region straddles the I-70 corridor between Denver and Glenwood Springs, crossing over some of the highest regions in the US Rocky Mountains. Mt. Elbert, the tallest peak at 14,440 feet, scrapes the sky in Lake County. American settlers arrived early in the gold rush; as the lower areas ran out of gold, prospectors moved ever higher. Some of the richest strikes in state history were located in this region, particularly Leadville's mid-1870s silver boom, followed closely by Georgetown's silver lodes. Today these mountains are known primarily for world-class ski areas and quaint old mining towns. There are no large cities, and ghost towns outnumber the current existing communities.

IDAHO SPRINGS

Idaho Springs was the first community established in Clear Creek Canyon during the gold rush days, and remains Clear Creek County's largest town. Prospector **George A. Jackson** located placer gold here, giving the location its first name, Jackson's Diggings. The town went by several other names before settling on the current one. It is jammed between I-70 on the south and canyon walls to the north. The

Idaho Springs Cemetery is southwest of town along the Mt. Evans Scenic Byway (CO 103, the highest paved road in North America), and occupies a steep, rocky slope best visited after the snow melts—a slow process on this northwest-facing site. The oldest graves date to the early 1860s. Now, more than three thousand interments fill the long, narrow property in sections with names such as Placer, Titanic, Miner's Bluff, Golden Hill, and Log Cabin.

The town's first mayor, **"Elder" Robert B. Griswold** (1830–1917), is buried in the Golden Hill section alongside his wife, **Eleanor M. Hooper** (1832–1888). His grave is unmarked, but Eleanor has a standard gabled pillar marking hers. Robert was born in New York, part of a large farming family. He had little education, but he had wanderlust and wound up in Wisconsin. Then the gold rush lured his family to Colorado in 1861.

The Griswolds worked as a team to make Idaho Springs a thriving, family-friendly community. Robert was a justice of the peace, county commissioner, and postmaster. He personally received the government grant for the town land from the US president and in turn deeded town lots to the settlers. He had great success in mining and real estate and was highly esteemed in the community. The Griswolds had a daughter and two sons. The younger son, **Harry Griswold**, was born in Idaho Springs in 1872, but contracted diphtheria in February 1883, dying after a four-day illness. His grave is not marked. Son **Scott Griswold** (1860–1928) is also in an unmarked grave. He followed his father into the mining business, at which they were sometimes partners, and lived in Idaho Springs all his life.

Daughter **Temperance "Tempe" J. Griswold** married twice, marrying her second husband a day after her divorce from the first. She lived in Idaho Springs at times and other times in Central City, Golden, and Denver. Tempe performed in a variety of theatrical productions at the Idaho Springs opera house. In 1887, she obtained the post of associate editor of the *Colorado Mining Gazette,* published in Georgetown. She also published an article about early days in Denver in the *Rocky Mountain News* in 1888. Perhaps this led to her position at the *Denver Sunday Graphic* as the society reporter. Her death date and burial location are unknown.

GEORGETOWN

Georgetown began as a mining camp started by brothers **George and David T. Griffith**, who came to Colorado soon after the 1858 gold strikes. They had no luck staking claims in Central City, so they came up the Clear Creek drainage, bypassing overcrowded Idaho Springs to the east. George struck gold in June 1859 and built a cabin at what would later be Seventeenth and Main in the town named for him. The initial influx to Georgetown after the gold discovery waned because of the Civil War. But afterward, veterans and others found their way to the small, triangular valley in the mountains west of Denver.

From 1859 to 1869, of the thirty or so deaths recorded in Georgetown, eleven were gun murders, or shootings by lawmen; two were accidental shootings; and one a lynching.

Then in 1873, the town suffered the horror of a murder-suicide. **Arden Shea** (1834–1873), a successful miner, became jealous of his lover, madam **Mollie Dean** (?–1873). After drinking heavily and quarreling most of the evening at Dean's brothel, Shea pulled his Colt pistol, shot Dean through her right temple, then put the gun to his right ear and ended his life, too. They were buried in the **Old Georgetown Cemetery**, located just north of town near the base of a west-facing slope.

Old Georgetown Cemetery was used into the 1870s, then largely forgotten when the **Alvarado Cemetery** opened about two and half miles north. Some graves were moved from the old burial grounds at that time. Soon the old cemetery was hidden behind the town dump with monuments going to ruin. An inspection in 1966 revealed only four extant headstones, all damaged. Before the Georgetown reservoir flooded the site in 1972, the remaining bodies were removed to a parcel across from the Alvarado Cemetery and given a single monument with not one name to recall those souls who endured Georgetown's embryonic period.

One veteran buried at Old Georgetown was **George A. Carns** (1839–1871) of Pennsylvania. He served in the Fourth Pennsylvania Cavalry and was captured by Confederates and put in the notorious Andersonville prison camp (Camp Sumter) in Georgia for nine months. He arrived in Georgetown by 1867 and worked as a laborer and a writer. For an adventure that year, perhaps for a tale to tell, he and several other young men traveled to Middle Park near Kremmling. They planned to bury the bones of a German prospector named **Joseph Hahn** who had died over the winter when he and two other miners decided to stay at their mining camp at the base of a large mountain in

An unknown number of bodies were moved in 1972 from the Old Georgetown Cemetery to this site near Alvarado Cemetery. No individual markers remain.
AUTHOR'S COLLECTION

Routt County. One had gone for supplies and never returned. Hahn and his companion, **William Doyle**, decided to try to make it back to Clear Creek. Hahn starved near Kremmling (his bones were buried where they lay) and Doyle was rescued. The peak where Hahn struck gold now bears his name (see chapter 8, Hahns Peak).

Carns belonged to the Grand Army of the Republic (GAR) in Georgetown, serving as the post's Sergeant Major. He also belonged to the Irish Republican Brotherhood of America (IRB of A). In 1870, he lived at a boarding house along with a younger man named **Henry Carns**, likely his brother. The following year, he intervened in an altercation at the boarding house. Someone pulled a knife and stabbed him. The **Rev. Mr. Amsbary** delivered Carn's eulogy in which the man's many virtues were enumerated. Four "brothers" from the IRB of A and four members from the GAR served as honor guards and fired a three-round salute over his grave.

The funeral of **Mrs. Elizabeth Jackson** (?–1873) at Georgetown was held on December 3, 1873. She came to Denver from New York before the war, a free Black woman, one of only a handful among five thousand residents in 1860. Her life is shrouded in mystery, as are those of many Black people of the time. What is known is that she was the mother of Mary (Jackson) Randolph, the noted restaurateur (see chapter 4, Denver, Riverside Cemetery).

The Alvarado Cemetery originally served not only Georgetown but many other communities in Clear Creek County, such as Empire, Dumont, and Silver Plume. Begun by the Masonic and Odd Fellows lodges, other organizations added to the grounds over the years. Since the early 1900s, Masonic Lodge #12, Ancient Free and Accepted Masons (AF & AM) has cared for the cemetery. The graves that date to the 1860s were probably moved from the Old Georgetown Cemetery. It has little formal organization and blends into the landscape with native pine, aspen, and spruce. The grassy open spaces and glades invite visitors to wander and ponder the people laid to rest here. The entrance to the cemetery is on the east side of the frontage road parallel to I-70, about four miles north of Georgetown.

David T. Griffith (1839–1882), one of Georgetown's founding brothers, lived there only part-time at the time of his death. Though David and his brother George had located gold at Griffith Mountain (named for them), they left town a few years later in 1862. Though their mine contained silver ore, which Georgetown would later become known for, the Griffith brothers did not process it. They sold out to Wilson & Cass Company. David lived in Denver, but traveled to Leavenworth, Kansas, where he married widow **Lovina (Wood) Smith** and became a stepfather to her daughter, **Mary B. Smith**. (Lovina is buried in Denver's Fairmount Cemetery.) David returned to Georgetown in 1867 and went to work for Wilson & Cass for a time.

David was in Georgetown in 1882, with plans to head to Arizona on business, but he suffered from pulmonary edema (dropsy) and died at age forty. Lovina and Mary remained in Georgetown, where Mary wed **Charles H. Morris**. Lovina married a third time to respected Georgetown banker **Charles R. Fish** and later moved to Denver for life, outliving her third husband by eighteen years. She

David T. Griffith, a founder of Georgetown, with wife Lovina and
stepdaughter, Mary B. Smith.
PUBLIC DOMAIN

also outlived her daughter, Mary, to whom she had planned to leave
an estate (passing to Mary's sons) worth an estimated $30,000, mostly
in mining claims.

Three white marble headstones, with the three-link chain sym-
bolizing the Independent Order of Odd Fellows (IOOF), mark the

graves of English miners buried in 1877. Two—**John Pope** (1852–1877) and **Henry Walters** (?–1877)—were born in Cornwall. The third, **John Gregory** (1843–1877) was born in Devon. The three men worked together on the night shift in the Silver Ore Tunnel near Brownville. No one else was in the tunnel at the time, but they clearly died from the effects of a premature blast of powder. Cornish miners were sought after for their skills at hard-rock mining and welcomed in the Colorado Rockies. The Cornish had a mining heritage dating to Roman times and were known around the world as "Cousin Jacks." The three men were members of the Brownville IOOF, and the Georgetown branch joined the funeral procession as it moved down

These headstones mark the graves of three Cornish miners, members of the Odd Fellows. They died in a mine blast.
Author's collection

the Silver Plume Road to the cemetery. A band playing a dirge led the way, followed by the three hearses, a number of carriages, and horsemen. The tragedy brought a large turnout for the ceremony.

Civil War veteran **Charles Osborn Townsend** (1846–1911) was a Black pioneer in Georgetown. His veteran's marker is in a section set aside for the GAR. Born in Alabama, he was the son of an enslaved woman and a white plantation owner. He was freed upon his father's death in 1856 and sent to Xenia, Ohio, to attend Wilberforce University and to keep him from being returned to slavery. Townsend enlisted in the Fifth Colored Heavy Artillery unit and held the rank of Quartermaster Sergeant. He moved to Georgetown after the war, along with his older brother.

Townsend married a niece of Aunt Clara Brown (see chapter 4, Denver, Riverside Cemetery), **Josephine Smith**, in 1873 at a ceremony attended by both white and Black citizens of town. Townsend was a respected barber (one of the few professions open to Blacks). He married a second time in 1877 to **Margaret Hall**. He had a ranch in Little Hamlin Gulch, a patented mining claim in Clear Creek County, and other mining properties, which may have brought him some income. Margaret died in 1905 and was buried in Denver. Townsend, who continued operating his barber shop, passed away suddenly in August 1911.

Downieville-Lawson-Dumont

Further up Clear Creek Canyon from Idaho Springs is the village of Dumont, first called Mill City, then later named for the founder, **Col.**

John M. Dumont. Dumont was a stage stop and had stamping mills and a smelting operation to serve the local mines. The **Dumont Cemetery**, established in 1864, is on Trails End Lane, which dead ends at the cemetery gate. This small cemetery incorporates natural granite rubble and bedrock within a peaceful ponderosa pine forest carpeted with grama grass and dotted with ball cactus.

On a chilly January day, **Anthony Joseph "A.J." August** (1842–1895) was laid to rest next to his son, **Willie C. August** (1866–1882), who died at fifteen after eating too many unripe chokecherries and green apples. A.J. August was a metallurgist and building contractor from Buffalo, New York. He came to Georgetown around 1865 and worked for the Stewart reduction works until fire destroyed it in 1877. He spent some months doing mill work in California, then came back to Clear Creek County. He was a successful miner, but his primary business was a lumber, feed, and hardware store in Lawson, a small community west of Dumont.

The Chinn family has a lot in Dumont Cemetery that includes Hoosier **Raleigh W. Chinn** (1927–1912) and his mother, **Susan (Smith) Chinn** (1797–1891). Raleigh headed overland to California in 1850 with two other men, six yoke of oxen, and food for four months. He returned home after a couple years and wed **Theresa Marie Eger** in 1855 (she is buried in Wheat Ridge). The family relocated to Missouri, and Raleigh began running freight across the plains, heading to Denver once the gold rush began. He settled his family, including his widowed mother, in Breckenridge around 1862,

Willie August's grave is made up to resemble a child's bed and pillow. His father, A.J. August, is buried next to him.

and later moved to Golden. Raleigh had a reputation as a most reliable and prompt freighter.

In late November 1875, Raleigh and a party of men from Golden headed out to the plains to hunt buffalo, something he had experience with. While he guarded the camp, the others went out and made a kill but lost their bearings in a sudden prairie snowstorm. One man made it back to camp the next morning and Raleigh loaded a pack horse with supplies to rescue the others, but one died of exposure.

Raleigh prospected in the mountains and developed several mines that he leased out. By the late 1870s, his family moved to Clear Creek County, where he went into the lodging business. He had a roomy boarding house in a mining camp called Chinnton. By the 1880s, he operated a hotel in Dumont, The Unadilla House, with Theresa heading up the victuals department. The hotel remained a fixture in town until burning to the ground in the 1940s. Raleigh's other civic involvements included building a lyceum in Dumont, organizing the Masons in Colorado, and publishing the short-lived *Dumont Courier*.

Other members of Raleigh's family interred in the lot include his brother, **Hezekiah J. Chinn** (1829–1900), a veteran; son **Richard Chinn** (1858–1929), his wife, **Myra Andrew** (1861–1885), and their infant son, **Noel Chinn** (1885–1885); and **Cuthbert H. Chinn** (1870–1930) and his young bride, **Zoe Lawson** (1882–1900), who died at age eighteen, two weeks after giving birth. She was the daughter of **Alexander "Alex" Lawson** and **Katherine "Kate" Coburn** (see below).

The Alvarado (Georgetown) and Dumont Cemeteries hold many members of the extended Coburn family, who are responsible for the development of Lawson and Downieville, west of Dumont. **John Coburn** (1822–1888) came to America from Ireland about 1839 and practiced the shoemaking trade in Pennsylvania. He married **Margaret Wilfong** (1823–1903) and they had four surviving daughters: Kate, Maggie, Hannah, and Annie. John came to Colorado to work for the Sterling Mining Co. of Pennsylvania. He purchased the 160-acre Downieville Ranch and brought his family out. He built a hotel and a schoolhouse and developed mining properties as well. All four daughters married and reared their families in the area.

Lawson began as a mining camp at the edge of the Coburn ranch and was named for Kate (Coburn) Lawson (1854–1907). She and her husband, Alex Lawson (1844–1902), were among the earliest to settle there and develop mines. Alex was born in Delaware and joined the Michigan Cavalry during the war. Kate and Alex had ten children together. They had close connections to the Chinn family of Dumont and the August family in Lawson. One child, daughter **Puss Lawson** (1886–1892), died at age six and is buried in Alvarado. Of their adult children, five are buried in Dumont.

Margaret "Maggie" Coburn (1857–1895) married Cornish miner **James Hoskins** (1851–1889) in Lawson in 1876, and they had five children before James committed suicide. They are buried in Alvarado, along with a son, **John Chester Hoskins** (1880–1954), but only James has a headstone, provided by the Masons. James suffered delusions of persecution related to his handling of the late John

Coburn's business affairs, a house fire, and the disappearance of his business partner. He shot himself in the head on March 20, 1889, and died nine days later.

Hannah M. Coburn (1859–1932) married a miner from Illinois, **Stephen Easley Cadwalader** (1848–1906). They had eight children born in Clear Creek County. Steve, who worked at unloading mine tram cars, died in an accident at the Jo Reynolds mine and mill on July 2, 1906. Almost three years later to the day, a family friend, **Ida Emma Green**, died suddenly, leaving a widower and three children. In August 1915, Hannah married the widower, **Thomas H. Green** (1861–1940). Thomas and Hannah had been friends for forty years or more, having performed together in a trio in 1882 at Mr. Chinn's lyceum in Dumont when in their twenties. At one point, Thomas had contemplated opening a meat market with James Hoskins. But, like the other men in the family, he worked in the mines for a living. Both of Hannah's husbands, and her baby boy **Reese Cadwalader** (1886–1887), have memorials in Dumont Cemetery, but there is no known marker for Hannah.

The youngest of John Coburn's daughters, **Annie H. Coburn** (1864–1919), married **Daniel J. Hooley** (1855–1924) in 1885. Only one of their three children, **Margaret "Madge" (Hooley) Johnson** (1891–1975), survived to adulthood. The entire family is buried in the Dumont Cemetery. Daniel and Annie have only metal mortuary markers. Their stillborn baby and six-year-old son, **John Coburn Hooley** (1886–1892), share a faceted headstone topped by two lambs.

JOHN
COBURN,
DIED
Dec. 2, 1892,
AGED
RS. 7 Ms. 16 Ds

BABY,
BORN
Nov. 1, 1893,
DIED
Nov. 1, 1893.

CHILDREN
OF
P. J. & ANNIE HOOLEY

Lambs frequently adorn children's headstones, but they are also found on adult headstones. This marker for the Hooley children is in Dumont Cemetery.
AUTHOR'S COLLECTION

The Coburn family held a reunion at Lawson in 1896 and commandeered the opera house for the celebration. It was the twenty-sixth anniversary of their move to Clear Creek County. The entertainments included a prophecy about the family fortunes twenty-five years in the future. They had some ambitions!

Mrs. Coburn had rounded out her hundred years, and like a Christian and a true woman, she looks without fear on the future and is ready to meet her creator. Mr. and Mrs. Lawson and son Howard reside in their brown-stone front, and Lawson contains a population of over 100,000. Charley and Phil are managers of the Brown Palace; Luella is editress of The Lawson Daily News; Ethel and Zoe are wallowing in connubial felicity, each content to remain home managing their large households. . . . Mrs. Cadwalader has a fortune sufficient to enjoy life as well as to make others happy, while her husband is now "Congressman Steve"; . . . Anna is mayor while Ida and Rhoda are authors of no mean repute; Mr. and Mrs. Hooley have just returned from a trip around the world, content to be at home after an absence of three years; their daughter Madge is an elocutionist and the wonder of the world.

. . . and more in a similar vein.

The Coburns organized a wide variety of social events, from dances and recitals to plays and picnics. They stepped up to console bereaved parents and mourning widows and widowers. Many a card of thanks in the Georgetown papers mentioned the kindness of Mrs. Lawson, in particular, who managed the family hotel. It is fitting to call the Coburns the "First Family of Lawson."

LEADVILLE

The highest incorporated city in the nation is Leadville, situated in a subalpine valley ringed with some of the highest peaks in America. Though gold was found in the area known as California Gulch in the early days of the rush, it soon panned out. By the mid-1870s, though, Leadville's silver ore had ascended to prominence and for nearly two decades drove incredible growth in this difficult place to live. With a population approaching twenty thousand at one point, it became Colorado's "second city" for a time. Fortunes were made and lost. Horace Tabor's share of the Little Pittsburgh Mine brought him a million dollars—and he lost it all by the end of the century. But pity the buyer: the mine ran out of ore just a year after the sale.

Leadville's **City Cemetery** was established in 1877 and used for under two years. A reporter for the *Leadville Chronicle* described it on May 26, 1879:

At the foot of Chestnut street, a little distance from the Leadville smelting company's works, is an acre plot of ground unfenced, and with the carbonate-like earth thrown up into little heaps. On a closer inspection the stranger will see that many of these carbonate mounds are marked by pieces of boards, slabs and sticks. . . . There were no flowery lawns, spouting fountains, shady nooks, grassy plats, nor artistically carved marble. . . . In short, there is nothing about the burry-ing [*sic*] place for the dead of Leadville to make a well man desire to die.

The article gives a detailed listing of the known burials at that time, many of them young children, few over forty. The graves that remained after some bodies were moved to **Evergreen Cemetery** are unmarked and rest under a football field with only a plaque to commemorate them.

Capt. Sullivan Breece (1815–1877), a Mexican War veteran, died in November 1877 to become the first City Cemetery interment. He was a miner and surgical instrument manufacturer. He arrived in California Gulch by 1860, leaving his family in Philadelphia, and part-nered with two brothers, **Thomas and Joseph Wells**. They took out $25,000 in gold in their first season and sold the Shamrock Mine for a considerable sum. Breece was one of Lake County's first commission-ers when the major town and county seat was Oro City. Breece Hill in Leadville was named for him, as was the Breece Iron Mine, which he located. A few months before his death, the mine came under the ownership of Jerome B. Chaffee, David H. Moffat, and others.

Evergreen Cemetery, a 131-acre parcel in a pine forest on the west edge of town off McWethy Drive, opened for burials in 1879. The trustees sold sections to various organizations, some now defunct. Originally, fences could only be used to delineate the sections—no family lots could be fenced or marked by shrubs. That restriction went away and now, in the more formal areas of the cemetery (i.e., paid burials), many lots have fencing. Free sections allowed for pauper graves, accounting for about six thousand burials in total. One that has drawn recent attention is the Catholic Free section, where roughly 1,400 Irish immigrants and other Catholics are buried, mostly in unmarked graves. Nearly half are children under five and stillborn babies. Many of the grave sites are simply rectangular depressions in the earth, the result of decomposition, as the bodies had basic coffins or shrouds when interred.

A memorial to the Irish and others buried in the Catholic Free section was unveiled in 2022. It echoes a traditional Gaelic burial mound and features a miner holding a pick and an Irish harp. He looks to the east, in remembrance of his homeland and in hopefulness for a brighter future. Names of the dead have been resurrected from Catholic Church records, and some burials have been identified. The Irish plight is a moving one: fleeing poverty and famine in their home country, they wound up in places like Leadville and Butte, Montana, living in rudimentary conditions at best, working for low wages, and suffering the pneumonia and other scourges common to the high-elevation, frigid camps. Their average death age in Leadville was a scant twenty-two years.

One person who moved to Evergreen from the old cemetery was Marshal **George E. O'Connor** (1848–1878). Reportedly born in Nova Scotia and reared in Maine, he came to Colorado in 1863. He lived in Georgetown and Lake City before arriving in Leadville, where he was appointed town marshal. He had been on the job just a

THE GOOD GUYS?

Marshall George O'Connor of Leadville planned to have Officer James Bloodworth fired by the town council for gambling and visiting dance halls. On the night of April 25, 1878, the two men came face to face at Billy Nye's Palatial saloon. After a brief exchange of words, Bloodworth drew his gun and coolly fired several rounds, killing O'Connor. Then the murderer slipped back out of the saloon, mounted his horse, and rode away, escaping justice.

In Colorado mining camps, recruiting good men to command law and order was a tough sell. Sometimes the only man willing to take the job was a gunslinger of questionable morals. Many a lawman gunned down innocent civilians and other officers. Among the most notorious of the good guys gone bad was **Tom Horn** (1860–1903). He was convicted for murdering Willie Nickell, just fourteen, in Wyoming in 1902. On November 20, 1903, Horn was hanged at the Laramie courthouse, using a rope he had woven himself during his months of incarceration. He is buried at **Columbia Cemetery** in Boulder, Colorado.

Horn moved west as a teen and became a scout for the US Cavalry. Able to speak both Spanish and Apache, he interpreted at the capture of Geronimo. He sometimes worked as a deputy in the Arizona borderlands. After a rustler stole all his livestock there, bankrupting him, Horn became a lifelong foe of rustlers and thieves. He had no scruples about shooting or hanging them, without benefit of a trial.

He was known as a range detective but in reality was a gun for hire. In the conflicts between sheep men and cattlemen, or between large cattle companies versus homesteaders, he most likely worked for those with the deepest pockets. He tracked and arrested outlaws for the Pinkerton Agency in the 1890s. He even packed mules for the Rough Riders in Cuba during the Spanish-American War.

During the range wars in Browns Park, Horn is believed to have been responsible for murdering two ranchers (see chapter 8, Browns Park). The Willie Nickell killing took place during a range feud between the Nickell and Miller families at Iron Mountain. Horn allegedly confessed to the crime while drunk. Many believe he was wrongly convicted for this murder, but there is no question that many a man died by Horn's hand. Some of them may have even "needed killing." But his death proves the adage: "live by the sword, die by the sword."

For more about "The Good Guys?" see Tin Cup and Telluride in chapter 7.

few weeks when he was gunned down by Leadville policeman **James Bloodworth**. He left a widow and young daughter.

A well-known but unmarked grave at Evergreen is that of madam **Mollie May** (?–1887), alias Virginia "Jennie" Mickey. She purchased her first property in Leadville under the name Melinda May Bryant. A journalist working on a book in 1879 proclaimed Mollie was the daughter of Morris Pendill of Herkimer County, New York. Whoever she really was, she achieved notoriety out West in Cheyenne, Deadwood, and parts of Colorado before winding up in Leadville, where she rose to prominence as a madam of her own bawdy house. Frequently in the news, Mollie elicited the most outrage when she "adopted" (some said "purchased") a young girl called **Ella Moore**.

After selling her first establishment, Mollie built an ostentatious replacement on Harrison Avenue, allegedly with Horace Tabor as a silent partner. She befriended **Mindy Lamb**, the widow of **Lewis Lamb** (1840–1880), when he was shot and killed in 1880 by former marshal Martin Duggan. She contributed generously to charitable causes in Leadville. When Mollie died of heart disease in 1887, a large procession, including Mindy, accompanied her to Evergreen. Mollie's coffin lay in the most expensive hearse in the country and several other fancy carriages followed. Her estate was estimated at $25,000, with $8,000 of that in diamonds. The city purchased her building to serve as a courthouse.

A more "respectable" citizen of Leadville is buried with members of his family in Block 29. **Jeremiah "Uncle Jere" Irwin** (1834–1893), a war veteran and accomplished builder from Cincinnati, came to Leadville in 1879. During the Civil War, he enlisted in the Navy, became acting master of the steamer *Judge Torrence,* and fought in the Mississippi River theater. He married **Harriet Rose** (1840–1899) in 1855, and they had three daughters and four sons. **Charles Irwin** (1861–1901), **Albert Irwin** (1869–1900), and **Edward Irwin** (1877–1904) are also interred in the family lot. Jere Irwin was the Leadville mayor twice, spent six years as county commissioner, and ran for sheriff in 1883. His residence on West Third Street had one of Leadville's early telephones.

Irwin became mayor due to an odd accident. During a Fourth of July parade, a wagon in the procession contained fireworks. A rocket went off by surprise and blasted into the crowd of several thousand spectators. It broke the leg of then-mayor Bowers, who later died from the injury. A convention called to replace him named Irwin to be Bowers's successor.

Prior to his Colorado days, Irwin constructed asylums in Illinois and Missouri, and rebuilt in Chicago after the great fire in 1871. Upon arrival in Leadville, he opened brickyards that provided materials for the city's substantial buildings. He built the American National Bank on Harrison Avenue and Fifth, a Romanesque Revival–style building of brick with red sandstone trim and a bell-shaped dome. He also did the excavation, brick work, and plastering on the Odd Fellows Hall at Harrison and Eighth. In 1890, Irwin started another brick factory in Salt Lake City. In addition, he had a brickyard and building contracts in Aspen. It may have been all these extensive and widespread business interests—plus some lawsuits, including one brought by his Aspen

The large headstone for Jeremiah and Harriet Irwin in Leadville's Evergreen Cemetery.
COURTESY OF THOMAS GROSS

business partner—that strained his constitution. Upon a return trip from Salt Lake, he suffered a stroke and soon passed on, just fifty-nine years old. Harriet Irwin also lived to just fifty-nine, coming to Evergreen in December 1899.

The Irwin family was wealthy. Jere and Harriet sent their sons to college in the East. Back in Leadville, Charles, Albert, and Edward led lives of leisure and dissipation, particularly after the deaths of their parents. Albert, who had many run-ins with the law in Leadville, died suddenly in May 1900 in Carbondale, and his siblings provided him a private burial. Charles, who had been working as a card dealer in Denver, became despondent over relationship troubles and gambling away his inheritance. He committed suicide in late December 1901, and his body was not discovered for more than two weeks. Edward, an actor, also chose the suicide route at his cabin in Leadville in February 1904. The fourth son, **Robert H. Irwin**, who also had trouble with the law, followed his father's footsteps and worked as a bricklayer. He died in Cripple Creek in 1909. Thus, four young brothers, who had every advantage in life, all died and were buried over the course of a single decade.

Red Cliff

Red Cliff, clutching the side of a mountain above the Eagle River, developed during the silver-boom years when miners from Leadville began exploring outlying areas to the north. Settled in 1879, it became Eagle County's first town in 1883 and was county seat until 1923. The settlement benefited from the arrival of the Denver & Rio Grande

Railroad in 1881, enabling ore to be shipped to Leadville's smelters. Situated on a narrow bench of land, Red Cliff's growth is limited geologically. The road to **Greenwood Cemetery** crosses the river and climbs a narrow alley to Knob Hill above town.

The most prominent monument in Greenwood is that of **Arthur H. Fulford** (1856–1891), who was a dark-haired man with wide-set eyes and a luxuriant handlebar mustache. He was born in Canada to **Edward J. Fulford** and **Sarah McLaughlin**. Edward was a Methodist minister who traveled with his family across the American West. In 1880, Arthur arrived in Leadville, where he met **Mary Quirk** of Wisconsin, living with her family. They married in 1883 in Red Cliff, as

Portrait of miner Arthur Fulford.
EAGLE VALLEY LIBRARY DISTRICT 1982.001.115.

His tree-style monument in Red Cliff's Greenwood Cemetery signifies a life cut short. He was killed in an avalanche on New York Mountain.
AUTHOR'S COLLECTION

the mines there developed. Arthur had a knack for discovering paying lodes and managing mining operations. He is credited with finding the quartzite in the Eagle River mining district. He was also the Red Cliff town marshal for a time.

The Fulfords had five boys and two of them are buried with Arthur in Greenwood, having died as infants. Arthur, along with his parents, had a ranch about fifteen miles west of Red Cliff (as the crow flies) at the base of New York Mountain. This area is still called Fulford today.

Arthur kept tabs on a variety of gold and silver mines in Eagle County. One of these properties drew Arthur up New York Mountain on New Year's Eve 1891. The next day, reports of a massive snowslide on the mountain alarmed the Fulford household. Search parties went looking for Arthur, fearing he could be buried under hundreds of feet of concrete-like snow. They found him in just eighteen inches, but his neck had been broken by the avalanche's impact. He was thirty-five.

Pioneers often had to assume many roles, and **Dr. Thomas N. Evans** (1831–1899) was no exception. In addition to being the community doctor, he did some mining work, served the town as marshal and deputy sheriff, and was county surveyor for many years. In his capacity as surveyor, along with two others, he settled a boundary dispute between Eagle and Garfield Counties that benefitted Eagle. As a physician, he and his wife, **Sarah "Sallie" C. Huston** (1832–1908) attended the first birth in Red Cliff. When smallpox broke out in 1883 at the Star Hotel, he quarantined the afflicted in a log cabin above the railroad water tank. Dr. Evans faithfully cared for the three sick men. Two perished, but one did recover. Dr. Evans also had to patch up some knife wounds when an altercation between sheep men and cattle men broke out in Wolcott.

Thomas and Sallie Evans were both born in Missouri and married there in 1855. Sallie graduated in 1853 from the Columbia Female Academy in Boone County, a high-school-level institution that "fit her for her mission as a ministering spirit wherever she goes," according to the school catalog. Thomas spent time working as a carpenter in Denver, while Sallie worked as a seamstress. They moved to the mountains around 1878.

Another doctor buried in Greenwood Cemetery, **Dr. Joseph Gideon Gilpin** (1845–1920), was a benevolent fellow in service to humanity. His grave is marked by a metal mortuary sign and a legible wooden headboard once painted with his name and death date. Dr. Gilpin worked as a pharmacist and went to medical school in Baltimore before moving to Colorado. He arrived in Red Cliff in 1881 and practiced his profession for a time, left for the mines, then returned and continued ministering to the sick and injured for nearly forty years (he never gave up mining, though).

He treated all and would make the hard trek through the mountains to help miners. He even went up New York Mountain on January 1, 1892, when Arthur Fulford went missing. When Gilpin had not returned in a week, the town feared him dead from a slide, but he was found safe. Dr. Gilpin charged based on what his patients could pay, which was sometimes nothing. Because pneumonia was one of the deadliest diseases in the Rockies, he became a specialist and others sought him out for his treatment expertise. Ironically, he once had to be hospitalized for that very condition. He was county coroner beginning in 1905, being well qualified for the position. One of the worst cases he had to attend was twenty-six people killed in a Denver & Rio Grande wreck in January 1909, involving a head-on collision of two trains at Dotsero.

Dr. Gilpin remained a bachelor until late in life but married a widow in 1904. Perhaps he was spurred by a 1903 state legislative attempt to pass a bachelor tax of $50 per year to fund schools. He said of the proposal, "I would not pay the tax. I'd leave the state first, hanged, if I wouldn't." Fellow Red Cliffer **Ben Cress** said, "They ought to tax the old maids, too." Dr. Gilpin's bride, **Mrs. Ida E. (Silver) Kesecker**, came out to Colorado from West Virginia and was reported to be an old friend of the doctor. The *Eagle County Blade* speculated the romance had been percolating for some time. A year after their marriage, Dr. and Mrs. Gilpin suffered a bad buggy accident on Battle Mountain Road. If they had not landed on a tailings pile fifty feet below, they would certainly have been killed by a much further fall.

When Dr. Gilpin passed in 1920, he was much mourned. He was known for his Santa-like appearance and demeanor. One person said they remembered "his beautiful horses and his mean dog. The doctor responded to calls for help at any time, and under any conditions. He made medicine from powders, and had a secret concoction guaranteed to cure the flu."

In 1901, Dr. Gilpin was called upon to treat a nine-year-old boy who had been injured while sledding. The children, released from school, would coast the high bridge across the Eagle River and down into town. **Harold Tague** caught a runner on a bare spot, whirled around and slid out under the railing, falling thirty feet to the railroad tracks below. Not only did he survive the drop, but he did not break a single bone.

Harold was the son of **Judge Patrick "Pat" Tague** (1852–1911) and his wife, **Lydia (Berkley) Tague** (1868–1937). Pat Tague, born in New York, came to Red Cliff, Colorado, in 1883, where he was a newsdealer and by 1888, a justice of the peace. He spent a dozen years as district clerk and was elected to three terms as county judge. Lydia was born in Boulder to **Judge Granville Berkley** and his second wife, **Annie Mason**. Lydia's older sister, **Josephine (Berkley) Mays**, lived in Red Cliff, where her husband was a doctor. When their father died, Lydia moved to Red Cliff and worked as assistant postmaster.

Lydia had many suitors, but in 1889, she accepted Pat Tague's proposal. When he died from tuberculosis in February 1911, the county commissioners appointed Lydia to take his place as county judge, she having served previously as court clerk. Lydia Tague thus became the first female county judge in the United States. She continued to be elected to the post until she insisted on retirement in 1924. She spent some additional time again as a court clerk until health issues compelled her to give up the position. She spent the final two years of her life as an invalid in Montrose, and after her death from a stroke in 1937, was interred next to her beloved husband in Red Cliff.

Portrait of Lydia Berkley Tague, who became the first
female county judge in the United States in 1912.
BAIN NEWS SERVICE PHOTOGRAPH COLLECTION, LIBRARY OF
CONGRESS, PRINTS & PHOTOGRAPHS DIVISION, LC-B2-1305-11

Three prominent granite markers stand near the cemetery
entrance—a father, mother, and daughter—little revealing that two
of the three were shot to death in a fit of passion, a result of love gone
wrong. The two separate but tragic incidents took place a dozen years
apart. **William Henry Nottingham** (1851–1896) married **Nancy**

Angeline Tracy (1853–1928) in Iowa in 1874. They moved to Morrison, Colorado, in 1879 and later relocated to Red Cliff. One child born to the couple was **Grace V. Nottingham** (1882–1908). Angeline and her daughter were both striking women who turned men's heads. William had a jealous streak and a temper. He was a silver miner and a county commissioner. A boarding house kept Angeline busy. William began accusing boarders of turning his wife's affections away from him. One allegedly committed suicide. Another was **Ernest V. Hurd**, who resided with the Nottinghams for several years.

William took a shot at Hurd one day and missed, but he vowed to try again. On December 20, 1896, the two men crossed paths and a chase ensued. Cornered in a stable, Hurd fired in self-defense, killing William instantly. Angeline married Hurd in 1899, but it was a short-lived relationship. On a trip to New York in 1901, Hurd passed away at age forty.

Grace Nottingham moved to Denver, where she worked as a bookkeeper. She met traveling salesman **Harry Adler,** and they married in Los Angeles, California, in June 1906. Within six months, she filed for divorce in Denver, claiming that Adler was a bigamist and had another wife in California. When the court dismissed the case, she filed again on grounds of cruelty and received her decree. A full year later, Adler, determined that no other man should have Grace, came to her lodgings and shot her, then himself. In his murder-suicide note, he expressed a wish that they be buried together. It was not granted.

MATERIAL MATTERS

Some headstone carvers in Colorado used locally available sandstone, which is hard and attractive but not enduring. These weathered monuments frustrate many a descendant today. Some Front Range monument carvers quarried a crystallized limestone that looked like marble. Sandstone and limestone make good building materials but simply do not hold up to the elements as grave markers. Granite does well, particularly in the state's dry climate, and marble was most in demand for the discerning monument purchaser. Yule marble was discovered in aptly named Marble, Colorado, in the 1870s. Though its quality rivaled that of eastern quarries, its remote setting and lack of transportation options made it too expensive. Even importing marble from Italy was cheaper.

Stone, without engraving, was also used to mark graves. Sometimes just a chunk or slab of sandstone served as a marker, or a ring of rock surrounded or covered a burial. Less permanent but common were wooden memorials. Most that remain are no longer legible, but in some cases faint lettering can still be read. The lead in paint, long ago flaked away, permeated the cellulose, leaving a visible record of the names and epitaphs. Wood markers are the most susceptible to theft, vandalism, and destruction. Boys playing with matches in 1985 set fire to the Animas City Cemetery in Durango, burning every last remaining wood memorial.

An inexpensive material sometimes used is concrete. While wet, lettering is stamped or crudely etched to create a long-lasting message to the world. But this substance, too, erodes more quickly than marble or granite.

Aside from stone, a durable substance is metal. Some are simple mortuary markers, small and inconspicuous, often vandalized or buried under layers of dirt and sometimes grass. But in the latter part of the nineteenth century, people could order prefabricated zinc memorials (sometimes called "white bronze") every bit as elaborate as carved marble. They are hollow inside and sometimes the name/date panels are broken or missing. However, they remain legible today, though in some cases the metal is becoming brittle and subject to deformation, particularly at the seams. In urban areas, pollution has caused pitting and other degradation, but this is much less common in Colorado's clean air.

CHAPTER 7

MOUNTAINS AND MESAS

Southwestern Colorado is characterized by a diverse landscape. From the Colorado River and soaring mesas in the Grand Junction area, to the watersheds of the San Juan Mountains. From the scorched Colorado Plateau desert of Paradox Valley, to the sky-scraping peaks of the Elk Mountain range. As with the terrain, diverse cultures shaped present-day communities.

Ancestral Puebloans, with ties to modern Pueblo and other tribes, settled the area for over a thousand years. Large numbers of their dwellings are preserved in Mesa Verde National Park, Ute Mountain Tribal Park, and many national monuments. Bands of Ute Indians roamed all of Colorado and were eventually relegated to reservations. The state's only reservations are found here: Ute Mountain Ute and Southern Ute.

Spanish Franciscan priests/explorers **Atanasio Domínguez** and **Silvestre Vélez de Escalante** crossed the area in 1776, searching out a route to Monterey, California, but they never made it further than southwestern Utah before returning to Santa Fe. Their difficult trek was only made possible by the assistance of tribes in the area. They were preceded by **Juan Maria Antonio de Rivera**, who was sent by the New Mexico governor to find silver and designated the Spanish landmark names still used in the region.

In the early 1870s, miners began prospecting the San Juan Mountains and a few farmed in the flat-bottomed Animas Valley to provide food to the miners. Major settlement did not begin until after the Brunot Agreement was ratified in 1874 and bands of northern Utes were removed from the state.

The latter portion of the nineteenth century was characterized by rapid development aided by the building of railroads through this mountainous section of the state. The trains hauled ore to smelters, hauled agricultural goods to markets, and provided a link to Denver.

Tin Cup

Tiny, old mining communities dot the gulches east and northeast of Gunnison. The first placer mining in Tin Cup Gulch, above 10,000 feet elevation, began in 1859, but no town existed until 1879 after lode deposits were found. Called Virginia City at first, confusion with other places by that name led to the name Tin Cup (sometimes Tincup). The **Tin Cup Cemetery** occupies a forested hill south of town off FR 765, bordered by alpine wetlands. It contains a "Jewish Knoll," "Catholic Knoll," and "Protestant Knoll."

The Keyes family arrived early, opened a hotel, and established the Abbey ranch (Abbeyville) to raise hay. **Landon Harrison Keyes** (1840–1918) fought for the Confederacy, and had extensive experience building railroad grades back East. **Adaline A. (Rice) Hensley** (1831–1908) had been widowed about a year when she married Keyes in Iowa in 1873. They arrived in Colorado about 1881. Though neither had children of their own, Adaline adopted her first husband's orphaned niece, **Lillian Louisa Vaughn**. In November 1882, Lillie married miner **Andrew Jamison** (1856–1883), who was the sixth town marshal.

Tin Cup, like other start-up mining camps, had a rough element holding sway over the entire place. The first town marshal, a position held in name only by one of the toughs, tolerated rowdy drinking and violent quarrels. The second town marshal, **Tom Leahy**, murdered the one who succeeded him, **Frank Emerson** (1838–1882). **Marshal Harry Rivers** (?–1882) was killed by a prisoner he was escorting to jail. A subsequent marshal went insane from the pressure of the job and died in an Illinois asylum. Finally, Andy Jamison was persuaded to wear the badge. Jamison was shot to death by **William Taylor**, while the marshal was beating on Taylor's friend. Unlike the previous murderers, Taylor was arrested and sent to prison. Jamison's widow, Lillie, gave birth to their daughter, **Aileen Jamison**, three months after the killing. None of the three dead marshals have a known grave marker.

Adaline, after thirty-five years married to Landon Keyes, died of stroke in April 1908. She has a wooden headboard in the Tin Cup Cemetery. Keyes's fortunes declined after his wife's passing. He lost some Tin Cup properties in a lawsuit in 1912. Nearing the end of life, he wound up in the county poor house, where the county doctor undertook to find his family back in Virginia. Keyes went back East to spend a final few days with a niece and her family before dying. His remains were returned to Tin Cup for burial, where he has a marble Confederate headstone.

Sheltered inside a wooden pole fence on the Protestant knoll is the grave of **Kate Fisher** (?–1902), a Black woman who ran a popular hotel and restaurant in Tin Cup. Stories indicate she escaped from slavery, leaving behind a husband and child. She headed west seeking a life of freedom and opportunity. She made stops in Leadville and Buena Vista before settling permanently in Tin Cup. Her establishment became known as "Aunt Kate's Hotel" and served rich and poor alike. Being entirely uneducated, she asked patrons to sum their own tab—but even those who could not pay did not leave with an empty stomach. She died of cancer in April 1902.

Ohio City

Ohio City came into being when miner Jacob Hess found silver in Ohio Creek in 1879. The town made news in May 1880 when two men had a quarrel. Believed to be from good families in Louisville, Kentucky, **James Reid** aka **James Oakley** (?–1880) and **James Edwards** (?–1880) came to Colorado in the mining era and lived "wild and dissipated," according to the report in the *Gunnison Review* on May 29. The disagreement seems to have begun during their time in Leadville.

The two men had a partnership in a tent restaurant. Reid learned while away on business that Edwards had been drinking heavily. Reid wanted his money out of the business, he confided to another partner. This third partner warned Edwards, who borrowed a gun stating that "a man would be killed before breakfast." Reid was in the restaurant in the morning and greeted Edwards as he walked in. Edwards responded

THE SAN JUAN PATHFINDER

No discussion of developments in southwestern Colorado is complete without mention of mighty-mite **Otto Mears** (1840–1931). A scant five-feet-five-inches tall, this orphaned Russian immigrant possessed the will and abilities to reshape the state in a brief timespan. Relatives in New York shipped him to California when he was just ten, ending his formal education and setting him on a path to self-determination.

After banging around California selling newspapers, learning the tinsmith trade, and mining, Mears joined the first California regiment in the Civil War. The regiment held off Texan rebels in New Mexico and battled the Navajo under Kit Carson. After his discharge in 1864, Mears made his way to Santa Fe and worked for several mercantile businesses. He started his own store in Conejos, Colorado, in 1865. He built the San Luis Valley's first sawmill and grist mill to supply Fort Garland. The local wheat crops being insufficient, he homesteaded near present-day Saguache, founded the town, the county, and a newspaper to promote them.

When his crop matured, wheat prices had crashed at the fort, so he forged a road over Poncha Pass to the Arkansas Valley and California Gulch. With encouragement from William Gilpin (first territorial governor and long-time owner of the Sangre de Cristo land grant), Mears improved the route and chartered it as a toll road. Another 300-plus miles of toll roads followed, opening the San Juan Mountains for mining and homesteading, even though the land still belonged to the Utes. Mears became friends with Chief Ouray, learned to speak fluent Ute (the only white man known to do so), and sat on the commission that created the Brunot Agreement of 1873, which richly rewarded Ouray at Mears's urging. A later agreement with the Utes that Mears crafted is characterized as a deliberate swindle (with probable forged Ute signatures), a deed that will forever mar his legacy.

Mears turned to railroad development, building the Rio Grande Southern between Ridgway and Durango. Other railroads radiated from Silverton. The roads and railroads in this section of the mountains were engineering marvels, for which Mears was rightly lauded. Other ventures and incidents involving Mears included the founding of Lake City and Montrose, mail contracts from Lake City to the town of Ouray, and the state legislature. He also sat on the Board of Commissioners that oversaw construction of the Capitol in Denver, where his stained-glass likeness hangs.

(continued)

Mears is astonishing for having his fingers in so many pies and mastering so many complex skills. He made and lost several fortunes but never detoured from his ambitions. Poker was his only recreation. After the Silver Crash of 1893, he spent a decade in the East, building the Washington & Chesapeake Railroad before returning to his beloved San Juan Mountains and settling with his wife, **Mary Kampfschulte** (1849–1924), in Silverton. Mary's health necessitated a move to lower-altitude California in 1917. After Mears's death in 1931, their ashes were scattered in the mountains outside Silverton. Both have cenotaphs in Silverton's **Hillside Cemetery**.

The Ouray toll road, now US 550 over Red Mountain Pass, is one of Otto Mears's most well-known and impressive feats of road building.

angrily and drew the gun. Reid jumped up, pulling his revolver, but Edwards fired and missed. Then they both fired two shots apiece, guns touching chests at the hearts, with predictable results.

The two are buried, boot-hill style in Illinois Gulch, just west of town, opposite the **Ohio City Cemetery**. The coroner's jury verdict stated that Edwards murdered Reid and was killed himself by Reid's self-defense. Not that either one cared by then.

Animas City

This agricultural community, situated on the Animas River between Animas Mountain on the west and a series of glacial moraines on the east, arose to supply the miners, who could not produce their own food at high elevations. The residents anxiously awaited the arrival of the Denver & Rio Grande Railroad. Unfortunately, the railroad board found the Animas City government disagreeable to terms and they laid out their own rival town two miles to the south and named it Durango. Animas City declined while Durango thrived, eventually annexing the former.

On high ground, partway up the side of what became known as Reservoir Mesa, the citizens established the **Animas City Cemetery**, the oldest documented cemetery in La Plata County. The first burials likely occurred in 1877. The oldest extant stone dates to May 1878. Like other pioneer cemeteries, this one has suffered vandalism and neglect. Though some efforts have been made to protect and preserve it, development pressures currently threaten it. Use of the Animas City Cemetery declined after the Durango Masonic Lodge

This recent photo taken at the Animas City Cemetery shows evidence of vandalism in this endangered pioneer cemetery.

purchased twenty acres closer to the city, which is now Durango's **Greenmount Cemetery.**

The entire Culver family is buried at Animas City. **Daniel Culver** (1837–1881) married **Permelia Arabella "Bell" Gaines** (1850–1921) at her parents' pioneer homestead in Fountain, El Paso County, in 1873. Daniel was a trader and sheep man. He had large flocks in the Pueblo area and in northern New Mexico at Tierra Amarilla, where he had a store. Daniel preempted land north of Hermosa in 1876, and settled his wife and daughter **Bessie** (1874–1941) in Animas City in 1877. Sons **Albert** (1877–1880) and **Clifford** (1878–1880) soon arrived. Daniel opened another mercantile business there, later

(Top) Bessie Culver c. 1890s, the last of her family to be interred at Animas City Cemetery. The Animas Museum in Durango houses a collection of Culver family photographs, though many are not identified.

Courtesy of La Plata County Historical Society

(Bottom) This badly eroded and broken headstone marks the graves of Bessie's younger brothers, Albert and Clifford Culver, who died of scarlet fever.

Author's collection

partnering with Bell's brother, **Richard E. Gaines**. He continued his business interests in New Mexico. Hired herders took care of the Culver sheep.

The Culvers suffered a devastating shock when the two young boys died of scarlet fever in December 1880. The little ones were laid to rest in the cemetery under a double headstone. Just prior to their deaths, Daniel developed "softening of the brain." He was committed to the asylum in Pueblo; one report stated that he "is only slightly demented." Another brother-in-law, **Cyrus C. Gaines**, assumed control of Daniel's business affairs. Bell was left to deal with her daughter and her grief. A year later, Daniel died at the asylum. His headstone has been shattered to pieces. He was remembered in Caroline Westcott Romney's *Durango Record* for his "peculiarly generous and noble nature . . . Many are the miners throughout the San Juan who are indebted to him for food . . . for he knew not how to refuse the needy."

Bell's daughter Bessie married **Robert L. Dale** in 1892 and remained in Animas City. Bell had the pleasure of watching her grandchildren grow, though Bessie lost several infants, too. Bell was buried in Animas City Cemetery, presumably near Daniel and the boys, but she has no marker. Bessie Culver Dale died in 1941 and has one of the later graves found in this cemetery.

A child buried here lost his life when many residents of Animas City still lived in tents. Three women, whose absent husbands were teamsters, shared a tent, along with their children. One night, a burglar breeched the canvas and **Mrs. Duncan** pulled a gun to defend the sleeping families. However, she accidentally discharged the gun before aiming and some of the buckshot shattered the femur of Mrs. Ackerman's two-year-old son. Doctors removed a portion of the bone, but little **Nelson LeRoy Ackerman** (1878–1881) suffered a slow, painful passing about fifteen hours later. Nelson has a marble headstone carved with a hand pointing heavenward with the words, "Gone Home." Nelson was the son of **Theron and Augusta Ackerman**, a transient family. They lived in Kansas when he was born, and had been in Colorado only a short time. They moved on, winding up in British Columbia, Canada, probably never to see their son's grave again.

Victims and perpetrators of violent crime are buried here "with their boots on." The most notorious is **Isaac "Ike" Stockton** (1852–1881), of the Stockton Gang, a Texas outlaw bunch that included his older brother, **Porter Stockton**, who was a remorseless killer. The Stocktons migrated to Lincoln County, New Mexico, where Ike operated a saloon. They also spent brief periods in Colfax County, New Mexico, and Trinidad, Colorado. The gang rustled cattle in the Animas Valley, operating out of Silverton. The Stocktons presented themselves in Animas City as legitimate cattlemen, and Porter even served as town marshal. Their rustling activities led to Porter being killed in Flora Vista, New Mexico, in early 1881, during a feud with the Simmons family known as the San Juan County War. Ike died later that year after being shot in the leg by La Plata County **Sheriff Barney Watson** and **Deputy James Sullivan** when they attempted to arrest him on an outstanding warrant. An amputation failed to save him. Ike's marble headstone, broken and lying flat, has an incorrect death date.

FORT LEWIS POST

Potential problems with their Ute neighbors and the Navajo (Diné) in the Four Corners area worried southwest Colorado residents. As a consequence, Fort Lewis Post relocated from Pagosa Springs to western La Plata County, south of present-day Hesperus. The troops included a segregated company of Buffalo Soldiers. The Army selected a large section of level land with a mix of pine forest, meadows, and cottonwood riparian habitat along the La Plata River. In the eleven-year period that Fort Lewis existed as an Army post, the soldiers engaged in no battles.

After the Civil War, young men joined the service for a variety of reasons, but many from economic necessity. They often found the terms of their commitment unpleasant at best. The post surgeon spent considerable time evaluating medical complaints from men who hoped for a discharge from their duties, either temporarily or permanently. Suicide as an exit happened regularly at the fort. One man, after repeated attempts, was sent to an asylum. Most commonly, the doctor treated sexually transmitted diseases and alcoholism. Those who died at the fort were buried in the **Fort Lewis Post Cemetery**. Not all the soldiers were American-born. Among the deceased were men from Germany, Ireland, England, Canada, and France, serving as a reminder that our nation's military has a long tradition of reliance on immigrants.

One foreign soldier was musician **Julius Griesner** (1844–1882) of Germany. He arrived in America in 1874 and enlisted in St. Louis in March 1875 as a band member for the Seventh Cavalry—of which five companies under Lt. Col. George A. Custer were annihilated at the Battle of Little Big Horn. After Griesner's term of service expired in 1880, he reenlisted at Santa Fe. He died two years later of paralysis brought on by "softening of the brain."

Enoch Wood (1858?–1884) of England drowned in the shallow La Plata River, about two miles north of the fort. **Henry Sallmann** (1860–1886), another German, froze to death the day after receiving a discharge for chronic rheumatism. Alcohol may well have played a part in these latter two deaths.

A few officers at the post were married. Probably none suffered more than **Sgt. George Mornwig**, a German immigrant (who died elsewhere). He began his service with the Army in 1854 and was stationed in California during the war. While at Fort Lewis, his wife and three of his six children died of unknown causes.

When the fort was decommissioned in 1891, twenty-eight soldiers, a dozen of their children, and one wife were disinterred and reburied at Fort McPherson National Cemetery in Nebraska. From 1891 to 1910, the fort buildings were repurposed as an Indian boarding school focused on industrial trades.

COLORADO'S INDIAN SCHOOLS

When Fort Lewis became an Indian Boarding School, it joined three others established seven years earlier: Southern Ute Boarding School in Ignacio, Grand Junction Indian School in Grand Junction (aka Teller Institute), and Good Shepherd Industrial School in Denver. A fifth school opened on the Ute Mountain Ute reservation in 1907. All operated into the twentieth century.

At the time, the federal government's official policy was to assimilate Indian children into white American culture and sever them from their own cultural history. In the words of Carlisle (Pennsylvania) Indian School founder, Richard Henry Pratt, "Kill the Indian; save the man." Children were often sent to schools far from their families to facilitate this process. Forced to cut their hair, wear non-Native apparel, and forbidden to speak their tribal languages, the students suffered abuse, identity crises, and homesickness. Hundreds of children died at these schools across the country, according to a recent study.

In May 2022, Colorado Governor Jared Polis signed a bill to initiate investigations into the abuses and trauma that occurred at the Colorado Indian Schools, and the impacts to the students' families. The signing ceremony took place at Fort Lewis College in Durango. At the Old Fort Lewis site south of Hesperus, a search has been conducted to determine if any burials occurred during the two decades it was an Indian school. At least twenty-one students died at the school in Grand Junction; the location of the burials is currently unknown.

Fort Lewis underwent several transformations after the Indian school closed and the property transferred to the State. It first became a high school, then a two-year college, and finally a four-year institution of higher learning. Since 1911, it has offered free tuition to Native Americans and Alaska Natives. The college relocated to Durango in 1956. The State leased the Old Fort property to various entities until finally reconnecting ties to Fort Lewis College in 2010. It now serves as a site for agricultural studies and an incubator for new farmers.

Mancos

Settlement in present-day Montezuma County began in the Mancos Valley. Some pioneers came to prospect the La Plata Mountains. They found the rich grasses along the Mancos River to be excellent forage, so they brought in herds of cattle. Utes were displeased to find white settlers on their doorstep, but diplomacy and good-faith dealings averted any major crises. The first death among the early arrivals was prospector **Dick Giles** (?–1877), who built the first house in the valley in 1875. He survived a self-inflicted gunshot to the neck but died of pneumonia and was buried on his property along the West Mancos River. Giles sold the land to **William Andrew "Andy" Menefee** (1830–1902), whose family lived with him during his final illness. The precise location of this burial ground is no longer known, though a few others were buried there and all were later removed to the **Cedar Grove Cemetery**. The Menefee family is credited with the having first white boy born in the valley when **William Monroe Menefee** (1877–1964) came along, joining three older brothers, including **John W. Menefee** (1870–1892). The long, steep mountain bordering Weber Canyon south of their ranch bears the family name to this day.

Cedar Grove Cemetery was established south of Mancos about 1886, on land owned by the Ratliff family. Prospector **James H. Ratliff** (1842–1882) of Kentucky died at age forty. His body, along with Dick Giles and others, was later moved from the Menefee ranch to Cedar Grove. His widow, **Samantha (Viets) McGeoch Ratliff**, received her homestead patent in 1887 and purchased an additional

Monument for John W. Menefee, early Mancos settler, in Cedar Grove Cemetery.
AUTHOR'S COLLECTION

160 acres, which included the cemetery land. Her marriage to Ratliff in 1877 was the first in the Mancos Valley. She later relocated to Routt County in northwest Colorado and is buried in Steamboat Springs. Andy Menefee and his wife, **Sarah Ann (DeMaris) Menefee** (1850–1936) were buried in Cedar Grove, though they do not have markers. When they were moving to Mancos, Andy was thrown from a horse and broke his collar bone. Sarah then drove the wagon team and created her own path in places, lowering the wagon by rope down the steep slope now known as Mancos Hill.

The grave of **Benjamin Kite Wetherill** (1831–1898) is here. Originally from Pennsylvania, this restless wanderer fathered five sons and a daughter. Two sons, **Richard** and **Clayton Wetherill**, are credited with being the first whites to find the cliff dwellings at Mesa Verde, particularly the spectacular Cliff Palace, which they spotted in 1888. Mesa Verde is sacred to the Indians, who tried to keep white ranchers off the land, without success. The Wetherills and others grazed their cattle among the piñon-juniper forests on this high plateau. Mesa Verde became a National Park in 1906.

Mormons from the San Juan (Utah) Mission settled in Mancos in 1881. Members of the so-called Hole-In-The-Rock expedition founded Bluff, Utah, in 1880, finding the harsh red-rock-canyon terrain could not support them all. Some headed east to colonize the Mancos and San Luis Valleys in southern Colorado. They homesteaded south of Mancos and down into Weber Canyon (originally spelled *Webber*). The first to arrive was **Joseph Stanford Smith**, who came to Mancos in 1880 and returned with his family to work for

James Ratliff the following year. Smith homesteaded land adjacent to the Ratliffs and encouraged other Mormons from Bluff and Montezuma Creek to join him. The Mancos/Weber community was one of the first permanent settlements by the Latter-Day Saints (LDS) in Colorado (Manassas in the San Luis Valley being slightly earlier).

Mormons **Lafayette and Phebe (Perkins) Guymon** buried their son, **John Francis**, who died of whooping cough shortly after birth in 1882. Thus began the **Old Mormon Cemetery** (aka **Mancos Pioneer Cemetery**) on the edge of a knoll located on their property.

Joseph S. Smith's wife, **Jane Arabella (Coombs) Smith** (1853–1883) died the following year, and Smith buried their daughter, **Mabel Smith** (1882–1885), not long after.

The Guymons lost another son, ten-year-old **Heber Guymon** (1874–1885), to diabetes.

Lafayette Guymon grew up near Nauvoo, Illinois, the early home of the Mormons. When just a child, he met LDS founder Joseph Smith. His parents converted and moved the family to Utah. Lafayette's first wife, Anne Margrette Mortenson, with whom he had seven children, died in 1875. Two years later, he married Phebe Perkins, who was just fourteen. Phebe lost a set of newborn twins and went on to give birth six more times. Though the family endured many sad events, Lafayette enlivened the LDS community gatherings with his fiddle and Phebe played the organ. Though five of the Guymon children rest in Mancos, Lafayette and Phebe are buried in Springville, Utah.

By the turn of the century, approximately four hundred LDS members lived in the verdant valley and narrow canyon to the south.

This granite headstone in the Old Mormon/Mancos Pioneer Cemetery honors five children in the Guymon family and their grandmother, Jane Benson Perkins. AUTHOR'S COLLECTION

They farmed the land, developed a community, and built a log church in 1888 on the Joseph S. Smith farm. Up until 1928, nearly all LDS in Weber were buried in the Old Mormon Cemetery. Other family names found here include **Decker**, **Ellis**, **Fielding**, **Lamb**, and **Willden**.

RICO

Finding the **Valley Rico Cemetery** is no difficult matter. CO 145 runs smack through the middle of it, dividing it into a west section (older) and east section. The sites occupy a west-facing slope covered in spruce and aspen just before you reach Rico when driving north. Rico incorporated in 1879, but some miners and prospectors were in the area before then. Previous names for the settlement include Carbonate

City, Doloresville, and Lead City. The town created its cemetery upon the occasion of the murder of **Julius "Frenchy" Burgen** on August 31, 1879. His killer, **George "The Kid" McGoldric**, who did not know Frenchy, was found not guilty by reason of self-defense.

This high-altitude community near Lizard Head Pass in the San Juan Mountains was the Dolores County seat before being overtaken in size by Dove Creek in the twentieth century. The population has always been in the hundreds, currently under three hundred. As with most Rockies mining camps, keeping safe and healthy proved difficult for the residents. But life improved measurably after the arrival of the Rio Grande Southern Railroad in 1891.

The monument marking the grave of **Fannie Burghardt** (1849–1900), who died of pneumonia, reveals the story of a typical pioneering family in these harsh mountains. Fannie was born Frances Cart in Covington, Kentucky. Her parents had a roaming spirit, moving the family to Iowa, Missouri, and finally Golden, Colorado, though the original destination had been California. In Golden, Fannie married a Civil War veteran, **Benjamin McConnell**, in 1870. They had two daughters, **Emma Jane** and **Lillie Maud McConnell**, before the marriage collapsed. Fannie, her daughters, and her older brother, **James Cart**, arrived in Rico the year of the town's founding. James was the first town marshal in Silverton and took on the same role in Rico. Marshal Cart brooked no nonsense, enforcing everything from the no-carry law to the dog law.

Fannie remarried in 1881 to a miner, **Samuel H. Burghardt**, from Massachusetts. He and many male relatives had traveled out to

Carte de visite portraits of Fannie (Cart) Burghardt and her second husband, Samuel H. Burghardt.
COURTESY OF AL ROTHE

Colorado in 1859. Burghardt had been mining in Central City when he enlisted to serve Colorado in the war. He was a sergeant in Chivington's Third Colorado regiment at Sand Creek in 1864, where he was wounded (probably by another soldier). He did his civic duty as a Dolores County commissioner, Rico trustee, and juror. He continued mining, bought and sold claims, and superintended the Rico Silver Mining Co. His fortunes declined with the 1893 silver crash.

The Burghardts suffered the loss of two young daughters, **Ida May Burghardt** (1888–1890) and **Fannie L. Burghardt** (1890–1890), who have a double headstone in the west part of the cemetery. A third daughter and two sons survived childhood. After the grievous loss of her baby girls, Fannie celebrated her two older daughters' marriages in Rico. Maud McConnell's husband, **Robert "Bob" P. Heyer** (1870–1906), worked as a brakeman for "the Southern." Their first-born, a boy named **Robert Heyer** (1899–1899), lived only a few months and was buried near Fannie's girls. Fannie herself joined them all in 1900. She was much loved in the community: a member of the Episcopal church, the Seventy-Niners, and the Order of the Maccabees (a women's auxiliary to the Knights of the Maccabees fraternal organization). The Maccabees supported the funeral arrangements and put together a funeral booklet for the family. After Fannie's death, Sam Burghardt found relatives to help care for his children. His daughter, **Stella**, attended school at the convent in Durango. In 1906, he and his sons moved to Oregon.

Bob and Maud Heyer lost their second child, daughter **Lucile Heyer** (1900–1905), in March 1905. The next month, Bob badly injured a foot in a train derailment. The newspapers offered expressions of concern and followed his medical care and recuperation, as he had many friends. The following year, another train accident took his life. He is buried next to his children.

Close to the Burghardt/Heyer graves stands a granite pillar erected on the grave of a fourteen-year-old boy, **Claude J. Adams** (1887–1902). Though he appears to be alone, both his parents are buried by his side, though lacking markers. **Jefferson Davis "J.D." Adams** (1852–1924) moved his family from steamy, lowland Mississippi to cool, high, and dry Rico in the early 1890s. J.D. set up a dry goods and grocery store in town, where he ran the post office. He became involved in local politics and joined the Masons. He served a term as representative in the state legislature. Though he threw his hat in the ring for other offices, he won none. His wife, **Martha Adams** (1859–1921), tended the home and their two sons, **Ethelbert "E.B."** and Claude, who attended the local school.

During school break, Claude helped his father by making deliveries to customers. On a late June day, after returning the wagon to the barn, he began unhitching the large horse, a tame family pet that had been reshod the day before. Neighbors heard a commotion and saw the horse run from the barn. The horse had kicked Claude in the head and chest, mortally wounding him. Rico citizens grieved for a boy who was "greatly beloved by the entire community because of his manly, upright bearing and his gentlemanly qualifications," according to the *Telluride Journal* on July 3, 1902.

The older son, E.B., went to college in Boulder, where he obtained a law degree . . . and a wife, **Elizabeth Fonda**. They returned to the southwestern mountains, where E.B. set up his law practice in Telluride.

J.D. and Martha purchased a ranch in Arriola, in Montezuma County, though they only visited occasionally for years before moving there permanently in 1914. Martha fell ill and died there in 1921, with her funeral and burial held in Rico. J.D. visited Telluride in 1924 and suffered a stroke at the local barber shop, and later passed away at the hospital. He, too, was buried by his son in the Rico cemetery.

At least nine Civil War veterans are buried in Rico. **Sgt. Jacob Wyant Winkfield** (1843–1905), born in Pennsylvania, was a member of both the Grand Army of the Republic (GAR) and the Masons (along with J.D. Adams). After the war, Winkfield went to Dakota Territory to fight Indians. By 1870, he moved to Iowa, married, and began his family. In 1877, he moved to Trinidad, Colorado, and operated The Overland Hotel. He then moved to nearby El Moro to manage the New State Hotel. A guest described him as "a jolly hotel keeper."

He relocated to Rico in 1879 and took up yet another hotel, purchased a wholesale liquor and cigar business, and joined the mining boom. He was elected mayor of the town in 1881; Sam Burghardt was also elected to the board that year. Winkfield's wife, **Anna Belle (Acker) Winkfield**, organized a Christmas charity ball in December that year to ensure even the poorest children in Rico received a decent present and a festive holiday. This may have taken place at the O.B.B. hall, a unique Rico lodge. One wag joked that the initials stood for "old busted bummers," but the real name was Order of Benevolent Bachelors.

Winkfield invested in a number of local mines with a variety of partners, including his father-in-law. The Pigeon Mine was the most successful. His acquaintance with railroad-builder Otto Mears proved fortuitous. According to family lore, Mears built a spur from the Rio Grande Southern line to the Pigeon, enabling an easy transfer of ore to the smelter in Durango.

As a senior member of the community, Winkfield adopted the honorific rank of Major. In January 1905 he came down with pneumonia and developed nephritis; within two weeks he was dead. According to the *Telluride Journal*, attorney E.B. Adams attended Winkfield's funeral, attesting to the close relationship between the families in this tiny mining town.

*T*ELLURIDE

San Miguel County settlers consisted first of prospectors, followed by homesteaders. The first known prospector and Civil War veteran, **Lindley M.L. "Lon" Remine** (1846–1928), visited the area in 1873 with several others. The following year this native of Virginia built a dugout in the box canyon that would later hold the communities of San Miguel City, Columbia (now Telluride), and Pandora. He illegally squatted on Ute land along the San Miguel River looking for precious metals. Many others followed, and as transportation improved in the 1890s, national and international conglomerates from as far away as China acquired the rich mine properties. The remote owners hired local managers whose business practices provoked union action to improve working conditions. The conflicts between labor and management incited violence on both sides around the turn of the century.

San Miguel City was established in 1876, and Columbia/Telluride came into being two years later. Being closer to the mining activity, Telluride grew and became county seat. Many San Miguel City businesses and residents relocated a mile east to the newer town. Most of those interred in the **San Miguel Cemetery** were moved to **Lone Tree Cemetery**, east of Telluride, on land **George S. Andrus** provided when he buried his baby boy, **Edwin Andrus** (1884–1885). The cemetery rises above the valley floor, ringed by shear rocky peaks soaring over 13,000 feet. The burial grounds slope throughout, each grave forming its own mini-terrace. Early burials consisted of easily decomposed, simple wooden boxes covered in black calico. The remains are engaged in a snail-paced race to the valley floor. Gravity acting on cemetery soil sometimes reveals human bones.

Telluride was not a place to grow old. Looking at the stunning blue skies, snowcapped peaks, thriving green pastures, and million-dollar condos of today, it is difficult to imagine the gritty reality of the nineteenth-century version. Wood and coal smoke filled the air. Sewage ran in the streets, not to mention garbage. Homes lacked insulation, plumbing, sometimes even floors. Due to its remoteness, residents had trouble getting the basic necessities of life that had to be brought in over the mountains. Diseases, avalanches, mining accidents, murder, and suicide took a grim toll on the population. Fueled by alcohol and miniscule comforts, residents had to be tough. You will not find grannies and nattering grandpas in Lone Tree before 1900. Living to forty could be considered a major accomplishment.

Lon Remine, the valley's first settler, and his brother, **William "Bill" Remine** (1844–1916), are buried beside one another in a family concrete crypt. During the Civil War, the brothers fought on opposite sides and were not on speaking terms. After the war, Bill and Lon worked in Central City, where Bill lost an arm in the stamp mill. Bill lived on Deep Creek, Last Dollar Mountain, near the **Tom Wilson** ranch, where he was developing some quartz claims in 1916. Wilson asked Bill to take care of his cattle for a couple days. Wilson found Bill's badly gored body in his field with a bull. All the old timers mourned his untimely death—he was known as a kindly man.

Lon Remine had a reputation as a hermit, but he remained friendly to visitors and did show his face in Telluride each month to get mail and supplies. He reportedly never discarded anything. When his cabin became full of refuse, he would build another and move. Several small abodes dotted his homestead. He died in 1928 and was placed next to his brother, per his request.

The mines drew European labor: Tyrolians from the Alps, Swedes, Finns, and Cornish and Welsh miners from the UK. These groups tended to live in segregated clusters within Telluride. By 1900, more than 180 residents of San Miguel County had been born in Italy, the vast majority being men living in boarding houses, though there were some families. Over 350 hailed from England, again, most without families. Twenty-five nationalities are represented in Lone Tree, their headstones offering some flavor of the various homelands, with their foreign-language inscriptions.

Mining is by nature a dangerous occupation, and Lone Tree contains graves of those who suffered accidents or died from lung diseases. A particularly devastating fire at the Smuggler-Union mine in November 20, 1901 took the lives of twenty-four men, some of whom perished trying to save others. The fire began outside the mine, but air currents drew the toxic smoke into the tunnels and shafts. Norwegian **Thorvald Torkelson** (1868–1901), took his job as crew boss seriously. In his efforts to save others, he gave his life. The *Telluride Journal* credited Thorkelson and tram foreman **Carey Barkley** with saving many who escaped the mine, though they were not the only heroes. Others who died in the incident with marked graves in Lone Tree are cousins **Marco Zadra** (1868–1901) and **Frank Zadra** (1879–1901), **Alex Fellman** (1877–1901), **William Jones** (?–1901), and **August Kaanta** (1855–1901). Some of the miner's bodies were transported elsewhere, including Barkley, who was taken to Delta. Others were likely interred in a mass grave. This Telluride funeral has probably never been surpassed in the number of mourners (well into the thousands) who accompanied the bodies to their resting place.

Mining accidents and labor practices drove the Telluride Miner's Union to go on strike many times from 1901 to 1904. One union tactic was to round up scabs and drum them out of town. In July 1901, 250 men marched up to the Smuggler-Union and waited for the night shift to exit. A Finn named **John Barthell** (1874–1901) stood on a rock and announced to the non-union workers "that they were under arrest." Someone fired a shot, killing Barthell. Two others were killed and several injured in the skirmish. The union erected an elaborate monument in Barthell's honor (see front cover).

In that era, even lawmen could not be trusted. A tall, ocher monument draped in rufous lichen, engraved with "We loved him but he left us" commemorates the murder of **William Wearing** (1859–1888) by a deputy marshal on November 6, 1888, shortly after the polls closed. The prominent monument is visible from the cemetery entry gate, because of its height and unusual coloring. The unwarranted killing of this Cornish man caused an uproar in the San Miguel Valley communities. The paper described Wearing as "one of the most quiet, inoffensive, industrious miners in this section."

The monument in Lone Tree Cemetery for William Wearing, a young Cornish miner murdered by a deputy marshal.

OURAY MEMORIAL PARK

In the 1873 Brunot Agreement, **Chief Ouray** (1833–1880) of the Utes received an annual stipend and a ranch near present-day Montrose. Today this is the site of the Ute Indian Museum and **Ouray Memorial Park**. This park contains the re-interred remains of Ouray's second wife, **Chipeta** (1843–1924). Though Ouray is buried in Ignacio, where he died of kidney failure, he is also memorialized here.

Ouray was born in Abiquiu, New Mexico. His father was Apache and his mother a Tabeguache Ute. They named him "Arrow" because of the Leonid meteor shower that took place at the time of his birth. His parents sent him and his brother to Taos to be criados in the powerful Martinez family. He learned Spanish and Apache, as well as a little English. Learning the Ute language came later. Because of his association with the Martinez family, Ouray understood power politics and land control in the Southwest. He was an influential leader among the Tabeguache, but not recognized as a spokesman by other Ute bands.

The federal government bestowed the "Chief of the Utes" title on Ouray in 1868, preferring to negotiate with a single individual over many tribal leaders. Thus, he was responsible for later agreements in which the Utes lost about twenty million acres of their homeland. In exchange, he kept the Utes from experiencing the type of genocidal events some other tribes suffered. It is a complex legacy still debated among Utes and students of history. Clearly, the stress of the responsibility he carried contributed to Ouray's declining health and death at a young age. The Southern Utes buried him in a secret location south of Ignacio but moved his bones to the **Ouray Memorial Cemetery** in 1925. He is memorialized in stained glass in the Capitol, an honor that received a unanimous vote.

Chipeta was born an Apache and reared by Utes after the death of her parents. She took care of Ouray's son after his first wife's death. They married in 1859. She accompanied her husband on peace negotiations and helped care for Nathan Meeker's abducted wife and daughter after their release. The Tabeguache considered her a tribal leader after Ouray's death, an unusual honor for a woman. Not inheriting the ranch or Ouray's annual stipend, she accompanied the Tabeguache to a Utah reservation. She lived out her life in poverty but in a traditional manner. Though first given a tribal burial in Utah, her remains were exhumed a year later, brought to her former homestead, and placed in a mausoleum. A twelve-foot-tall granite memorial stands in the park to honor Chipeta and Chief Ouray. Chipeta is depicted on the Women's Gold Tapestry in the Capitol.

Chief Ouray of the Tabeguache Utes and his second wife, Chipeta.
BRADY-HANDY PHOTOGRAPH COLLECTION, LIBRARY OF CONGRESS, PRINTS & PHOTOGRAPHS DIVISION, LC-DIG-CWPBH-04477

Fruita

Fruita came into being in 1884, though homesteaders arrived a couple years before. The town was the brainchild of **William E. Pabor** (1834–1911), a newspaperman from Harlem, New York, who came west with the Union Colony. He also helped found Fort Collins and Colorado Springs. He later moved to Longmont, where he ran an agricultural paper. He envisioned a fruit-growing, family community in the Grand Valley with its mild climate and ample water from the Colorado (formerly Grand) River. To promote it, he wrote a three-hundred-page volume, *Colorado as an Agricultural State,* and created the Fruita Town and Land Company to lay out and sell town lots.

The **Elmwood Cemetery**, established in 1895, has a small park area dedicated to Pabor. It is located on North Mesa Street and Elmwood Avenue. Pabor started a number of newspapers around the state and was also the state poet laureate in 1888. He was largely self-taught, having worked at an India-rubber factory to support his family when he was in his teens. He was a founder of the Colorado Editorial Association and poet laureate of the national organization. Pabor lived for twenty years in Florida, but returned to Denver just before he died of a stroke. He visited his old eastern Colorado stomping grounds at Greeley, Boulder, and Fort Collins on that trip. After he passed away in August 1911, his remains were shipped to Fruita, where a large funeral was held on September 6.

Jennie Knox (1876–1895) had only recently relocated to Fruita with her family when she accepted a ride from a suitor that would be her last. She may have been engaged to one man, but another was desperate to claim her hand. Jennie's parents objected vehemently to **James Powell**'s proposal. But Jennie never suspected that his passion could turn violent. On August 3, 1895, she was walking to town to make purchases. Powell pulled up alongside in his buggy, offering her a ride, which she accepted. While she bought household goods at one counter, Powell purchased a handgun and ammunition at another, then hid the weapon under his left arm.

As they rode back out of town, Powell reiterated his proposal and Jennie stated firmly the answer was no. Powell pulled the gun and fired two shots at Jennie. She managed to jump from the carriage and flee, as horrified onlookers began to converge on the bloody scene. Powell soon caught up to her and, while Jennie heartbreakingly pleaded for her life, Powell fired another round into her head. He contemplated making an escape, but saw the men surrounding him and shot himself in the forehead. His survival was touch and go for days, and he experienced partial paralysis and mental disturbances. But he recovered sufficiently to stand trial, was convicted, and sentenced to life in prison at Cañon City. He committed suicide in July 1896 while incarcerated.

GRAND JUNCTION

The Grand Valley, home to Fruita, Grand Junction, Palisade, and other communities, remained firmly in Ute control until 1880. At the time, the valley was part of Gunnison County. The land opened for a rush on September 4, 1881, and among those vying for development property were **George A. Crawford** (1827–1891) and his partners. They staked their claims later that month, platting a town site at the confluence of the Gunnison and Colorado Rivers.

Crawford died of consumption in January 1891, still a single man. He had plans for a mausoleum on Orchard Mesa, south of the city he founded from whence he first viewed the valley. His casket remained in a temporary Masonic vault for seven years while they constructed his stone tomb. A hundred years later, the mausoleum, alone on its promontory, had fallen into disrepair. Young residents found the area a perfect place for "parking" and general mischief. In 2006, a journalist pushed for a commission to restore the city founder's resting place, and today it is a refreshed and fitting monument. A statue of Crawford was removed from City Hall and installed next to his crypt.

Crawford was born in Pennsylvania, the son of a judge, and he studied law. He moved to Kansas in 1857 and, along with others, founded the town of Fort Scott. Crawford was a Free Stater and got caught up in the "Bloody Kansas" events involving Abolitionist John Brown and the Border Ruffians, nearly losing his life. He was elected to be the first governor of Kansas in 1860, but the Kansas Supreme Court declared the election invalid and he never took his post. Crawford lost considerable property and fell into debt when an uninsured flour mill that he owned burned to the ground. After coming to Colorado, he helped bring in the railroad and lobbied for the creation of Mesa County. Access to his monument is via County Road 26-1/4, which winds past the nearby **Orchard Mesa Cemetery**.

ONLY THE LONELY

In previous centuries, if people died indigent or unknown, with no family to claim their body, they typically wound up in a "Potter's Field." These burials lacked grave markers and often went unrecorded. Particularly if it was a John or Jane Doe, they were forever forgotten. It still happens that people die anonymously, or without funds or family to cover the cost of burial. What happens then?

In Colorado, the state Department of Human Services provides $1,500 toward the burial cost. A county agency may add to that amount. But first, the coroner and law enforcement attempt to identify the person and any assets or family they may have. Sometimes a family member is found but does not have the means (or willingness) to cover the cost. The La Plata County coroner states they keep a body for thirty days, then they contract with a local mortuary to handle the remains. State statute dictates these be kept for three years prior to burial, so the bodies are cremated and the cremains are held instead. In La Plata County, they remain with the coroner's office.

At the end of three years, the cremains are buried in Greenmount Cemetery in Durango in a plot set aside for the purpose. The burial sites are unmarked but well-documented in case any family comes forward in the future.

CHAPTER 8

THE GREAT WEST

Northwestern Colorado features far more open space, wilderness area, and scenic vistas than people. It was the last portion of the state to see permanent pioneer settlement, due to its remoteness and the fact the land belonged to the Utes until the Meeker Incident. Even today, few major highways exist, and backcountry exploration is best done with a full tank of gas and plenty of water. The area's history is as dramatic as the backdrop it occurred in. Home to the Utes when the territory formed, the constant push by land-seekers from the east led to inevitable strife.

After Ute removal, ranchers arrived. And where there were cattle, there were cattle rustlers . . . and plenty of places for outlaws to hide. The Yampa and Green Rivers converge in present-day Dinosaur National Monument, a land where the prehistoric behemoths once roamed and left their bones embedded in sandstone. Home to headwaters of the Colorado River, much of the region features grazing land. Desert canyons give way to soaring peaks as you head eastward.

GLENWOOD SPRINGS

On a tour of pioneer cemeteries, one thing is nearly constant: most of the people you will encounter are underground. **Linwood Cemetery** in Glenwood Springs, tiny and perched above a tolerant residential neighborhood, attracts a steady flow of tourists. They are undaunted by the steep hike through piñon-juniper woodland on their pilgrimage to visit the memorial to **John Henry "Doc" Holliday** (1851–1887).

The consumptive dentist is famous for his connection to the Earp brothers and the storied shootout at the O.K. Corral in Tombstone, Arizona. Holliday's real talents were gambling and sharp-shooting. He spent his final days at Glenwood, perhaps to "take in the waters" at the mineral hot springs. Holliday began life in Georgia and

The location of John Henry "Doc" Holliday's grave is unknown, but he has this memorial and interpretive signage at the Linwood Cemetery in Glenwood Springs. AUTHOR'S COLLECTION

received his dental degree in Pennsylvania. He probably traveled west due to his health, as many tuberculosis sufferers did. He died a pauper and may have been buried in the Potter's Field section of this cemetery that had recently opened. If his grave had a marker at the time, it no longer exists and his burial location is unknown.

Glenwood Springs founder **James M. "Jim" Landis** (?–1885) is likely buried in Linwood, though no headstone marks his grave. At the time he passed, burials were made in the town's original cemetery at the base of the hill below Linwood. These bodies were exhumed and moved uphill in the late 1880s. Once Landis arrived at the hot springs valley in 1879, he grew hay to sell in his former home of Leadville. After the Ute removal, he acquired title to the land where the town of Glenwood would be incorporated the same year he was buried. Landis sold the land to developer **Isaac Cooper** in 1882. Cooper and his wife named it Glenwood in honor of their home-town in Iowa. Later "Springs" was added to the name to promote the hot springs resort.

A pioneer woman who was beloved in town is buried with her husband in a fenced enclosure at Linwood. **Catherine "Katie" C. (Mueller) Bender** (1846–1917) was born in Germany and came to America at age three, arriving in Philadelphia. Her family went to Gasconade County, Missouri, where Katie married **Joseph J. Bender** (1843–1888) in January 1868. They made their home in Randolph County, Missouri, in the early 1870s, then relocated to the new town of Salida, Colorado, where Katie ran a hotel and restaurant.

She claimed to be the first white woman in town, having set up camp nearby in 1878. Joseph opened a saloon next door to the hotel. Some townspeople were not happy about Joseph having a liquor license, but they thronged Katie's hotel and restaurant. She also contracted with the county to provide meals for jail inmates.

In 1886, the Benders moved to Glenwood Springs, where Joseph died of edema a couple years later. Katie purchased properties in Glenwood and later a farm near New Castle. The *Glenwood Post* published glowing stories about the kindly matron of the popular Commercial Restaurant at the corner of Grand Avenue and Seventh Street, across from the Colorado River and railroad tracks. In 1897, friends gave her a parrot that perched at the entrance, greeting patrons as they arrived and saying "Bye-bye" when they departed.

As a charitable and Christian woman, Katie offered a helping hand to many people in distress, tried to prevent young women from straying into prostitution, and offered guidance to those who struggled with alcoholism and poverty. She used her funds to lavish gifts on her friends and most valued employees, such as a $100 gold watch to her lead cook, and a fancy baby carriage for a friend's newborn. "Mother Bender" also contributed money to children's homes across the country. Though never a mother herself, she had a soft spot for children.

At Linwood Cemetery, a large marble headstone for Joseph is flanked by individual granite markers for Joseph and Katie. Katie's incorrectly gives her middle initial as J. instead of C.

THE MEEKER INCIDENT

In 1878, President Rutherford B. Hayes appointed **Nathan C. Meeker**, founder of the Union Colony (Greeley), to head the White River Indian Agency near the northern boundary of the Ute Reservation in western Colorado. Previously, agents had been in the mold of frontier entrepreneur, but the federal government increasingly encouraged missionary involvement with tribes in order to "civilize" them. Meeker had no firsthand knowledge of the Utes or any other tribe, but he was eager to preach Christian principles and Anglo farming methods to them, regardless of their desires. He was partially set up for failure due to years of undelivered payments and supplies to the Utes, promised by the federal government in the 1868 treaty. The Utes were prohibited from hunting off-reservation (which they did anyway, as they would starve otherwise).

Meeker's first misstep, after arriving at the agency in the spring of 1879, was to move the agency buildings onto a Ute horse pasture, with the goal of diminishing their reliance on the animals. The Utes resisted his unrelenting insistence that they take up farming. Meeker even withheld food supplies as punishment. He could tell that his methods were causing an antagonistic reaction, but he persisted, plowing up their horse-racing track. Meeker soon feared for his life and requested military support. **Maj. Thomas Thornburg**, stationed in Wyoming, began moving nearly two hundred troops toward the reservation in late September. He encountered a Ute party that warned him to stay off the reservation. If the Army breached the border, it would be seen as an act of war.

At first, Thornburg honored Meeker's request to stay off the reservation and advance to the agency with only a few men. The Army set up camp on Milk Creek. Thornburg, knowing that his troops outnumbered the Indians, decided to defer to his orders from Gen. George Crook to cross the reservation on September 29. He assumed the Utes would not attack, but they had prepared and immediately began firing as the cavalry crossed the dry creek marking the boundary. A sniper's bullet ended Thornburg's advance.

Word reached the agency of the battle at Milk Creek. The Utes killed Meeker and all the white male staff at the agency, mutilating their bodies. Meeker had a barrel stave driven through his mouth. The Utes took Mrs. Meeker and her daughter as captives, along with another family. On October 1, the Ninth Cavalry of Buffalo Soldiers arrived and prolonged the battle, but could not gain the upper hand. It finally took 450 troops under **Col. Wesley Merritt**, arriving from Rawlins, Wyoming, to turn the tide and end the conflict after five days of battle. Government agents worked with other Utes to negotiate the release of the captives from the White River Agency. As a result of the battle and the killings at the agency, the Utes were forced to relocate to Utah by 1881.

MEEKER

There are only two incorporated towns in Rio Blanco County, which was formed from Garfield County in 1889. The county seat is Meeker, named for the murdered White River Agency head. The town was platted in 1885, six years after the incident. Before that, a US Army camp occupied the site. The White River Museum is housed in one of the original camp buildings.

Reach the **Battle of Milk Creek** site by driving east of Meeker on CO 13, then north on County Road 15 for seventeen miles. Seventeen dead soldiers were buried on site and remain there today. There are two memorials at the site, one for the soldiers, and one for the roughly two dozen Utes who died in the conflict. Maj. Thomas Thornburg's body was recovered from the battlefield and is buried in Omaha, Nebraska.

The Battle of Milk Creek preceded the killings at the White River Ute Agency. Those killed in battle are buried here.

JEFFREY BEALL ON WIKIMEDIA COMMONS CREATIVE COMMONS ATTRIBUTION-SHARE ALIKE 3.0 UNPORTED CREATIVECOMMONS.ORG/LICENSES/BY-SA/3.0/DEED.EN, CROPPED

Head west from Meeker on CO 64 for six miles to Powell Park to visit the memorial at the White River Agency. The remains of the victims, hastily buried where they lay, were exhumed in the summer of 1880 by **George T. Dresser**, the father of two victims. He put them in coffins and buried them on a bluff above the agency site. They were removed to Meeker's **Highland Cemetery** in 1898 (aside from Nathan Meeker; see chapter 4, Greeley) and buried in the Potter's Field section without markers. The cemetery lies on level land atop a hill south of town, above the White River. The cemetery is formally planned, with paved roads and headstones facing east-west, and with a manicured lawn. The site provides an excellent panoramic view of Meeker and the mountains.

Most of the murdered men were from the Union Colony and close to Nathan Meeker. In fact, Dresser had been a friend of Meeker's. His sons **Harry S. Dresser** (1852–1879) and **Frank G. Dresser** (1858–1879) were both shot in the chest. Harry, the elder brother, was born in Canada and worked at the agency as a blacksmith. The family moved to Wisconsin, where Frank was born. He worked at the agency as a herder.

George W. Eaton (1845–1879), also of Greeley, was persuaded to join Meeker at the agency, where he worked as a farm laborer. Though his body was moved to Highland, there is a memorial for him with his parents in Greeley. Other young laborers were **Fred E. Shephard** (1859–1879) of Illinois, and **Arthur L. Thompson** (1858–1879) of Wisconsin.

Shadrach Price (1850–1879) was born in Indiana and lived for a time in Kansas before moving to Wyoming and later Colorado. He worked as a blacksmith at the agency. He may have been the one plowing the Ute's racetrack and been warned off by a shot over his head in the days before the killings. His wife, **Sophoronia "Flora" Ellen (Parker) Price**, and their two children were among the captives later released. Flora was just eighteen at the time.

In the southeast corner of the cemetery are the marked graves of three bank robbers. The citizens of Meeker did not take kindly to the daring, broad-daylight holdup at the bank inside **J.W. Hagus**'s general mercantile. After **George Bain** (?–1896) and his two companions gained control of the citizens in the bank and store, one of them fired two warning shots at assistant cashier **David Smith** (1854–1933), who was not moving fast enough to produce the cash. One bullet passed through his hat brim, the other hit a ledger. Those shots would prove to be the dastardly thieves' downfall.

Hearing the shots, the townspeople discerned a robbery was in effect, and every man with a gun surrounded the building, with most near the rear door. The burglars forced all the hostages out of the building ahead of them. The freed hostages scattered, running for their lives, leaving the bandits exposed. The townspeople and their barrage of gunfire cut down the three men, killing two immediately. The youngest one, known only as **"The Kid" Pierce** (?–1896), lived an hour longer and gave fictitious names for himself and his dead companions. The third man was **Jim Shirley** (?–1896). Both Bain and Shirley had known records as outlaws. The quick-thinking citizens of Meeker put an end to their depredations on October 13, 1896. Sadly, the robbers had hidden their horses and the unfortunate animals were not found until seventeen days later.

David Smith wore several hats (figuratively speaking) besides the one punctured by the gunshot. In addition to being cashier at the bank, he did the bookkeeping for the mercantile and ran his own lumber business next door. David was born in Scotland. He came to Colorado in 1885 to visit two married sisters already living in the state, one at Fort Lupton, one in Meeker. He spent time around the state working at a variety of businesses. He returned to his homeland and visited England, where he met **Mary Elizabeth Allsebrook** (1866–1945), a niece of his brother-in-law, and they married in 1891. They moved to Meeker and settled in. Mary knew nothing of cooking and pioneering ways, but they managed to make things work. They had seven children who all survived to adulthood.

David and Mary purchased a ranch just west of Meeker, which Mary and her sons mostly ran. David's strength was more in the business world. They ensured the children received a good education. Daughter Marion, in her brief memoir of Meeker days, recalled some of their favorite childhood outdoor games were "Run, Sheep, Run;

WILDLIFE SANCTUARIES

The custom of setting aside land for the dead has a side benefit for the living—living wildlife, that is. Those with forests provide habitat for a variety of birds and mammals. Open fields or sagebrush lands attract grazers such as deer, rabbits, and rodents. The latter can attract predators such as snakes, coyotes, foxes, and raptors. While animals are not usually factored into cemetery planning, their presence is appreciated and even encouraged. This is in keeping with the historic garden/park cemetery movement begun in the 1800s.

Mule deer and squirrels are probably the most common cemetery residents and visitors in Colorado. At the Highland Cemetery in Meeker, sandhill cranes sometimes stop in during migration. Migratory turkey vultures roost in the many trees at Durango's Greenmount Cemetery. Geese congregate on the large irrigation pond at Pueblo's Roselawn Cemetery.

Denver's Fairmount Cemetery has offered birding walks in the past. It also happens to be the state's largest arboretum, containing seventy-three species. These were part of the cemetery design by **Reinhard Schuetze**. Schuetze also designed City, Congress, and Washington Parks in Denver. Riverside Cemetery in north Denver, along the South Platte River, has wetlands vital to native plants and wildlife, including mink and migratory birds. Both cemeteries are recognized by the National Wildlife Federation as vital wildlife habitat.

Kick the Can; Pom Pom Pullaway; Sheep in My Pen; Ante Over; and Hide and Seek." Son Colin had the greatest educational ambition, attending law school. He worked as an attorney not just in Colorado but also in Chicago and Washington, D.C. Two daughters moved to England for life. Three sons are buried in Highland Cemetery.

David helped found the Episcopal Church in Meeker (though brought up Presbyterian, he went with the will of the town majority on denomination). He was a charter member of the Masonic Lodge, an organization he belonged to in Scotland. He had a term as mayor from 1894 to 1895. He embraced the life of community building in a rough and tumble corner of the state, and his sons followed in his footsteps.

BROWNS PARK

In the far northwestern reaches of Moffat County is a protected valley once called Browns Hole and changed to Browns Park, probably named for a fur trapper camped there in the early 1800s. The forty-mile-long park straddles the Utah and Colorado state line along a section of the Green River that curves into Colorado from Utah and back out again after capturing the flow of the Yampa River within Dinosaur National Monument. Protected by highlands to the north and south, it was a favored wintering ground for Shoshone and Ute and, in the early nineteenth century, for Rocky Mountain fur trappers.

The trappers built a raggedy fort in 1836 and named it for Davy Crockett, who had been killed at the Alamo that year. The trappers usually called it Fort Misery, though. It was abandoned around 1840. Cattle drovers on their way to California wintered their herds here in the 1850s. Later in the century, this remote area became a hideout for rustlers, most famous among them being **Butch Cassidy** and his Wild Bunch. Outlaws took advantage of the proximity of state lines to avoid various law officials who might attempt a pursuit. Venturing into this region today gives the visitor a sense of the wild and remote nature all of Colorado exhibited in the past but is now usually found only in wilderness areas.

On a bench with a view to the Gates of Lodore, where the Green River flows into canyon lands, settlers repose in the **Browns Park Cemetery**, also called the **Lodore Cemetery**. Long after the cemetery was established, a schoolhouse was built close by. The 1911 building is still used as a community center. Both school and cemetery are

The Lodore Cemetery and the community center built in 1911 in the background. Both are within the Browns Park National Wildlife Refuge.
AUTHOR'S COLLECTION

within the Browns Park Wildlife Refuge, just off CO 318. Within the cemetery is a large petroglyph-inscribed boulder, placed there by the highway department, that sports a plaque about Fort Davy Crockett. Many of the graves here are set with metal mortuary markers in concrete, some with inaccurate and incomplete information. One belongs to colorful Colorado pioneer **Dr. John Parsons** (1817–1881), whose marker says "Dr Parson 1877"—which was not the year he died.

Dr. Parsons was born in Indiana. He married in Illinois in 1849 and began his family. The year he arrived in Colorado is variously reported, but it was soon after the gold discovery. His daughter, **Helena Parsons**, was born in the territory in 1861. He was in financial straits and poor health at the time. He tried his hand in the South Park mining district near Tarryall as an assayer. He built a smelter and purchased coin-minting dies, with which he converted gold dust into $2.50 and $5.00 coins; only a handful still exist. One side had his name (missing the final S) and the image of a small ore-stamping mill. The obverse bore a crude eagle image, the words "Pikes Peak Gold," and the denomination.

He next ventured into dairy farming, and by 1865 had 120 acres adjacent to what is now Denver's Riverside Cemetery on the South Platte. He conceived an irrigation plan on the river that he called the Denver Aqueduct Company, but it failed. By the late 1870s he had moved to Brown's Park in Utah, following the trail of his son, **Warren D. Parsons**. Warren and his wife, **Annie**, arrived in Browns Park in the summer of 1874. "Snappin' Annie," as she was called by early settler **Samuel C. Bassett** (1836–1910), may have been the first white woman in the park. Dr. Parsons became the park's first postmaster in 1878. After his death in 1881, he was buried in the Colorado portion of the park at Lodore. His cabin complex—including a springhouse, bunkhouse, and blacksmith shop—later became an outlaw hideout and historic landmark. Shortly after receiving the historic designation in 1976, a fire destroyed the cabin.

Following Dr. Parsons's death, another Browns Park settler filled his shoes as the local doctor, undertaker, ferry operator, and postmaster. The Jarvie Ranch (formerly Parsons') is now a historic site managed by the Bureau of Land Management, located in Utah on the Green River at Sears Creek. **John Jarvie** (1844–1909) was born in Scotland and eventually followed his father into the iron mines. He arrived in America in 1865 and migrated to Rock Springs, Wyoming, where he became a saloon keeper. In 1880 he wed **Nellie Barr**, also a Scottish immigrant, and they left Wyoming to settle in Brown's Park. Nellie was known for her nightingale voice.

Jarvie opened a trading post to serve a large surrounding area of sparse settlement. The store carried an admirable array of goods from Indian flour to saddles, lodge poles to liquor. Though arrested in 1892 for selling the liquor without a license, the jury acquitted Jarvie after sampling the evidence, possibly concluding it was undrinkable. In 1890, Nellie died from tuberculosis and was buried in Ogden, Utah, where her parents resided. Jarvie was left to rear their four sons alone. He expanded his landholdings to include property in Colorado.

Jarvie's acquaintances included outlaws. They were tolerated in the park, and most of the settlers engaged in some cattle rustling as

Like many of the pioneer graves in the Lodore Cemetery, John Jarvie's has a simple mortuary marker set in concrete.

(they felt) a matter of necessity. Only the largest operators were considered criminal if they attempted to do the same. According to **Ann Bassett**'s memoirs, Jarvie presided over an "Outlaw's Thanksgiving Dinner" in 1895, the park's one known formal event. Jarvie, white-haired and full-bearded, seemed like Santa Claus to the younger set. He had an array of hobbies that set him apart from the rough crowd: sewing clothes for his sons, mathematics, phrenology, and playing the organ and concertina.

Though he suffered financial setbacks over the years, rumors persisted that Jarvie had a large fortune stashed at his ranch. These tales may have led to his untimely death. On July 6, 1909, **George Hood** and his brother-in-law, **Bill McKinley**, stopped at the ranch and Jarvie set out plates to serve them dinner. But instead of joining him to dine, the men forced him to open his safe, which was nearly empty. Jarvie escaped, briefly, but the robbers killed him with two gunshots and set him adrift on the Green River in a boat, thinking rapids would destroy the evidence. Jarvie's son **Archie** found the body eight days later. The killers had long since escaped.

Across CO 318 and due east from the Lodore School, the **Bassett Cemetery** is located on private land. The small fenced burial ground sits on an undeveloped bluff above the irrigated lands that the family of scholarly **Herbert Bassett** homesteaded. Herbert, Samuel Basset's older brother, had little in the way of pioneering skills, but his wife and children had the determination it took to survive in Browns Park. **Mary Eliza Chamberlain** (1855–1892) was born in Little Rock, Arkansas, and brought up to be a genteel southern lady. She married Herbert in Arkansas in 1871, and two children, **Josie (Bassett) Morris** (1874–1964) and **Samuel Bassett** were born there. After arriving in Brown's Park, Eliza had another daughter, the first white child born in the park, delivered by Dr. Parsons. She was named **Ann Bassett** (1878–1956), and she gained fame as "Queen of the Rustlers." Several biographies have been written about Ann's rambunctious life.

Eliza Bassett took up some of the slack in the medical department after Dr. Parsons's death. Eliza managed the ranch and was handy with her Winchester rifle. The family's ten-room log cabin served as a stopping point for travelers needing hospitality. This remote outpost of people relied on one another and looked out for their own. Some raised cattle, others sheep or horses. Large cattle outfits from Wyoming or Utah were unwelcome to bring their herds into the park. The Bassetts and others would use sheep to strip the range of vegetation as a tactic to drive the outfits elsewhere, and rustling was part of business as usual.

A cowboy whom Eliza relied upon for assistance was an ex-slave from her home state. After **Ned Huddleston** left the slaughtered **Tip Gault** cattle-rustling gang, he shed his slave name and adopted **Isom Dart** (1849–1900), the name on his lonely grave site in Moffat County. Dart was born in Arkansas. During the Civil War, Confederate soldiers sent the teen out to forage (i.e., steal) food and supplies. A pattern was set that the young Black man never fully shed. He moved to Mexico after the war and learned bronc busting (said to be the best) and became a rodeo clown. With a partner, he stole Mexican horses and sold them in Texas. He came to northwest Colorado on a cattle drive, where he met the Gault gang.

A gang member was killed by a horse and, while the others were burying him, cowboys bent on revenge ambushed them. Only Dart survived by jumping into the open grave and playing dead. To get away, he stole a horse from a rancher, who shot him. He managed to escape, though, and recovered. Years later he returned to Browns Park.

Dart was fifty-one years old and by then a legitimate rancher, when hired gun Tom Horn shot him dead as he walked out of his cabin on October 3, 1900. Though arrested numerous times for cattle rustling, Dart was never convicted. He was known as a kind, fun-loving fellow and well liked. He was buried near his cabin, which is located on private ranch land north of Browns Park on Cold Spring Mountain. Dart was not Horn's only victim. Ann Bassett's fiancé, **Mat Rash**, head of the Browns Park Cattlemen's Association, was killed the previous July in a similar manner. Bassett believed Horn (who used the alias Tom Hicks, horse buyer), had been hired by **Ora Haley**'s Two Bar outfit. She took revenge against Two Bar whenever it suited her, allegedly driving hundreds of head of cattle over a cliff into the Green River.

CRAIG

In the Yampa River Valley in eastern Moffat County is the county seat of Craig. The town was laid out in 1889 by **William H. Tucker**, a speculator from Glenwood Springs. He heard rumors of a railroad to be built in the area and staked out a town with financial backing from

Rev. William Bayard Craig and **Frank Russell.** Though the town grew and thrived, the railroad did not arrive until 1913. The **Craig Cemetery** is located on Ashley Road east of town and north of US 40. The oldest section is a narrow spit overlooking the valley to the south.

The first burial occurred in the spring of 1876, long before the town existed. **Martha Jane (Curtis) Banks** (1829–1876), died at age forty-seven. Her burial is marked by a broken sandstone slab, a rough tombstone, and a memorial plaque set in concrete. Martha married **L. William Henry Eubanks** (aka **Banks**) in Missouri in 1848. After living for some time in Arkansas and Missouri, the Banks family relocated to Custer County, Colorado, then later came to the Yampa River Valley. As winter 1875 approached, the story goes that the Indians left, warning settlers the game would all depart. The Banks family decided to stay, anyway. They survived on trout from the river. The spring thaw caused flooding and they moved uphill to camp near the base of what is now the cemetery bluff. Martha, perhaps suffering from malnourishment and exposure, fell ill and died. Though a plaque is laid here for her husband, he was buried in Idaho, where he died in 1900.

Homestead land settled by two Ranney brothers became part of the City of Craig, and Ranney Street is named for them. **Frank B. Ranney** (1854–1939) and **Alvor M. Ranney** headed for California from their home in Michigan. Arriving by train in Denver, via Pueblo, they bought a wagon and team to cross the Rocky Mountains. On July 4, 1883, they happened to camp on the **Ezekiel Shelton** ranch northeast of Hayden. They met there with some men from Golden and headed on to Fortification Creek on the Yampa and decided to stay. Some of the land there had been recently surveyed by **William H. Rose** (1844–1930), an engineer from Leadville. The two brothers took up their homesteads on the sagebrush plain near the mouth of the creek and built log cabins, relishing the bachelor life. At that time, all their supplies had to be brought from Rawlins, Wyoming.

Alvor Ranney left Craig after 1900, lived in Michigan for a time, and finally returned to Colorado to live in Denver. Frank stayed in Craig for life. He married twice, first to **Mary Agnes Sturdevant** (buried in Denver). Agnes was born to a pioneer family in Fort Collins that later resided in Steamboat Springs and Walden. The wedding was held at the home of Frank's sister and brother-in-law, **Cora Ranney** (1865–1946) and **Archibald "Archie" McLachlan** (1847–1917), Archie being one of the men from Golden who Frank had met on first arriving. Per the *Craig Courier*, "The groom is one of the county's most prosperous young men and was among the first to locate in the Craig valley. His ranch adjoins the town of Craig and in the near future he will erect a cosy new residence." Being trained as a carpenter, the house-building project would be a snap for Frank. Though not exactly "young" at forty-four, he retained a youthful-looking face all his long life.

After Agnes died of cancer in 1907, Frank resumed his bachelor ways until marrying **Sarah Jane "Sadie" (Gregg) Salter** (1859–1919) in 1918, a second marriage for both. Sadie died a short time later after surgery for appendicitis.

Frank was a founder of the Craig Masonic Lodge and served in the state legislature. He raised cattle and hay. Though he had no children, one of the first Craig schools was located on his property, built in 1888 with **Miss Rose Johnson** teaching. He participated in gun club activities and the creation of irrigation districts. He liked to entertain, acting in play productions at the Craig Opera House. After retiring from farming and ranching, he enjoyed botanical and geological research in summer and practiced his taxidermy art in winter, adding to his extensive collection of mounts.

Archie McLachlan, a carpenter like Frank, was born in Nova Scotia to Scottish immigrants. He moved to Golden, Colorado, in 1872 after an early building career in Boston and Chicago. He set up on land south of the Ranney brothers and opened a sawmill and lumber business in addition to his stock-raising enterprise. Cora Ranney came to Craig in 1890, joining her brothers Frank and Alvor, and accompanied by brother **Charles A. Ranney** (1867–1937), and **Louden J. Ranney** (1858–1912), who are also buried in the Craig Cemetery.

Archie and Cora wed in 1895 and had four children together, only two daughters surviving to adulthood. One son, **Edwin McLachlan** (1901–1910), drowned in the Bear River after breaking through the ice while skating. His older brother, **Archie "Hunt" McLachlan Jr.** (1898–1918) attempted to save him with the help of their dog. Hunt nearly drowned himself and the dog did not survive. Hunt died in the influenza epidemic at age nineteen.

Archie Sr. was on the school board and in the state legislature as a Democrat. After his death in 1917, Cora married twice more and died in California. Her daughter, Audrey, brought her back to Craig for burial.

The Craig Cemetery has many unmarked graves, some of them belonging to children. **Ethel Shaw** (1888–1899), who died after a brief bout of typhoid fever, is one. The *Craig Courier* reported, "She was ill for several days before she was confined to her bed, but her desire to prepare for the approaching examination at school nerved her to fight against her illness." She was borne to her grave by six classmate pall bearers, all girls. That she was popular and well-loved shines

Ethel Shaw was a popular schoolgirl who died young of typhoid. All the pall bearers at her funeral were female classmates.
COURTESY OF PATRICIA JOY

through in her extensive obituary. She left behind an older brother and her divorced parents. Her mother, **Eudora "Dora" Shull**, died a few years later in Michigan. Her father, **Wilber "Cap" Shaw** (1852–1922) was buried in Craig after drowning in his hot springs at Juniper.

Hayden

Along the Yampa River in western Routt County is the small community of Hayden, named for US Geological Surveyor **Ferdinand V. Hayden**, who mapped much of Colorado in the 1860s and 1870s. At one point he allegedly camped near the place that became the town. Ranchers holding large spreads populated the area. The Utes named the Yampa River for an edible root they found growing along its bank. Yampah (*Perideridia gairdneri*) is a member of the parsley/carrot family.

There are two cemeteries in Hayden. The earlier is the **Hayden Pioneer Cemetery**, tucked between cattle pastures east of town on County Road 69. The first burial dates to 1881. Prior to the 1990s, the cemetery almost vanished into the elements. Since then, it has been cleared of overgrowth, marked with a sign, and is maintained by a local 4-H club.

Veteran **Adrian Jackson Marshall** (1833–1902), his daughter, **Katie Lavina (Marshall) Smith** (1870–1899), and a granddaughter, **Ciccely Smith** (1891–1892) are buried here. Marshall came from New York and joined the Third Colorado Regiment (Chivington's 100-day group). He married **Mary A. Thompson** in 1866. They settled in Routt County sometime after 1881. Marshall provided

The Hayden Pioneer Cemetery long suffered neglect but is now maintained by a local 4-H group.

homes to indigent people in the Hayden area, for which the county reimbursed him. This included caring for his father-in-law, **Simeon J. Thompson** (1810–1896), until his death. Thompson selected and cleared his own grave site prior to his death, but it is unknown whether it was in a cemetery or on the Marshall homestead, which straddled the Yampa River east of the pioneer cemetery.

The more formal **Hayden Cemetery** is in the town limits with access from Shelton Street on the north and Crandell Street on the south. **Samuel B. Reid** (1833–1919) and his wife, **Mary E. Denney** (1847–1920), have graves marked with concrete rectangles, stamped with the letter "Q," next to the stylish headstone of their murdered son-in-law, **Ephus Donelson** (1856–1908). The Reids are examples of Colorado pioneers who did not arrive from eastern states or foreign countries. They met and married in Walla Walla, Washington Territory. Reid has an interesting footnote in history. He was in the prospecting party led by Capt. Elias D. Pierce that trespassed on Nez Perce lands to find gold in 1860. The expedition sparked a gold rush that led to the creation of Idaho a few years later.

The Reids are believed to be the first permanent settlers in the Hayden area. Their homestead is now the western edge of town. Samuel first went west from his home state of North Carolina, heading to California, in 1856. He mined and moved north to Washington Territory. He came to the Routt County area in 1874, but did not remain, returning to Idaho for a time. After hauling produce from Idaho to Hahns Peak to supply miners, he decided to return to the area. He opened the first store at Hayden, built the first irrigation ditch, and hired the first schoolteacher. He decided to roam the country a bit more in the 1890s and returned to Hayden to live out his life in 1900.

The Reids' daughter, **Martha J. Reid**, was born in Montana. She married Ephus Donelson in 1887 in Hayden, and they had three children. Martha, her niece, and a ranch hand witnessed Donelson's callous killing by a neighboring rancher.

From the beginning of settlement, homesteaders were aware that irrigation was essential to cultivate the land in this area. **Simp Tipton** purchased unirrigated land in Hayden in 1903, knowing his only water would be wastewater from other properties. He quarreled with Donelson about fencing and ditches and, on the day of the murder, came to the Donelson ranch demanding the ditch water be turned onto his dry land. Donelson explained the ditch situation. Tipton would not be mollified. He pulled his rifle from his saddle and threatened to shoot. Donelson, perhaps unwisely, said "Well, blaze away." Tipton immediately fired, the soft-nosed bullet severing Donelson's aorta, leaving him to rapidly expire in front of the shocked witnesses. Tipton served a life sentence until released from Cañon City in 1922 due to poor health. He died soon after in Georgia.

The Donelson murder shocked the entire county. The victim was especially admired and his funeral largely attended, where "the old timers who have known him so long, were overwhelmed with sorrow and strong men shed tears like children." Martha never remarried.

Hahns Peak

Hahns Peak Village was the first permanent settlement in northwestern Colorado and is sometimes called a ghost town, though people still live there. It served as the first Routt County seat, but lost the honor to Steamboat Springs in 1912. The village began as a mining camp at the base of Hahns Peak, an extinct volcano, around 1865 (see chapter 5, Old Georgetown Cemetery). Gold mining continued until the early 1900s. Some mining interest resurged in the 1950s.

The small **Hahns Peak Cemetery**, the oldest in Routt County, is on private land but publicly accessible via a short drive from County Road 129, which follows the Elk River north of Steamboat Springs. Interest in the cemetery also revived in the 1950s, and **Herman F. Mahler** (1875–1969), whose mother and grandfather are also buried here, had a fence built to enclose the space, and he identified the unmarked graves, many of which now have metal plaques identifying them. The subalpine aspen-spruce-fir habitat sprouts numerous glacier lilies and other wildflowers in springtime's soggy ground, in addition to the daffodils and irises that have been planted on the graves.

A 1911 photograph shows the wintertime funeral cortege for Irish miner **Michael Condelin** (1851–1911), who had likely suffered a couple years from the effects of a stroke. Condelin operated a sawmill business and, along with a partner, made a nice sum selling a well-producing gold claim. His grave is enclosed by a sturdy iron fence.

Joseph Morin (1850–1932) came to the United States in 1864. He worked in the east for a time (allegedly some years for Andrew Carnegie) and came to Hahns Peak around 1879 to work as a blacksmith. He made the community his permanent home and held a variety of jobs, including miner. He was a musician and organized local groups to provide entertainment. According to **Judge C.A. Morning**, Morin's closest friend (who performed Morin's funeral service), Hahns Peak in the early days was like one big, happy family. The residents certainly counted as family to Morin, who never married but who loved the local children. His granite headstone simply gives his name and years.

Two of the added metal plaques are for women identified only by their husbands' names: **Mrs. Floyd Reynolds** (?–1903) and **Mrs. James Young** (1854–1921). Mrs. Reynolds married an older bachelor in 1902. She was known at the time as Margaret Jarvis. Judge Patrick Tague performed the ceremony at Red Cliff (see chapter 6, Red

Funeral, Mine Condelin Hahns Peak, Colo. 1910

Funeral of Michael Condelin showing his casket, accompanied by men from the community, dogs, and one child, apparently a girl. The initials "J.M." and an arrow indicate Joseph Morin, a French-Canadian miner and friend of Condelin.

Cliff). Margaret died about a year into the marriage, after an unsuccessful operation, and was buried at Hahns Peak.

Much like Margaret Jarvis Reynolds, Mrs. Young had married just a year before her death, at age sixty-six. Her first name was Mary, and Young was at least her third husband. She immigrated from Germany in the late 1850s. Prior to Young, she married German immigrant **George Frey;** they lived in Rifle, and George died in 1912. Mary and George wed in 1890 and she was known as Mrs. Mary Shrader at the time. James Young was a bachelor lodger in widow Mary Shrader Frey's home shortly before their 1920 marriage.

An old-style wooden grave marker that is still legible, though aspen trees have sprouted around it within a decaying wooden enclosure, is that for **George W. Cross** (1843–1907). Like many a bachelor at Hahns Peak, Cross was a war veteran and dedicated miner, married to his mineral pursuits. His final illness, pneumonia, was precipitated by a fall in which he broke his hip. He had nearly convalesced from the injury when he died.

Yampa

The valley south of Steamboat Springs was named Egeria Park by **Capt. Edward L. Berthoud** in 1861 while he surveyed for a railroad route. The region has an ancient volcanic history, and the valley is dotted with erosion-resistant basalt necks. The most prominent of these is Finger Rock, two miles south of the town of Yampa. The town is the eastern gateway to the Flat Tops Wilderness. White settlers arrived in 1881. Men from the Breckenridge mining camp rode into

Manhunt

In March 1898, the justice of the peace in Lodore District, **James S. Hoy**, issued warrants for the arrest of **P.L. Johnstone** and **Bennett** (known only by his last name) for stealing cattle. Johnstone was also wanted in Wyoming for murder. Knowing he needed more than just a local posse, Hoy called in Sheriff Neiman. Neiman had an intimate knowledge of Routt County, having worked for many years as a range cowboy, including in Browns Park. Heading west, he gathered additional members to his crew and they converged at Herbert Bassett's ranch. As they approached the park, they spied three men fleeing on horseback with pack horses. Neiman intuited that the two men they sought were among them.

Neiman deputized a number of local men, including V.S. Hoy, to join the pursuit. The lawmen managed to deprive the fugitives of their horses and food, but still the chase took nearly a week. In the process, they managed to bring in Bennett, who had not been with the fleeing three. While he was held prisoner at the Bassett ranch, a group of hooded men arrived, told the guard to remain quiet, and lynched Bennett. Up in the mountains, the outlaws and deputies faced off on either side of a large split boulder. Hoy made an approach, exploring the crevice, when he was summarily gunned down.

Johnstone had become acquainted with two men who met at, and escaped from, a prison in Utah: **Harry Tracy** and **David Lant**. Though they had not been included on the original warrant, they were now wanted for murdering Hoy. The bedraggled fugitives were finally brought in on April 5, and after a night at Bassett's (Neiman foreclosed on the lynching option), Lant and Tracy were taken to jail in Hahns Peak. Johnstone was taken to Wyoming.

After Neiman served his prisoners supper, they managed to momentarily distract him by asking for a match. Lant, a large man, began brutally beating the sheriff. Neiman finally feigned unconsciousness. Lant wanted to finish the job but, held back by Tracy,

(continued)

gave the miming sheriff a final, forceful kick. They locked him up and fled, stealing two stage horses to get to Steamboat Springs.

Neiman had heard the prisoners discussing their plans, so after giving them several hours to leave the area, he raised a ruckus until neighbors came and freed him. They set off for Steamboat. Tracy and Lant had stopped at a ranch to wait for the stage to take them to the railroad. As daylight approached, so did the stage. Opening the stage door, they beheld several guns pointed at them. Tracy spied the sheriff and said, "Hello, Neiman, I thought you would be just waking up."

Egeria Park in 1883 looking for homestead land. They played cards to determine who would get the first choice of sites. Yampa was founded soon after. Ranching became a way of life then and still is today. The **South Routt Cemetery** (aka **Yampa Cemetery**), established in 1898, occupies a gentle, east-facing slope a little north of town.

A celebrated local pioneer in the cemetery is **Charles W. Neiman** (1861–1947), former Routt County sheriff. Neiman's moment of fame occurred in 1898 when Routt County included present-day Moffat County, and the county seat was at Hahns Peak. One of Neiman's temporary deputies was **Valentine Shade "V.S." Hoy**, who resided in Browns Park. Sheriff Neiman headed to the park to serve warrants on two wanted men.

HOT SULPHUR SPRINGS

Hot Sulphur Springs is the county seat of Grand County, home of Grand Lake (headwaters of the Colorado River) and the area known as Middle Park. Middle Park lacks the wide open, fairly level spaces of North Park and South Park. *Rocky Mountain News* editor William N. Byers founded the hot springs resort in 1860, calling it Saratoga West. The area had been used as hunting grounds, primarily by the Utes. Fur trappers arrived in the 1820s, and by the 1850s they were bringing hunting parties in from the settlements east of the mountains.

The **Hot Sulphur Springs Cemetery** occupies a sagebrush-covered hill east of town with commanding views of the surrounding mountains and canyons. Modern-day developers would salivate to put McMansions on it. But this knoll belongs to the pioneers and

The Hot Sulphur Springs Cemetery sits atop a hill with a grand view of the surrounding area.
Author's collection

those who followed them. The first burial occurred upon the death of
Nathan Stockton Bangs (1854–1875). While hunting elk along the
Muddy River in December 1875, his untrained hunting dog began
barking at the herd. Bangs struck the dog with the butt of his gun and
it discharged into his leg, which resulted in his death the following
day. Bangs was a native of New York State and just twenty-one years
old. His headstone is partially buried, covering the dates.

Two Grand County pioneers, **Thomas J. Dean** (1826–1883)
and **Barney B. Day** (1832–1883), became officers in the nascent
county government, and paid for it with their lives. They each have
pioneer markers on their graves, and though both fought for the
Union, only Dean also has a veteran headstone. Day had a splendid
ranch about twelve miles west of the Springs on the Colorado River
at a place called Troublesome. His sheep herds brought him good
money, and he also ran cattle. In December 1882, Governor Pitkin appointed him to the county commission, along with attorney
Edward P. Weber. The harsh winter of 1882–1883 saw four Grand
County miners lose their lives in snow slides. But tragedy did not
bring political harmony.

Troubles probably began with the moving of the county seat
from Hot Sulphur Springs to Grand Lake. An election to send Grand
County representatives to the state legislature compounded matters.
The county government was in turmoil by February 1883. Weber and
Day headed a group that turned on the county treasurer and county
clerk, who were backed by Commissioner **John G. Mills** and the
county sheriff, **Bill Redman**. The Mills group kept the commissioners

from holding meetings, under threat of a bloody riot. Dean's son arrested Treasurer **W.S. Chamberlain** and two others for illegally collecting taxes, which led to a hearing in Georgetown in early June. By then, Dean had been appointed acting county clerk, replacing **Lem Pollard**. Tempers ran high on both sides of the conflict, which culminated in the July 4 events.

Commissioners Weber and Day, and Clerk Dean left the Fairview House in Grand Lake after breakfast, heading to the county office, and walked into an ambush. Three masked men shot Weber first, through the lung. "Oh, I am shot," he said to his companions, who lowered him to the ground while drawing their weapons to return fire. They managed to kill one masked attacker, who turned out to be Commissioner Mills. Mills died at the scene. Weber died the same day, near midnight. Dean was shot through the head and hip, but managed to linger nearly two weeks before dying. He was able to relate his account of the ambush. Day was killed instantly by undersheriff **Charlie Royer**. The third masked man was Sheriff Redman. Royer and Redman fled the scene and Royer shortly after committed suicide, despondent over killing his friend Day. Redman is also believed to have committed suicide. Though Dean and Day are buried in Hot Sulphur Springs, Weber was buried on his ranch. Mills is in the **Grand Lake Cemetery**.

By 1883, Grand County had turned the corner from mining to tourism. The fishing, hunting, and scenery proved a greater draw than minerals. But the violence of that year dimmed the fortunes of Grand Lake for almost a decade to come.

Grave of Grand County Commissioner Barney Day, who was killed in an ambush due to a political battle. All three commissioners died in the gunfight on July 4, 1883. AUTHOR'S COLLECTION

FRASER

William "Billy" Zane Cozens (1830–1904) came to Colorado with the rush of Fifty-Niners and wound up in the gold camp at what became Central City in Gilpin County. He was born in Quebec, along with two sisters and three brothers. Their grandfather had been a Loyalist during the Revolution, and their father obtained land in Canada for that reason. But Billy wanted to live in America. He went there to learn the carpentry trade then traveled westward.

Tall, steady, and sober, Billy was tapped to be deputy sheriff in Gilpin County. When the elected sheriff went to fill a state position, Billy rose to the office and was re-elected several times. He was a good shot, but not known as someone who drew his gun. At six-foot-two, he carried himself with the air of a man with brass balls. It seemed to do the trick. He became legendary as a lawman who not only caught the bad guys, but also ensured they were not lynched by a mob.

In Central City, he met the shy, orphaned Irish-Catholic girl, **Mary York** (1830–1909), who had been rescued by a successful prospector. Mary had been brought west by her guardian, who allegedly intended to sell her in the brothels. Mary was as tiny and plain as Billy was tall and handsome, but they made a lifetime match and were married by Bishop Joseph Machebeuf (see chapter 4, Wheat Ridge) in 1861. They had three surviving children by 1870. Billy obtained land in Grand County in 1872, just below Berthoud Pass, at what later became the town of Fraser. After their stint at civilizing Central City—he with law and order, she with religion—the Cozens quit the sooty charm of the city for the refreshing emerald environs of the

Fraser River Valley. They were the valley's first permanent residents, arriving in 1874.

The Cozens expanded their ranch to 400 acres or more where they had a hotel, stage stop, and postal center. Mary and her daughters worked day and night running the place, never taking a vacation. Billy was often called on to deal with local troubles. As a Republican, he served on the party committee with Barney Day and others after Grand County was formed in 1874. Governor Routt appointed him to the county commission in 1877. He retained the position of postmaster until his death.

When Billy died in 1904, the family began the **Cozens Cemetery** on the ranch. Mary joined Billy there in 1909. Their three offspring never married nor had children, so Billy and Mary's line ended with the deaths of **William Cozens Jr.** (1862–1937), **Mary E. Cozens** (1864–1928), and **Sarah Cozens** (1866–1923).

Unlike the elevated cemetery at Hot Sulphur Springs, upon which luxury-home builders may cast a longing eye but not construct homes, the Cozens Ranch became a high-end development after the last of the family had died and the property transferred to the Jesuits in Denver. The Cozens allowed the Jesuits to hold a camp there for many years. With no descendants, it seemed fitting they should donate the property to Mary's church friends. Money from the sale of the land funded the construction of buildings at Regis University. The family headstones, surrounding iron fence, and an Ave Maria shrine, all sit within a ring of new condominium buildings. In life, the Cozens hosted many friends and strangers in their home, and so they do now in death.

The Cozens Cemetery was surrounded by fields and forests until recently. The family donated their land to the Jesuits in Denver who sold it to a developer.

ACKNOWLEDGMENTS

ompiling a work that covers a large geographical area and many individuals involves reliance on many previously published works, but also behind-the-scenes curation of museum exhibits, archive material, and on-the-ground work, particularly in documenting cemeteries. I wish to thank the special collections librarians at the Denver Public Library for pulling a ton of material for me from their stacks and archives over a busy two-day period.

Some individuals I wish to thank: Molly Daniel at the Telluride Museum for a personal tour of Lone Tree Cemetery; Patty Tharp of the San Juan County (NM) Historical Society for providing material on the Arrington family; Gretchen Gray of the Center for Southwest Studies at Fort Lewis College for help accessing material from their collection and online databases; Lynn Sinclair for providing lodging and friendship on my Denver trip; Richard Guenther for records from the Colorado State Insane Asylum, articles from the Pueblo Historical Society magazine *The Pueblo Lore*, a tour of the Colorado Mental Health Institute at Pueblo Museum, and cemetery photographs; Susan Jones for help with material from the Animas Museum library; Nancy Cristofferson for information about La Veta pioneers;

Al Rothe for family stories and photographs about the Burghardt and Cart families; and Patty Joy for family history on the Shaws of Craig.

I'd also like to mention, in general, those who work in cemetery offices for providing plot information and maps, and for confirming unmarked burials; the Find a Grave volunteers who provided photos to illustrate this volume; county clerks who searched for records; and museum, historic site, and historical society volunteers.

A note of gratitude to my critique group: Judith Lethin, Cyndie Zikmund, Tami Richards, Andrea Jones, Alice Trego, and Janice Kirk. I appreciate all your feedback and encouragement. Thank you to my editor Debra Murphy at TwoDot. And most of all thanks to my husband, Pat Lyon, for taking on extra dog walks, getting me out for ski days and bike rides, and tolerating my ambitious work schedule.

BIBLIOGRAPHY

ONLINE DATABASES SITES (INDIVIDUAL ITEMS NOT CITED)

Ancestry: www.ancestry.com
Find a Grave: www.findagrave.com
Family Search: www.familysearch.org
Colorado GenWeb: cogenweb.org
US GenWeb: www.usgenweb.org
Colorado Encyclopedia: coloradoencyclopedia.org
Colorado Historic Newspapers Collection: www.coloradohistoricnewspapers.org
Newspapers: www.newspapers.com
Bureau of Land Management—General Land Office: glorecords.blm.gov

ONLINE ARTICLES, BLOGS, AND VIDEOS

"A Colorado Panorama: Mary Rippon and Joseph Henry Stuart." Accessed August 24, 2023. your
　　hub.denverpost.com/blog/2020/03/a-colorado-panorama-mary-rippon-and-joseph-henry
　　-stuart/258615/.
"Adeline Warfield Hornbek—Florissant Fossil Beds National Monument (U.S. National Park Service)."
　　Accessed July 29, 2023. www.nps.gov/flfo/learn/historyculture/adeline-warfield-hornbek.htm.
Aker, Jr., Martin. "San Luis Valley Land Grants." Accessed December 13, 2022. www.kmitch.com
　　/Huerfano/sanluis.html.
"Akron, Colorado Collection Mss.00005.Pdf." History Colorado. Accessed May 29, 2023. www.history
　　colorado.org/sites/default/files/media/documents/2018/mss.00005.pdf.
"Alkaline Hydrolysis—Cremation Association of North America (CANA)." Accessed October 10,
　　2022. www.cremationassociation.org/page/alkalinehydrolysis.
Anderson, Robert N. "A History of Guadalupe—a Thesis." Accessed December 13, 2022. cogenweb.com
　　/conejos/Towns/A%20History%20of%20Guadalupe.html.
Armijo, Patrick. "Funerary Objects Will Be Returned to Native American Tribes," *Durango Herald*.
　　Accessed September 29, 2022. www.durangoherald.com/articles/funerary-objects-will-be-returned
　　-to-native-american-tribes/.
Bayer, Ethel. "Early Day History: Red Cliff." Mesa County Libraries. Accessed July 2, 2023. mesa.marmot
　　.org/Archive/evld%3A7581/Book?bookPid=evld:7581&pagePid=evld:7582&viewer=transcription.

Brewer, Garry. "GJ History: Grand Junction Town Founder George A. Crawford—A Witness to Early American History," *Post Independent,* September 26, 2013. www.postindependent.com/news/local/gj-history-grand-junction-town-founder-george-a-crawford-a-witness-to-early-american-history/.

———. "History: A Witness to History at George Crawford's Tomb," *Post Independent,* August 20, 2014. www.postindependent.com/news/local/history-a-witness-to-history-at-george-crawfords-tomb/.

"A Brief History of the Hardscrabble Area and Wetmore, Colorado." Wetmore-Hardscrabble Genealogical & Historical Society. Accessed August 5, 2023. www.wetmorehistoricalsociety.com/my-blog/brief-history.html.

"Burial & Cremation Laws in Colorado." Nolo. Accessed October 10, 2022. www.nolo.com/legal-encyclopedia/burial-cremation-laws-colorado.html.

Butler, Ann. "Respect 'Above and Below the Ground,'" *Durango Herald.* Accessed September 29, 2022. www.durangoherald.com/articles/respect-above-and-below-the-ground/.

Case, Linda Saulnier. "Monumental Happenings and Histories: David McShane, Early Pioneer to Monument," *Colorado Springs Gazette,* March 19, 2019. gazette.com/thetribune/monumental-happenings-and-histories-david-mcshane-early-pioneer-to-monument/article_c441633e-4a73-11e9-ab95-0faa0c03f204.html.

"Catholic Encyclopedia: Los Hermanos Penitentes." Accessed December 14, 2022. www.newadvent.org/cathen/11635c.htm.

Catholic Funeral and Cemetery Services—CFCS of Colorado—Mt. Olivet Cemetery Virtual Tour—Episode 04 Bishop Joseph P. Machebeuf, Facebook. Accessed August 26, 2023. www.facebook.com/watch/?v=1316072455392830&paipv=0&eav=AfbxeJqDkI6ljIVKzDCcV_RuSgkVnoDl7q Hgz1l5FhMHKP9-naZdh588vUhx_P0cLFM&_rdr.

"Cemetery Monuments Made of Zinc." Accessed August 25, 2023. mci.si.edu/cemetery-monuments-made-zinc.

"Cleora Cemetery." History Colorado. Accessed October 10, 2022. www.historycolorado.org/location/cleora-cemetery.

Collins, Jan MacKell. "Mollie May, Early Sweetheart of Leadville." *Jan MacKell Collins* (blog), April 24, 2018. janmackellcollins.wordpress.com/2018/04/24/mollie-may-early-sweetheart-of-leadville/.

"Colorado State Insane Asylum: Cemetery." Accessed December 3, 2022. scalar.usc.edu/works/colorado-state-hospital/cemetery.

"Colorado's Early Monument Makers, Feat. Annette Stott—YouTube." Accessed October 17, 2022. www.youtube.com/watch?app=desktop&v=xkQkZWu4e_E.

Cooke, Kyle. "Polis Signs Bill to Investigate History of Abuse and Death at Colorado's Indian Boarding Schools." Rocky Mountain PBS. Accessed July 29, 2022. www.rmpbs.org/blogs/news/colorado-indian-boarding-school-investigation-bill/.

Decker, Gwenlyn I., and Fern Ellis. "Old Mormon Cemetery for Montezuma County Colorado." Genealogy Trails, October 10, 1992. genealogytrails.com/colo/montezuma/oldmormoncemetery.html.

"Document 3: Joseph Projectus Machebeuf, 'Woman's Suffrage: A Lecture Delivered in the Catholic Church of Denver . . .'" Alexander Street Documents. Accessed August 26, 2023. documents.alexanderstreet.com/d/1000669805.

Draper, Electa. "A Proper Reburial at Mesa Verde," *The Denver Post* (blog), April 24, 2006. www.denverpost.com/2006/04/24/a-proper-reburial-at-mesa-verde/.

"Elizabeth Piper Ensley and the 100th Anniversary of the 19th Amendment." History Colorado. Accessed October 12, 2022. www.historycolorado.org/story/womens-history/2020/02/18/elizabeth-piper-ensley-and-100th-anniversary-19th-amendment.

BIBLIOGRAPHY

"Evergreen Cemetery: Chronicle of Leadville History." SKJ Travel (blog). Accessed July 20, 2023. skjtravel.net/index.php/15-features/489-evergreen-cemetery-chronicle-of-leadville-history.

Fleming, Barbara. "History: Fort Collins Cemeteries Have Storied History," *Fort Collins Coloradoan.* Accessed June 10, 2023. www.coloradoan.com/story/news/local/fort-collins/2018/10/28/history -fort-collins-cemeteries-have-storied-history/1756237002/.

"Friends of Historic Riverside Cemetery." Accessed August 31, 2023. friendsofriversidecemetery.org/.

"Fruita History—Go Fruita," September 25, 2022. gofruita.com/things-to-do/fruita-history/.

"General William Jackson Palmer & the Founding of Colorado Springs" Palmer Land Conservancy. Accessed September 21, 2023. www.palmerland.org/blog/general-william-jackson-palmer-the -founding-of-colorado-springs.

Gilbert, David. "Colorado's Oldest Business Just Sold. Its Future Could Help Preserve a Community's Way of Life," *The Colorado Sun,* March 20, 2022. coloradosun.com/2022/03/20/rr-market-sells -co-op/.

Haile, Bartee. "Outlaw Too Smart for His Own Good," *Plainview Herald,* September 2, 2014. www .myplainview.com/opinion/editorials/article/Outlaw-too-smart-for-his-own-good-8395227.php.

"Headstone Symbols and Meanings: A Guide to Cemetery Symbols," Memorials.com (blog). April 18, 2022. www.memorials.com/info/headstone-symbols-meanings/.

Heicher, Kathy. "Red Cliff: Ghosts in the Graveyard," *Vail Daily.* Accessed July 2, 2023. www.vaildaily .com/news/red-cliff-ghosts-in-the-graveyard/.

Hernandez, Esteban L. "'Heartbreaking' Report on Native Schools Cites Colorado Sites." Axios, May 13, 2022. www.axios.com/local/denver/2022/05/13/report-native-schools-abuse-colorado.

"History of Elizabeth," Elizabeth, Colorado. Accessed November 20, 2022. www.townofelizabeth.org /community/page/history-elizabeth.

"History of Ft. Collins Cemeteries." Accessed July 29, 2022. www.fcgov.com/parks/history.php.

"History of Silver Cliff." Silver Cliff, Colorado. Accessed August 3, 2023. www.silvercliffco.com /history.

"Hole-in-the-Rock Pioneer Biographies." Accessed August 14, 2022. www.hirf.org/history-bio.asp.

Horgan, Paul. "Churchman of the Desert." American Heritage, October 1957. www.americanheritage .com/churchman-desert.

Horwitz, Tony. "The Horrific Sand Creek Massacre Will Be Forgotten No More," *Smithsonian Magazine.* Accessed July 28, 2022. www.smithsonianmag.com/history/horrific-sand-creek -massacre-will-be-forgotten-no-more-180953403/.

Jaros, Garret. "What Happens to Those Who Die and Have No Family or Money for Burial in La Plata County?" *Durango Herald.* Accessed February 12, 2023. www.durangoherald.com/articles/what -happens-to-those-who-die-and-have-no-family-or-funds-for-burial-in-la-plata-county/.

Jessen, Ken. "Los Ricones: Where the Salazar Family Took Root," *Colorado Central Magazine* (blog), January 1, 2005. www.coloradocentralmagazine.com/los-ricones-where-the-salazar-family-took -root/.

"John Parsons & Co." PCGS CoinFacts. Accessed June 25, 2023. www.pcgs.com/coinfacts/category /territorial/colorado-gold/john-parsons-co-1861/1744.

"Journalistic Notes," *The Publishers' Weekly.* September 4, 1897. archive.org/details/sim_publishers -weekly_1897-09-04_52_10.

Kelley, Debbie. "Manitou Springs Residents Offer Reward Money to Find Cemetery Vandals," *Colorado Springs Gazette,* June 8, 2021. gazette.com/news/manitou-springs-residents-offer-reward-money-to -find-cemetery-vandals/article_e4c2ddf8-c876-11eb-ad82-3bd2162024f8.html.

Leadville, Colorado—The Forgotten Irish—Evergreen Cemetery—Hidden History, S9:E3, 2022. www
.youtube.com/watch?v=esubBTuL6dI.

Lindner, Douglas O. "The Trial of William 'Big Bill' Haywood: An Account." Accessed August 6,
2023. famous-trials.com/haywood/236-home.

McMillin, Sue. "Pioneer Cemeteries Reveal Surprising Details of Colorado's History," *The Denver Post*
(blog), October 5, 2021. www.denverpost.com/2021/10/05/colorado-cemeteries-history-pioneer/.

Mimiaga, Jim. "Tribes to Rebury Ancient Remains Found by Hiker Near Dolores," *Durango Herald.*
Accessed September 29, 2022. www.durangoherald.com/articles/tribes-to-rebury-ancient-remains
-found-by-hiker-near-dolores-2/.

Mitchell, Karen. "Huerfano County Presents Our Lady of Guadalupe Deaths, Conejos, Colorado."
Accessed January 21, 2023. www.kmitch.com/huerfano/conejosdeaths.html.

———. "Pueblo County Doyle Settlement Cemetery." Accessed March 3, 2023. www.kmitch.com
/Pueblo/doylecem.html.

———. "Pueblo County, Colorado Terecita's Cemetery aka Dog Town Cemetery aka Plaza Cemetery."
Accessed March 3, 2023. www.kmitch.com/Pueblo/terescem.html.

Mogon, Marianne. "Teller County Guide: Florissant: Then & Now," *Colorado Springs Gazette,* March
3, 2021. gazette.com/pikespeakcourier/teller-county-guide-florissant-then-now/article_220d80e2
-6a75-11eb-8b06-bf4c8aa8cd4f.html.

Nadler, Alex. "Mastering Cemetery Iconography." The Academy at Penguin Hall, June 3, 2021.
penguinhall.org/mastering-cemetery-iconography/.

Neton, Jim. "History in Focus: To Name a Town." June 14, 2019. www.craigdailypress.com/news
/history-in-focus-to-name-a-town/.

"Officers of Navy Yards, Shore Stations, and Vessels, 1 January 1865." Accessed July 22, 2023. www
.history.navy.mil/content/history/nhhc/research/library/online-reading-room/title-list-alpha
betically/o/0fficers-navy-yards-shore-stations-vessels-1865.html.

Palmer Lake Historical Society. "Monument 1879," November 10, 2019. palmerdividehistory.org
/monument-1879/.

Phillips, Autumn. "Hayden Cemetery Tells Century-Old Tale," *Steamboat Pilot.* December 4, 2002.
www.steamboatpilot.com/news/hayden-cemetery-tells-century-old-tale/.

"Project Seeks to Identify Indian Students Who Perished While Attending Grand Junction Indian
Boarding School." The Southern Ute Drum. Accessed July 29, 2022. www.sudrum.com/top
-stories/2019/02/15/project-seeks-to-identify-indian-students-who-perished-while-attending
-grand-junction-indian-boarding-school/.

"Red Cliff Colorado—Historic Images." Western Mining History. Accessed July 2, 2023.
westernmininghistory.com/towns/colorado/red-cliff/.

Romeo, Jonathan. "Students: Fort Lewis College's Dark History Needs to Be Addressed," *Durango
Herald.* Accessed July 29, 2022. www.durangoherald.com/articles/students-fort-lewis-colleges
-dark-history-needs-to-be-addressed/.

Rudolph, Katie. "Cheesman Park's Past Life . . . as a Cemetery," Denver Public Library History.
October 5, 2015. history.denverlibrary.org/news/cheesman-parks-past-life-cemetery.

Scoles, Sarah. "What's Really Behind the Ghost Lights of Colorado's Silver Cliff Cemetery?" Atlas
Obscura, October 1, 2022. www.atlasobscura.com/articles/silver-cliff-ghost-lights.

Shepherd, Mrs. L.A. "1931 Tales of Evergreen Cemetery," *The Herald Democrat,* October 18, 2018.
www.leadvilleherald.com/free_content/article_8ea718f2-d2fc-11e8-829a-87cdcf4bf2cf.html.

"Silas S. Soule to Walt Whitman, 12 March 1862 (Correspondence)—The Walt Whitman Archive."
Accessed October 10, 2022. whitmanarchive.org/biography/correspondence/tei/loc.00587.html.

"Silas Soule: Witness at the Sand Creek Massacre." Accessed October 10, 2022. www.arcgis.com/apps
/MapJournal/index.html?appid=4319861c09144b2b8f31db8bec550134.

Simpson, Kevin. "Colorado Boarding School Listed as a 'Most Endangered' Place," *The Journal.*
February 10, 2020. www.the-journal.com/articles/colorado-boarding-school-listed-as-a-most
-endangered-place/.

———. "Echoes of a Buried Past Carry from the Pauper's Section of a Leadville Cemetery All the Way
to Ireland's Shores," *The Colorado Sun,* October 30, 2022. coloradosun.com/2022/10/30/leadville
-cemetery-irish-history/.

"Solid Muldoon, or the Cardiff Giant Heads West." Denver Public Library History. Accessed July 19,
2018. history.denverlibrary.org/news/solid-muldoon-or-cardiff-giant-heads-west.

"Temple Aaron and the Pioneer Jews of Trinidad, Colorado." Jewish Museum of the American West.
Accessed March 31, 2023. www.jmaw.org/temple-aaron-trinidad-colorado/.

"Testimony of Captain Silas S. Soule." Kansas Memory. Accessed October 10, 2022. www.kansasmem
ory.org/item/211149/page/1.

"The Hermanos Penitentes of Southern Colorado and Northern New Mexico." Denver Public Library
History. January 15, 2014. history.denverlibrary.org/news/hermanos-penitentes-southern-colorado
-and-northern-new-mexico.

"The Life of Silas Soule—Sand Creek Massacre National Historic Site." U.S. National Park Service.
Accessed October 10, 2022. www.nps.gov/sand/learn/historyculture/the-life-of-silas-soule.htm.

"The Officer Down Memorial Page." Accessed May 8, 2023. www.odmp.org/.

"Tribes Celebrate Mesa Verde Repatriation." Indian Country Today. Accessed September 29, 2022.
indiancountrytoday.com/the-press-pool/tribes-celebrate-mesa-verde-repatriation.

"Trump Administration Finalizes the Return of American Indian Ancestral Remains and Funerary
Objects from Finland," Indian Affairs. Accessed September 29, 2022. www.bia.gov/as-ia/opa
/online-press-release/trump-administration-finalizes-return-american-indian-ancestral.

"Tuttle Post Office." Travel Storys (blog). Accessed May 11, 2023. travelstorys.com/geotag/13025.

Udell, Erin. "Who's Who of Grandview Cemetery," *Fort Collins Coloradoan.* Accessed June 10, 2023.
www.coloradoan.com/story/life/2015/09/17/grandview-cemetery-th-cemetery-stroll/72366394/.

US News & World Report. "Indigenous Schools Leave Legacy of Generational Scars." Accessed July 29,
2022. www.usnews.com/news/best-states/colorado/articles/2021-08-08/indigenous-schools-leave
-legacy-of-generational-scars.

Books, Periodicals, and Archive Material

A. W. Bowen. *Progressive Men of Western Colorado . . .* Chicago: A. W. Bowen & Co., 1905. archive
.org/details/progressivemenof00awborich.

Abbott, Carl, Stephen J. Leonard, and Thomas J. Noel. *Colorado: A History of the Centennial State.* 5th
ed. Boulder: University Press of Colorado, 2013.

Aldrich, John K. *Ghosts of Lake County: A Guide to the Ghost Towns and Mining Camps of Lake
County, and Eastern Pitkin County, Colorado.* Lakewood, CO: Centennial Graphics, 1986.

———. *Ghosts of Park County: A Guide to the Ghost Towns and Mining Camps of Park County,
Colorado.* Lakewood, CO: Centennial Graphics, 1984.

Archuleta, Ruben E. *Land of the Penitentes, Land of Tradition.* Edited by Joe T. Ulibarri. Pueblo West,
CO: El Jefe, 2003.

Arnusch, Sarah. *Evans.* Images of America. Arcadia Publishing, 2014.

BIBLIOGRAPHY

Athearn, Frederic J. *Land of Contrast: A History of Southeast Colorado*. Cultural Resources Series (United States Bureau of Land Management. Colorado State Office), no. 17. Denver, CO: Bureau of Land Management, 1985. catalog.hathitrust.org/Record/000472509.

Bader, Roy, and Avis Bader. *History and Stories of the Kit Carson County Cattlemen and Women*. Burlington, Colo: Kit Carson County Cattlemen's Association, 1963.

Bassett Willis, Ann. "'Queen Ann' of Brown's Park." *The Colorado Magazine* 29, no. 2 (April 1952): 81–98. www.worldcat.org/title/29946550?oclcNum=29946550.

Baugher, Sherene, Richard F. Veit, and Michael S. Nassaney. *The Archaeology of American Cemeteries and Gravemarkers*. American Experience in Archaeological Perspective. Gainesville, FL.: University Press of Florida, 2014.

Bent County (Colorado) History. Las Animas, CO: The Book Committee, 1986.

Beshoar, Michael. *All about Trinidad and Las Animas County, Colorado: Their History, Industries, Resources, Etc.* Trinidad, CO: Trinidad Historical Society, 1990.

Black, Robert C. *Island in the Rockies: The History of Grand County, Colorado, to 1930*. Boulder, CO: Published for the Grand County Pioneer Society by the Pruett Pub. Co, 1969.

Bluemel, Elinor. *One Hundred Years of Colorado Women*. Self-published, 1973.

Boyd, David. *A History: Greeley and the Union Colony of Colorado*. Greeley, CO: Greeley Tribune Press, 1890. archive.org/details/historygreeleyun00boyd.

Bradley, Christine. "Grand Army of the Republic Section of Alvarado Cemetery." *Clear Creek Chatter* 7, no. 7 (July 2016): 8–9. www.clearcreekcounty.us/Archive/ViewFile/Item/1006.

Broadhead, Edward H. *Fort Pueblo*. Pueblo, CO: Pueblo County Historical Society, 1981.

Brown, Robert L. *Ghost Towns of the Colorado Rockies*. Caldwell, ID: Caxton Printers, 1968.

Broyles, C.E. "Autobiography," August 5, 1887.

Bueler, Gladys R. *Colorado's Colorful Characters*. Boulder, CO: Pruett Publishing Co., 1981.

Bullen, Mabel B. *Pueblo County History: Issued under the Sponsorship of the Pueblo Chapter of the D.A.R.* Pueblo, 1939.

Cairns, Mary Lyons. *Grand Lake in the Olden Days: A Compilation of Grand Lake: The Pioneers, and the Olden Days*. Denver, CO: Printed by World Press, 1971.

Clark, Bonnie. "Understanding Amache: The Archaeobiography of a Victorian-Era Cheyenne Woman." *Colorado Heritage*, June 2006, 12–17.

"Colorado Cemeteries and Vital Records 1800–197?," n.d. C MSS WH1184. Denver Public Library. Accessed November 3, 2022.

Colorado Historical Society. "Inventory: John M. Francisco Collection #248," November 1984.

"Colorado SP Jaffa Opera House." National Register of Historic Places Inventory—Nomination Form. Accessed March 31, 2023. catalog.archives.gov/id/84131623.

Corbett, Ethel Rae. *Western Pioneer Days: Biographies and Genealogies of Early Settlers, with History of Elbert County, Colorado*. Denver, CO: Corbett, 1974.

Cozens, Mary E., Alice Reich, and Thomas J. Steele. *Fraser Haps and Mishaps: The Diary of Mary E. Cozens*. Denver, CO: Regis College Press, 1990.

Eads High School Local History Project and Kiowa County Historical Society. *Kiowa County*. Images of America. Charleston, SC: Arcadia Publishing, 2010.

Eberhart, Perry. *Guide to the Colorado Ghost Towns and Mining Camps*, 4th rev. ed. Chicago: Sage Books, 1970.

Eberle, Jeff D. *Abandoned Southern Colorado: And the San Luis Valley*. America through Time. Charleston, SC: Arcadia Publishing by arrangement with Fonthill Media, LLC, 2020.

Ebright, Malcolm, Rick Hendricks, and Glen Strock. *The Witches of Abiquiu: The Governor, the Priest, the Genízaro Indians, and the Devil.* Albuquerque, NM: University of New Mexico Press, 2006.

Ellis, Darrell. *Serious and Grave Plots: A Listing and Look at the Individuals Buried in the Mancos Valley Cemeteries*, rev. Mancos, CO: Fifth Raccoon, 2004. www.familysearch.org/library/books/viewer /490088/?offset=&return=1#page=3&viewer=picture&o=&n=0&q=.

Espinosa, J. Manuel. "The Origin of the Penitentes of New Mexico: Separating Fact from Fiction." *The Catholic Historical Review* 79, no. 3 (1993): 454–77. www.jstor.org/stable/25024072.

Feitz, Leland. *Conejos County: A Quick History of Colorado's Land of Many Contrasts.* Colorado Springs, CO: Little London Press, 1995.

Fetter, Rosemary. *Colorado's Legendary Lovers: Historic Scandals, Heartthrobs, and Haunting Romances.* Fulcrum Publishing, 2004.

Freeman, Ira S. *A History of Montezuma County, Colorado, Land of Promise and Fulfillment.* Boulder, CO: Johnson Pub. Co., 1958.

Fremont County Heritage Commission and Fremont County Historical Society. "Cemeteries of Fremont County," 2016. fremontheritage.com/wp-content/uploads/2017/04/cemetariesonline.pdf.

Fry, Eleanor. "Joanna Swayzie Sperry," *The Pueblo Lore*, March 2006, 12–14.

Gardner, Natasha. "An Angel Silenced: Sixty-Five Years after Her Death, Emily Griffith's Legacy Still Influences Denver." *5280*, December 2012.

Green, Richard L. *A Gift of Heritage: Historic Black Pioneers.* Chicago: Empak Publishing Co., 1990.

Gulliford, Andrew. *Garfield County, Colorado: The First Hundred Years, 1883–1983.* Centennial ed. Glenwood Springs, CO: Grand River Museum Alliance, 1983. https://garfield-county.com/about -garfield-county/filesgcco/sites/32/2019/06/the_first_100_years.pdf.

Guthrie, B.B. "Elias Griffith Davis." U.S. Federal Civil Works Administration. Pioneer Interviews Collection. Kit Carson County, 1934. PAM.350.43. History Colorado. 5008.sydneyplus.com /HistoryColorado_ArgusNet_Final/Portal/portal.aspx?lang=en-US&p_AAEZ=tab2.

Hafen, LeRoy R. "Elbridge Gerry, Colorado Pioneer." *Colorado Magazine* 29, no. 2 (April 1952): 137–49.

Hall, Frank, and Rocky Mountain Historical Company. *History of the State of Colorado, Embracing Accounts of the Pre-Historic Races and Their Remains; the Earliest Spanish, French and American Explorations . . .* Vol. 2. Chicago: Blakely Print. Co., 1889. archive.org/details/historyofstateof02hall.

Haskell, Chas. W., ed. *History and Business Directory of Mesa County, Colorado.* Grand Junction, CO: The Mesa County Democrat, 1886.

Hector, Ann. "Raleigh W. Chinn a Dumont Pioneer." *Mill Creek Valley Historical Society Newsletter*, April 2012.

History of Clear Creek and Boulder Valleys, Colorado: Containing a Brief History of the State of Colorado . . . an Account of the Ute Trouble: A History of Gilpin, Clear Creek, Boulder, and Jefferson Counties, and Biographical Sketches. Chicago: O.L. Baskin & Co., 1880. archive.org/details/historyofclearcr00olba.

History of the Arkansas Valley, Colorado. Chicago: O.L. Baskin & Co., 1881. archive.org/details/cu 31924028878754.

Jocknick, Sidney. *Early Days on the Western Slope of Colorado and Campfire Chats with Otto Mears, the Pathfinder, from 1870 to 1883, Inclusive.* Glorieta, NM: Rio Grande Press, 1968.

Kaplan, Michael. *Otto Mears: Paradoxical Pathfinder*, 1st ed. Silverton, CO: San Juan County Book Co., 1982.

Katz, William Loren. *Black West*, rev. Golden, CO: Fulcrum Publishing, 2019.

Keleher, William Aloysius. *Maxwell Land Grant: A New Mexico Item*, 4th ed. Albuquerque, NM: University of New Mexico Press, 1983.

BIBLIOGRAPHY

Kelsey, Harry. "Background to Sand Creek." *Colorado Magazine* 54, no. 4 (Fall 1968): 279–300.

Kit Carson County History Book Committee. *History of Kit Carson County, Colorado*. Dallas, TX: Curtis Media Corp., 1988.

Lambert, Ruth. "The Study and Documentation of the Animas City and Hermosa Cemeteries," September 2014.

Lavelett, Lucille. *Monument's Faded Neighboring Communities and Its Folklore: Pring, Husted, Gwillimville, Table Rock, Spring Valley, Greenland*. Colorado Springs, CO: ABC Printing, 1979.

———. *Through the Years at Monument, Colorado*, 2nd print. Colorado Springs, CO: ABC Printing, 1975.

Laverty, Marion Smith. "David Smith (1854–1933) and Family," n.d.

Lawrence, John, and Bernice Martin. *Frontier Eyewitness: Diary of John Lawrence, 1867–1908*. Colorado: 1990.

Leckenby, Charles H., ed. *The Tread of Pioneers*. Steamboat Springs, CO: Pilot Press, 1945.

Lecompte, Janet. *Pueblo, Hardscrabble, Greenhorn: The Upper Arkansas, 1832–1856*. Norman, OK: University of Oklahoma Press, 1978.

Leyendecker, Liston E., Christine A. Bradley, and Duane A. Smith. *The Rise of the Silver Queen: Georgetown, Colorado, 1859–1896* (Mining the American West Series). Boulder, CO: University Press of Colorado, 2005.

Luzar, Retha Beebe. *The Animas City Story: A Forerunner of Durango, Colorado*, 1978.

Maddox, Michael R. *Porter and Ike Stockton: Colorado and New Mexico Border Outlaws*. 2014.

Magennis, Ann L., and Michael G. Lacy. "Demography and Social Epidemiology of Admissions to the Colorado Insane Asylum, 1879–1899." *Social Science History* 38, no. 1–2 (2014): 251–71. www .jstor.org/stable/90017031.

McAdow, Beryl. *Land of Adoption*. Boulder, CO: Johnson, 1970.

McGrath, Maria Davies. *The Real Pioneers of Colorado: Clear Creek, Gilpin, Jefferson and Park Counties with Index*. Colorado Genealogical Chronicles. Lakewood, CO: Foothill Genealogical Society of Colorado, 2011.

Mead, Frances Harvey. *Conejos Country*. Colorado Springs, CO: Century One Press, 1984.

Merrill, Kay R., and Colorado Council of Genealogical Societies. *Colorado Cemetery Directory*. Denver, CO: Colorado Council of Genealogical Societies, 1985.

Meyer, Richard E. *Cemeteries and Gravemarkers: Voices of American Culture*. Logan, UT: Utah State University Press, 1992.

Monnett, John H., and Michael McCarthy. *Colorado Profiles: Men and Women Who Shaped the Centennial State,* 1st ed. Evergreen, CO: Cordillera Press, 1987.

Mumey, Nolie. *History of Tin Cup, Colorado (Virginia City); an Alpine Mining Camp Which Refused to Become a Ghost Town*. Boulder, CO: Johnson Publishihng Co., 1963.

Murray, Robert A. *Citadel on the Santa Fe Trail: The Saga of Bent's Fort*. Bellevue, NE: Old Army Press, 1970.

Murray, Robert A. *Las Animas, Huerfano and Custer: Three Colorado Counties on a Cultural Frontier: A History of the Raton Basin*. Denver, CO: U.S. Department of the Interior, Bureau of Land Management, Colorado State Office, 1978. archive.org/details/lasanimashuerfan06murr.

Nardine, Henry. *In the Shadows of the Spanish Peaks: A History of Huerfano County, Colorado*, rev. ed. Walsenburg, CO: H. Nardine, 1988.

Noel, Thomas J. *Colorado: An Illustrated History of the Highest State*. Sun Valley, CA: American Historical Press, 2006.

BIBLIOGRAPHY

O'Rourke, Paul M. *Frontier in Transition: A History of Southwestern Colorado*. Cultural Resources Series, no. 10. Denver, CO Colorado State Office, Bureau of Land Management, 1980. catalog. hathitrust.org/Record/102337710.

Owens, Robert Percy. *Huerfano Valley as I Knew It*. 1975.

Perry, Phyllis J. *Colorado Vanguards: Historic Trailblazers and Their Local Legacies*. Arcadia Publishing, 2015.

Peterson, Freda Carley. *The Story of Hillside Cemetery: Burials, 1873–1988*. Oklahoma City, OK: F.C. Peterson, 1989.

"Petition from Public Officers—Conejos County," January 18, 1864. M91. Denver Public Library.

Pierce, Elladean. "Early Days of Craig, Colorado." *The Colorado Magazine* 5, no. 4 (August 1928): 152–58.

Pilato, Denise E. "Illumination or Illusion: Women Inventors at the 1893 World's Columbian Fair." *Journal of the Illinois State Historical Society (1998–)* 109, no. 4 (2016): 374–99. doi.org/10.5406 /jillistathistsoc.109.4.0374.

Portrait and Biographical Record of the State of Colorado: Containing Portraits and Biographies of Many Well Known Citizens of the Past and Present. Chicago: Chapman Publishing Company, 1899. archive.org/details/portraitbiograph00chaprich.

Prowers Hudnall, Mary. "Early History of Bent County." *The Colorado Magazine* 22, no. 6 (November 1945): 233–47.

Randall, J. S. *Annals of Clear Creek County, Colorado*. Georgetown, CO: Courier, n.d.

Rankin, James H. "The Founding and Early Years of Grand Junction." *The Colorado Magazine* 6, no. 2 (March 1929): 39–45.

"Record of Deaths and Burials, Fort Lewis, 1881," 1891. M118 Box 4 Series 7 Folder 25. Center for Southwest Studies, Fort Lewis College.

Rush to the Rockies!: The 1859 Pikes Peak or Bust Gold Rush. Colorado Springs, CO: Pikes Peak Library District with the Western Museum of Mining & Industry, 2013.

Sarah Platt Decker Chapter. *Pioneers of the San Juan Country*. Repr. Vol. I, II, III, IV. 4 vols. Bountiful, UT: Family History Publishers, 1995.

Schlissel, Lillian. *Black Frontiers: A History of African American Heroes in the Old West*. New York: Aladdin Paperbacks, 2000.

Shaputis, June, and Suzanne Kelly. *History of Chaffee County*. Marceline, MO: Walsworth Publishing Co., 1982.

Shirley, Gayle Corbett. *More than Petticoats. Remarkable Colorado Women*. Guilford, CT: TwoDot, 2002.

Simmons, Virginia McConnell. *Bayou Salado; the Story of South Park*. Denver: Sage Books, 1966.

———. *The San Luis Valley: Land of the Six-Armed Cross*, 2nd ed. Niwot: University Press of Colorado, 1999.

———. *The Upper Arkansas: A Mountain River Valley*, 1st ed. Boulder, CO: Pruett Publishing Co., 1990.

Simonich, Edward. "The Bloody Fort Massacre of 1854." *The Pueblo Lore*, July 2007, 1–4.

Smith, Duane A. *Rocky Mountain Boom Town: A History of Durango, Colorado*. Niwot, CO: University Press of Colorado, 1992.

Smith, Duane A. *Sacred Trust: The Birth and Development of Fort Lewis College*. Durango, CO: Fort Lewis College Foundation, 2005.

Smith, Duane Allan. *A Time for Peace: Fort Lewis, Colorado, 1878–1891*. Boulder, CO: University Press of Colorado, 2006.

Spencer, Frank C. *The Story of the San Luis Valley*. Alamosa, CO: San Luis Valley Historical Society, 1975.

Spurr, Dick. *Historic Forts of Colorado*. Grand Junction, CO: Centennial Publishing, 1994.

Stanton, Elizabeth Cady, Susan B. (Susan Brownell) Anthony, and Matilda Joslyn Gage. *History of Woman Suffrage, Volume III*. Accessed August 28, 2023. archive.org/details/historyofwomansu28556gut.

State Historical and Natural History Society of Colorado. *History of Colorado,* Vol. 5. Linderman Co., Inc., 1927. archive.org/details/historycolorad05stat.

Stevenson, Thelma V. *Historic Hahns Peak*. Collector's edition. Fort Collins, CO: Robinson Press, 1976.

Stone, Wilbur Fiske. *History of Colorado, Illustrated,* Vol. 3. Chicago: S. J. Clarke Publishing Co., 1918. archive.org/details/historyofcolorad03stonrich.

Stoor, Yvette Cohn. "Growing Up Cohn in New Mexico" New Mexico Jewish Historical Society *Legacy* 33, no. 2 (2019): 12.

Stott, Annette. *Pioneer Cemeteries: Sculpture Gardens of the Old West*. Lincoln, NE: University of Nebraska Press, 2008.

Taylor, Morris F. *O.P. McMains and the Maxwell Land Grant Conflict*. Tucson, AZ: University of Arizona Press, 1979.

———. *Pioneers of the Picketwire*. Trinidad, CO: Trinidad State Junior College, 1964.

Taylor, Ralph C. *Colorado, South of the Border*. Denver, CO: Sage Books, 1963.

Tennent, William L. "John Jarvie of Brown's Park: BLM Cultural Resources Series (Utah: No. 7)." U.S. Department of the Interior, September 1984. www.nps.gov/parkhistory/online_books/blm/ut/7/chap2.htm.

Territorial Daughters of Colorado, ed. *Pioneers of the Territory of Southern Colorado*, 1980.

The Ryssby Swedish Cemetery: Boulder County, Colorado. Longmont, CO: Longmont Genealogical Society, 2008. www.familysearch.org/library/books/records/item/224599-the-ryssby-swedish-cemetery-boulder-county-colorado?offset=.

The State Historical Society of Colorado. "San Luis Store Celebrates Centennial." *Colorado Magazine* 34, no. 4 (October 1957): 256–63.

Thom, Kaye, Mary Ann Ratlief, Shirley Ververs, Caradell Gerstenberger, and Wayne Sater. "The History of Elbert County," 1959.

Turner, Carol. *Notorious Telluride: Tales from San Miguel County*. Charleston, SC: History Press, 2010.

Tushar, Olibama López. *The People of "El Valle": A History of the Spanish Colonials in the San Luis Valley*. Denver, CO: Tushar, 1975.

Vandenbusche, Duane, and Rex Myers. *Marble, Colorado: City of Stone*. Denver, CO: Golden Bell Press, 1970.

Vickers, William B. *History of the City of Denver, Arapahoe County, and Colorado: Containing a History of the State of Colorado . . . a Condensed Sketch of Arapahoe County . . . a History of the City of Denver . . . Biographical Sketches . . .* Chicago: O.L. Baskin & Co., 1880. archive.org/details/historyofcityofd00inolba.

Vigil, Phillip Arnold. *Reminders of a Forgotten Past: Weston, Las Animas County, Colorado, the Legends and Lifestyles of a Community*. Las Placitas Publications, 2014.

Wallihan, Samuel S., and T. O. Bigney. *The Rocky Mountain Directory and Colorado Gazetteer, for 1871, Comprising a Brief History of Colorado . . . Together with a Complete and Accurate Directory of Denver, Golden City, Black Hawk, Central City, Nevada, Idaho, Georgetown . . . First Year of Publication*. Denver: S. S. Wallihan & Company, 1870. archive.org/details/rockymountaindir00wall.

Wallis, Mather C., and Russell A. Morse. *A Short & Informal Early Days History of Fairplay, Colorado.* Fairplay, CO: Centennial Times Publishing Co., 1975.

Washington County Museum Association. *The Pioneer Book of Washington County, Colorado.* Denver, CO: Big Mountain Press, 1959.

Weigle, Marta. *Brothers of Light, Brothers of Blood: The Penitentes of the Southwest,* 1st ed. Albuquerque, NM: University of New Mexico Press, 1976.

Rote, Dave J. and Western Slope Historic Preservation Services. "Lone Tree Cemetery Survey," Telluride, CO: 1996. www.telluride-co.gov/Search/Results?searchPhrase=Lone%20tree&page=1&perPage=10.

White, Katherine E. "Meenan Family History 1880s," n.d.

Williamson, Ruby G. *Otto Mears, Pathfinder of the San Juan: His Family and Friends,* 1st ed. Buena Vista, CO: R.G. Williamson, 1981.

"Women's Gold Tapestry." Accessed December 7, 2022. leg.colorado.gov/sites/default/files/images/lcs/womens_gold_brochure.pdf.

Wommack, Linda. *From Sand Creek to Summit Springs: Colorado's Indian Wars.* Caldwell, ID: Caxton Press, 2022.

———. *From the Grave: A Roadside Guide to Colorado's Pioneer Cemeteries.* Caldwell, ID: Caxton Press, 1998.

———. *Our Ladies of the Tenderloin: Colorado's Legends in Lace.* Caldwell, ID: Caxton Press, 2005.

INDEX

Page numbers in *italics* indicate photographs.

INDEX

INDEX

ABOUT THE AUTHOR

Eilene Lyon writes history from the perspective of family and ordinary people who make the world go round. Her work has appeared in various journals and can be found on her blog at Myricopia.com. She is a professional speaker on family history, genealogical research, and writing. She is the author of *Fortune's Frenzy: A California Gold Rush Odyssey*. She has lived in Durango, Colorado, for thirty-nine years. EileneLyon.com